STAFF, PARENTS, AND POLITICS IN HEAD START

STUDIES IN EDUCATION/POLITICS
VOLUME 4
GARLAND REFERENCE LIBRARY OF SOCIAL SCIENCE
VOLUME 1188

Studies in Education/Politics

Mark B. Ginsburg, *Series Editor*

The Politics of
Educators' Work and Lives
edited by Mark B. Ginsburg

Politics, Race, and Schools
Racial Integration, 1954–1994
by Joseph Watras

Politics and Education
in Israel
*Comparisons with the
United States*
by Shlomo Swirski

Staff, Parents, and Politics
in Headstart
*A Case Study in Unequal
Power, Knowledge and
Material Resources*
by Peggy A. Sissel

Whose Education For All?
*Recolonization of the
African Mind*
by Birgit Brock-Utne

Staff, Parents, and Politics in Head Start

A Case Study in Unequal Power, Knowledge, and Material Resources

Peggy A. Sissel

Falmer Press
a member of the Taylor & Francis Group
New York & London
2000

Published in 2000 by
Falmer Press
A Member of the Taylor & Francis Group
19 Union Square West
New York, NY 10003

10 9 8 7 6 5 4 3 2 1

Library of Congress Cataloging-in-Publication Data

Sissel, Peggy A.

Staff, parents and politics in Head Start : a case study in unequal power, knowledge, and material sources / Peggy A. Sissel.

p. cm. — (Garland reference library of social science ; v. 1188. Studies in education/politics ; v. 4)

Includes bibliographical references (p.) and index.

ISBN 0-8153-3103-7 (hard : alk. paper). — ISBN 0-8153-3110-X (pbk. : alk. paper)

1. Head Start programs—United States Case studies. 2. Head Start Program (U.S.) I. Title. II. Series: Garland reference library of social science ; v. 1188. III. Series: Garland reference library of social science. Studies in education/politics ; vol. 4.

LC4091.S49 1999

372/21—dc21 99-30496

CIP

Printed on acid-free, 250-year-life paper.

Manufactured in the United States of America

For Kevin, Patrick, and Erin

Contents

Given a Head Start, Should One Compete or Cooperate?

Series Editor's Introduction to *Staff, Parents, and Politics in Head Start: A Case Study in Unequal Power, Knowledge, and Material Resources*

MARK B. GINSBURG
University of Pittsburgh

"Take education out of politics!" "Education should not be a political football!" "Keep politics out of the schools!" "Educators should not be political!" These and similar warnings have been sounded at various times in a variety of societies. Such warnings, however, miss (or misconstrue) the point that education *is* political. Not only is education constituted by and constitutive of struggles over the distribution of symbolic and material resources, but education implies and confers structural and ideological power used to control the means of producing, reproducing, consuming, and accumulating symbolic and material resources (see Ginsburg 1995; Ginsburg and Lindsay 1995).

Political struggles about and through education occur in classrooms and nonformal education settings; school and university campuses; education systems; and local, national, and global communities. Different groups of students, educators, parents, business owners, organized labor leaders, government and international organization officials, and other worker-consumer-citizens participate (actively or passively) in such political activity. These struggles not only shape educational policy and practice; they also are dialectically related to more general relations of power among social classes, racial/ethnic groups, gender groups, and nations. Thus, the politics of education and the political work accomplished through education are ways in which existing social relations are reproduced, legitimated, challenged, or transformed.

The "Studies in Education/Politics" series is designed to include books that examine how in different historical periods and in various local and national contexts education *is* political. The focus is on what groups are involved in political struggles in, through and about education; what material and symbolic resources are of concern; how ideological and structural power are implicated; and what consequences obtain for the people directly involved and for social relations more generally.

The purpose of this series, however, is not only to help educators and other people understand the nexus of education and politics. It is also concerned with facilitating their active involvement in the politics of and through education. Thus, the issue is not whether education should be taken out of politics, nor whether politics should be kept out of schools, nor whether educators should be apolitical. Rather the questions are toward what ends, by what means, and in whose interests should educators and other worker-consumer-citizens engage in political work in and about education.

This volume by Peggy Sissel, the fourth book to appear in the "Studies in Education/Politics" series, takes the reader inside the workings of Head Start, a preschool program initiated in 1965 by the U.S. federal government as part of a "war on poverty." One thing that *Staff, Parents, and Politics in Head Start* demonstrates quite clearly is that the adults' game of politics in and about Head Start is anything but child's play—it is real in its consequences not only for those immediately involved but also for human beings more generally.

Sissel's compelling analysis, thick in its description and sharp in its theorizing, weaves together various levels. She draws attention to the inequalities in power, knowledge, and material resources that exist in contemporary society in the United States (and, I would add, the global political economy—see Ginsburg, 1991).[1] It is within this context that what Sissel terms the "public" political world of Head Start operates, involving debates, lobbying, and voting about program funding levels and policies regulating the scope and depth of program activities. After sketching the relatively well known story of such macro-political phenomena, including the roles played by researchers and evaluators, Sissel paints a vivid picture of the "micro-politics" of various units of a Head Start program. This portrait, based on a year-long participant observation study, features multiple perspectives on the ways in which administrators, "professional" staff, other personnel, and parents interact in the "private" political world of two Head Start centers and the county-level organization responsible for running the centers.

Moreover, Sissel effectively illuminates the daily lived experience that various adults associated with the program have both within Head Start activities and beyond, while avoiding the unfortunate tendency of some ethnographic studies to overly privilege micro-level accounts. This book helps the reader to get "inside" the heads and bodies of staff and parents (mostly mothers, and many functioning as single head of household), but also traces the dialectical relationship between (a) the thoughts and actions of staff members and parents and (b) the distribution of wealth and power in society. That is, the adults are not only portrayed as engaged in the social construction of a Head Start program, using the different degrees of power as well as material and symbolic resources available to them; they are also shown to be actively involved in accommodating to and resisting unequal power, knowledge, and material resources.

The parents of children in the program, who faced the material challenges of life in poverty, encountered an "inadequately resourced" federal government program publicized as being designed to meet their children's and their own social and psychological needs. One might imagine a scenario in which parents came together—with other parents and the staff—to seek increased funding for Head Start, or even to struggle for a redistribution of wealth in the local, national, or global society. (Indeed, during the early years of Head Start the parental involvement component of the program was organized around the rubric of "maximum feasible participation" not only within Head Start activities but also in community action for social change.)[2] What Sissel describes is a rather different scenario, one in which the relatively few parents who become involved beyond a cursory level end up competing with themselves as well as with program administrators and center staff for the limited power and the meager material and symbolic resources available within Head Start.

The conflicts among Head Start parents revolve around issues of who should assume leadership roles and how to spend the small amount of money the parent organization accumulated from fund raising. At times the lines of conflict developed along racial and class (or level of education) divisions, thus drawing on as well as reproducing the ideological and structural system of social stratification in which most adult participants in Head Start are relatively disadvantaged.

The social divisions among active parents—and between active and inactive parents—were reinforced by many Head Start staff. For these staff members some parents were more "worthy" than others, meaning that they had valued cultural capital (see Bourdieu and Passeron, 1977)—that is, their language, thought patterns, and behavior styles were similar to those of the staff—and could be expected to contribute to the effective functioning of the program.

The staff's conception of what made for an effective program, whether designed for children or for parents, was not necessarily the same conception held by parents. This, of course, led to tensions between the two groups. These tensions were exacerbated because of inadequate levels and forms of communication between the two groups and because staff often believed that only they (and not parents) had the expertise and authority to develop program activities and assess their effectiveness. Conflict between parents and staff also arose around the question of who was to blame for aspects of the program about which there was a shared view of program shortcomings. For example, parents would blame administrative and other staff for insufficient program funding for parent involvement activities, while the staff expected parents to devote more time to raising funds for this underfunded component of the program. Such intergroup conflict functioned to deflect joint pressure on the federal government for increased funding. Pressure for government action was also deflected as a result of parents blaming staff when limited funds made it difficult or impossible to replace staff members who left the program or to provide the quantity and quality of training staff members needed to perform their duties well.[3]

As with the case of parents, however, staff members were also divided and sometimes came into conflict with each other. Of particular interest were the conflicts between county-level and center-level staff, between center-level administrative and nonadministrative staff, and between "professional" and other nonadministrative staff. Such divisions were structured hierarchically, with one of the subgroups holding more formal organizational power than the other. That the respective pairs of subgroups differed in general with respect to formal education credentials as well as social class background was used by the "higher" group to legitimate their greater power within the organization and the somewhat more extensive material and symbolic rewards accorded to those in their position. For instance, center-level staff with more formal education considered themselves to be "professionals" (teachers, etc.), who should exercise more authority, receive higher wages, and be recognized as having higher status than aides and other "nonprofessional" staff, most of whom were current or former parents of children in the program.[4]

I should clarify that the various "actors" associated with this Head Start program are not playing out some simple "reproductive" script. As emphasized in the book's subtitle, this is a story of accommodation and resistance (see also Anyon, 1983). The staff members and parents have agency, but given the contradictory nature of their situation, even in their acts of (individual and, rarely, collective) resistance to unequal power, knowledge, and material resources at the local institutional level, they seemed to be accommodating to such inequalities at national and global levels (see also Ginsburg, 1988). From the perspective of those who dominate and benefit from the current political economic relations, it is propitious that staff members and parents acted (with agency) to divide themselves—making it easier to rule over them.

Sissel's thought-provoking volume leaves me wondering whether perhaps even the metaphor of "head start" is part of the problem. Head Start was (arguably) designed to help poor children and their parents—as individuals—compete in a race or other game within in which there are winners and losers. The goal of the political economic game (perhaps best named MONOPOLY capitalism—the patriarchal and racist version) is to accumulate as much wealth (and power) as one can, working to insure that at least some other individuals and groups will have less, or none, of the same. Giving some individuals a *slight* head start in a game in which the "rules and resources" (i.e., the social structure—see Giddens, 1979) are stacked against them may not be based on altruism. Indeed, as with the Milton Bradley game of Monopoly®, sometimes one player with a near monopoly of properties and money will loan or even donate some resources to other players—giving them a second, if not a head, start—in order for the game (and further accumulation) to continue. And if the other players can be encouraged to struggle to acquire or maintain some portion of these limited resources, the game continues without the "dominant" player—or the legitimacy of the rules of the game—being challenged.

Perhaps if the staff members and parents (among others) were less "invested" in gaining a share of the "head start" advantage, they might more seriously consider organizing a "new game" of global political economy (perhaps called "Just Community"),[5] in which the object is to cooperate (engage in power-with relations—see Kreisberg, 1992) and to work toward meeting the material and other needs of as many people as possible.

NOTES

[1] For example, Braun (1995, p. 73) reports that "358 billionaires have a combined net worth of $760 billion, which equals the net worth of the poorest 45 percent of the earth's people"!

[2] It is instructive that over a short time period a shift occurred in Head Start's parent involvement focus from this notion of individual and collective empowering of parents for engagement in "public sphere" activities to a concept of upgrading individual parents' capacity to perform the "private sphere" roles of child-rearing and household management.

[3] Given the low pay for most of the staff positions in Head Start, the individ-

uals hired into them tended to have little formal education. In these circumstances inservice training was perhaps particularly important.

[4] See Ginsburg (1997) for discussion of how the ideology of professionalism is drawn upon by educators in ways that serve to legitimate unequal social relations in schools as well as society.

[5] For those who may dismiss the notion of an egalitarian utopia, it is worth considering that the Japanese post–World War II "economic miracle" has been orchestrated without producing the great disparities in wealth and income that characterize the U.S. political economy. According to Kerbo (1991, p. 423), Japan has "the lowest level of income inequality of all major industrial societies. . . . In the major corporations of Japan the pay gap between top executives and the lowest-ranked workers is around 8 to 1. . . . This same figure in the United States is 37 to 1."

REFERENCES

Anyon, J. (1983) "Intersections of Gender and Class: Accommodation and Resistance by Working Class and Affluent Females to Contradictory Roles." Pages 19–37 in S. Walker and L. Barton (eds.) *Gender, Class and Education.* London: Falmer Press.

Bourdieu, P. and Passeron, J. C. (1977) *Reproduction in Society, Education, and Culture*. Beverly Hills, CA: Sage Publications.

Braun, D. (1997) *The Rich Get Richer: The Rise of Income Inequality in the United States and the World,* second edition. Chicago: Nelson-Hall.

Giddens, A. (1979) *Central Problems in Social Theory*. London: Macmillan.

Ginsburg, M. (1988) *Contradictions in Teacher Education and Society*. New York: Falmer.

Ginsburg, M. (ed.) (1991) *Understanding Educational Reform in Global Context: Economy, Ideology, and the State*. New York: Garland.

Ginsburg, M. (ed.) (1995) *The Politics of Educators' Work and Lives*. New York: Garland.

Ginsburg, M. (1997) "Professionalism or Politics as a Model for Educators' Work and Lives." *Educational Research Journal* 11 (2): 1–15.

Ginsburg, M. and Lindsay, B. (eds.) (1995) *The Political Dimension in Teacher Education: Comparative Perspectives on Policy Formation, Socialization and Society.* New York: Falmer.

Kerbo, H. (1991) "Social Stratification in Japan." Pages 421–59 in *Social Stratification and Inequality: Class Conflict in Historical and Comparative Perspective*. New York: McGraw-Hill.

Kreisberg, S. (1992) *Transforming Power: Domination, Empowerment, and Education*. Albany: State University of New York Press.

Acknowledgments

I would like to express my deepest appreciation to the parents, children, and staff at Head Start, whose work and lives made this book possible. I also need to acknowledge the support and encouragement provided to me by Hal Beder, Nobuo Shimahara, and Pat Dunn during the initial stages of this work. My deepest gratitude also goes out to Mark Ginsburg for his ongoing belief in the importance of this project. And finally, to my husband Kevin, whose unwavering support and high level of father involvement with our children (both at home and in their preschools) allowed me the time and the space to complete this work.

Staff, Parents, and Politics in Head Start

INTRODUCTION

The Public and Private Worlds of Head Start

Politics and Head Start. The linkage of these words conjures up images of congressional hearings, heated debates, federal budget battles, and newspaper headlines. Indeed, as is well known by policy-makers, children's advocates, human service workers, educators, and many in the general public, since its inception during the Johnson Administration's War on Poverty in 1965, the program has experienced highly public periods of controversy, uncertainty, and change. Despite periodic challenges to the program, however, over the past thirty-four years Head Start has typically led a "charmed life" (Skerry, 1983). Never has this been more true than today, for despite this era of conservative fiscal policy and welfare reform, this enduring holdover of the War on Poverty remains alive and kicking, serving more children and families than ever before. Since its inception, over sixteen million American children have been enrolled in the program; in fiscal year 1997 over $3.8 billion was expended to provide educational and social services to a record 793,809 children and their families (U.S. Department of Health and Human Services, 1998). And in October of 1998 Head Start was once again reauthorized by Congress for another five years.

Because of the program's high level of visibility, the "public" political world of Head Start — including aspects of its policies, allegiances, funding levels, and its relationship to other social institutions and services — has been examined extensively over the years by a host of scholars, politicians, and advocates (Donovan, 1967; Greenberg, 1969; Moynihan, 1969; Danziger, Haveman & Plotnik, 1986; Washington & Bailey, 1995; Kassebaum, 1994; Zigler, 1996). In fact, much of the debate about Head Start has been discussed in terms that are highly political. For example, Head Start has been congratulated for providing programming designed to compensate for and correct the "deficits" that exist in the lives of low-income children and their families (Zigler & Valentine, 1979), but has also been soundly critiqued for its deficit perspective of the poor and the lack of attention given to the economic systems that maintain their marginal status (Washington & Oyemade, 1987; Swadener & Lubeck, 1995). Likewise, Head Start has been promoted for its role as an innovative "social laboratory" and an "incubator of ideas" (U.S. Department of Health and Human Services, 1997) and censured as being a gendered institution that maintains the patriarchal status quo (Miller, 1990; Pearce, 1990; Ames & Ellsworth, 1997).

The program has also been a source of contention from the outset regarding the mixed results about its value and effectiveness for children (Westinghouse Learning Corporation, 1969; Zigler & Valentine, 1979; Collins & Deloria, 1983; McKey, 1983; McKey et al., 1985; Washington & Oyemade, 1987; Kotelchuck & Richmond, 1987; Houlares & Oden, 1990; Zigler & Muenchow, 1992; Kennedy, 1993; Zigler, Styfco, & Gilman, 1993; Washington & Oyemade, 1995; Zigler, 1995). Debates have raged in the literature regarding appropriate outcome measures, research methodologies, and the meaning of results. For example, while some have blamed Head Start itself for the well-known "fade-out" effect of student gains (Westinghouse Learning Corporation, 1969; Borden & O'Beirne, 1989), others have placed the responsibility for such diminishing effects on the unresponsive school systems which do not adequately serve minority or impoverished children (Washington & Oyemade, 1987). In fact, a recent study done by the U.S. General Accounting Office (1997) points out that very little is known about the actual "impact" of Head Start, due to the fact that there are too few studies that have actually addressed children's outcomes, early studies do not necessarily reflect conditions in programs and families today, no particular outcome area or population has been researched, and the studies that do exist are often methodologically flawed. As the "centerpiece of the federal governments' early childhood efforts" (p. 3), however, it is likely that this conclusion will not change the popular conception of Head Start as a tested, proven program for the 1990s and beyond.

The policy of involving parents in the program and what that means for communities, families, and individuals has also been publicly contested. While parent involvement in Head Start was initially envisioned as promoting leadership development and community action with the objective of collective change in communities and in the institutions that serve low-income families (Datta, 1970; Valentine & Stark, 1979), due to political pressure in communities Head Start eventually shifted its focus almost solely to individualistic therapeutic and educational offerings related to parenting and domestic functions, "ceremonial" (Ellsworth & Ames, 1995) leadership functions in programs, and some opportunities for economic advancement through the hiring of parents in the program.

In fact, while Head Start has always been a "two-generation" program focusing on both children and their parents, the focus on parents has typically been underfunded and overlooked. Zigler and Styfco (1993), Washington and Oyemade (1995), and other scholars and advocates have noted that parent involvement and support for families has been the most neglected aspect of Head Start programming nationwide. For example, the National Head Start Association reports that national training efforts in parent involvement were ignored in four out of five years from 1988 to 1992 (in Zigler & Styfco, 1993), and in 1990 only 49 percent of all Head Start programs provided the required parental involvement activities and met performance standards in that area. At many sites, no one is in charge of programming for parents (Washington & Oyemade, 1995), despite programmatic mandates. Caseloads at programs with staff who do provide parent programming and family-support services typically exceed levels of good practice. In 70 percent of Head Start programs the Family Service Workers had caseload rates of over sixty to one (Chafel, 1992), the mean caseload was 228 families, and 10 percent of programs had upwards of five hundred families per Family Service Worker (Brush, Gaidurgis, & Best, 1993, in Washington & Oyemade, 1995).

In the same way that parent involvement has been neglected programmatically, research on parents and on the outcomes of parent involvement has also been lacking. In fact, the past lack of rigorous research on parent involvement in the program has been described as a "serious omission" (Washington & Oyemade, 1987, p. 110). Despite the repeated call for a comprehensive research agenda that would "direct attention to parental involvement in Head Start as a means to assure a stable foundation for the educational, economic and social progress of the poor families served" (Washington & Oyemade, 1987, p. xv), very little systematic research has been undertaken that focuses on parental involvement and the attending social, educational, and economic outcomes that are purported to be achieved as a result of the program's policies of parental involvement (U.S. Department of Health and Human Services, 1993; Phillips & Cabrera, 1996.). The Head Start research panel convened in the mid-1990s depicted this disturbing situation convincingly and succinctly: "research to date has not given adequate attention to one of the most distinctive and potentially powerful components of the program — family involvement" (Phillips & Cabrera, 1996, p. 3).

The research that has been undertaken on parents and parent involvement in Head Start represents a varied approach, from studies that are descriptive to those that are experimental. Studies that have focused on the way in which the program has affected parents' attitudes about and interactions with their children have had mixed results (Kuipers, 1969; Willmon, 1969; Payne, 1971; Weld, 1973; Kinard 1975; Shapiro, 1977) due to conceptual or methodological flaws in the research (Levine, 1993; Washington, 1985; Phillips & Cabrera, 1996). For example, research has indicated that parents who participated in Head Start reportedly understand their children's needs better and are better able to communicate with their children's teachers (Andrews, 1981; Larrivee, 1982), although desiring contact with their child's teachers, feeling a need to have information about their child's development, and having higher expectations for their children's education was also found to be a contributing factor of Head Start parents' participation in the first place (Pyle, 1989). Researchers in the broad area of early childhood education agree that parental influence and interaction is essential to preparing preschool children for learning in school; accept the view that such parental interest and involvement in a child's schooling is academically beneficial to children. Many have documented the correlation between family and adult behaviors, parent educational attainment, and adult literacy levels to children's achievement (Taylor, 1981; U.S. Department of Defense, 1984, in Jongsma, 1990; Greaney, 1986; Shapiro & Doiron, 1987; Strickland & Morrow, 1989; Chall & Snow in Auerbach, 1989; Reynolds, 1989; Strickland & Morrow, 1990; Pelligrini et al. 1990; Reynolds, 1991; Reynolds et al., 1991; Nickse, 1990; Marcon, 1993), but the lack of Head Start research in this area is glaring.

Head Start has been thought to result in parents' economic improvement, job acquisition, and educational advancement (Zigler, 1973; Thompson, 1980; Washington, Oyemade, & Gullo, 1989), although most data in this area has been criticized as being largely anecdotal (McKey et al., 1985; Washington & Bailey, 1995). The lack of emphasis and rigor in this area is especially compelling given the founding rationale for the program, which stressed economic self-sufficiency and the elimination of poverty.

Studies that have investigated parents' psychological dispositions have been both more prevalent and rigorous. Parent involvement has been shown to help parents take greater control over their lives, feel more successful (Midco Educational Associates, 1972, in McKey, 1983), increase their self-confidence (Collins & Deloria, 1983; Skerry, 1983), decrease instances of depression, and increase feelings of control and life satisfaction (Parker, Piotrkowski, & Peay, 1987). Parker, Piotrkowski, and Peay also found that the program can help parents develop a sense of affiliation and community. New work in this area is promising, including current Head Start studies and demonstration projects by Jay Fagan (Temple University), Gwendolyn Davis (University of Pennsylvania), and Zolinda Stoneman (University of Georgia), as are new initiatives in staff development related to parent involvement by Faith Lamb Parker, Beryl Clark, Lenore Peay, Susan Young, Awilda Fernandez, Ruth Robinson, and Amy Baker (Columbia University).

Research also indicates that those who participate most actively, such as those on committees in Head Start, have been found to benefit the most (Adams, 1976; Andrews, 1981; Slaughter et al., 1989). Complicating this outcome, however, are the findings by Hruska (1993), which ascertained that involved parents were more likely to have had previous experience with other organizations, and Pyle's (1989) research, which also indicated that involved parents had been participants in ongoing community activities and felt greater levels of acceptance and involvement in their community. Furthermore, Washington and Oyemade (1987) caution that very extensive involvement such as leadership roles typically involves only small numbers of parents.

Relatedly, studies of participation rates at Head Start programs have found high reported levels of participation, with two-thirds of parents reporting that they were involved in some way, and half indicating that they participated on a monthly basis (Abt Associates, 1978; McKey,1983). In these same studies parents were reported to perceive the program as both helpful to themselves and their families, and satisfying. Only a few researchers have attempted to discern why parents get involved in Head Start and what social and material conditions promote their effective participation. Payne and his co-authors (1973), as well as Williams (1975), found that the roles taken on by parents were determined both by the training and preparation that the program provided to them, and by how they thought about themselves. Coleman's (1978) research indicated that parent involvement was tied to feelings of control over the program, as well as positive attitudes about involvement. Relatedly, Wilson (1977) and McKey (1983) have reported that parents who felt self-confident, respected by the staff, and comfortable were those most likely to participate. Morris (1974), too, found that parental involvement was related to the level of staff encouragement, and Lieblein's study (1988) determined that the most significant variable predictive of participation was regular contact with a supportive staff person. She also found that the staff's attitudes about parent involvement was more important than the parents' attitudes.

Yet, while staff and programmatic support have long been thought to be a factor that mediated parent involvement in Head Start, little has been written about the staff behaviors, values, and understandings that either promote or impede parent participation, and the way in which these staff and parent relations empower or disempower parents. The new critical perspectives of Ellsworth and Ames (1995, 1998); Ames and Ellsworth (1997); Spatig, Parrot, Dillon, and Conrad (1998); Mickleson and Klenz (1993, 1998); my work (Sissel, 1993, 1994, 1995, 1997; Bradley & Sissel, 1997); and others are only now beginning to provide much needed information that will help staff in Head Start programs begin to develop a critically reflective perspective regarding their practice with parents.

To summarize, little emphasis has been placed on implementation and evaluation of programming for parents. The program's funding levels for research, while historically scant overall,[1] have provided few resources commensurate to the importance and potential of research on parents. The reality is that too few resources are available for the development of a meaningful, interdisciplinary, systematic analysis of the range of issues and outcomes that are pertinent to parents as adult participants. While no one has attempted to explicate the structural factors that have contributed to the neglect of programming and research on parents, it is clear that little political clout has been applied on behalf of programming and research related to parents over the course of Head Start's tenure. It is also clear that when the difficult, "public" questions are not posed, then the messy, "private" outcomes remain shrouded. Thus, by not asking whether the program's explicit promise of "maximum feasible participation," personal and collective empowerment, development of economic self-sufficiency, and programmatic involvement of parents in all aspects of the program is actually being implemented effectively and changing people's lives and communities for the better, then silence becomes the status quo, and only simplistic answers are required.

THE PRIVATE POLITICS OF HEAD START

Thus, talk of politics in relation to Head Start has typically involved discussions of the very public life that Head Start has led. And yet, while this book is about politics and Head Start, it is not an analysis of the historical and contemporary partisan politics and scholarly debates that have shaped its course over the years. Rather, it is both description and critique of "the politics within Head Start." As an analysis of what Foucault (1980) termed the "microsocial" environment, it exposes and makes explicit the "private" world of Head Start; one that reveals the lived experience of parents and staff in relation to the program's "public politics": its material conditions, its ideological framework, and its corresponding programmatic objectives.

The politics of this private domain has largely gone unexamined. And yet, the day-to-day actions of Head Start staff members and the relationship of those actions to the individual lived experiences of Head Start parents and families must be examined precisely because those individual experiences with the program are inextricably linked to the public through the program's ideologies and policies. By examining private politics in relation to public realities, what is revealed are the often contradictory actions and results regarding the required involvement of parents in programs. As Apple (1982) reminds us, the "microsocial descriptions of our commonsense practices are essential" (p. 39) before any type of systemic change can result. Thus, it is only through such analysis of personal practices that the ramifications of public policy can be more fully understood.

Furthermore, while this work is about politics within Head Start, it is also about Head Start as an *educational institution.* Because the program is administratively placed within the federal Department of Health and Human Services and not the Department of Education,[2] Head Start is typically thought of as a comprehensive social service provider, and outside the purview of traditional contexts of "schooling." Yet it is important to recognize the multiple educational roles that the program has maintained. Head Start has always been a preschool program for children, a provider of adult education for parents, a site of workplace and on-the-job training, and an agent of the state that develops, prescribes, funds, and implements educational policy and curricula. Moreover, Head Start is staffed by a variety of individuals whose titles and roles — as well as the normative expectations we hold about them — mirror the staff found in schools: teachers, teacher aides, nurses, bus drivers, administrators, nutritionists, cooks, counselors.

Thus, Head Start, with its varied educational and human service responsibilities and objectives, has always been an institution that has straddled conceptual and programmatic borders and boundaries. While Gramsci (1991) believed that the greatest potential for bringing about change in society lay in the "the spaces between," the multiple "shifting identities" of the Head Start program and its varied obligations have complicated it programmatically and politically. This is particularly true today, when some question the efficacy of a program that was designed in the 1960s but that attempts to meet the needs of today's children and families (U.S. General Accounting Office, 1997).

In a similar way, contemporary schools also have a wide variety of expectations placed upon them which not only complicates their traditional mission, but necessitates critical reflection on how it should be articulated and implemented. Like Head Start, schools now also do much more than provide academic instruction to students. Schools must now offer a range of human services and comprehensive programs that attend to students' health and well-being, that involve parents, and that integrate into programming various neighborhood, business, and professional constituencies and communities. Because of the need to do "all things" — some of which may be contradictory in expectations and outcomes — staff within these institutions often engage in struggles over elemental issues of ideology, diversity of goals, interests, power, and access to resources (Ball, 1987). Uncovering the types of conflicts, disputes, and other types of political activities that take place are integral to understanding the micropolitics of education, and now, I would posit, the micropolitics of Head Start.

The connection between the social relations of education and the way in which material, cultural, and symbolic resources intersect with those relations via avenues of power and privilege is at the heart of the concept of the micropolitics of education. As educators negotiate the day-to-day realities of teaching, they either accommodate and reproduce the structural and ideological frameworks of the institutions in which they work (and by extension, the broader society in which they reside), or they engage in action that either resists the institution or seeks to transform it (Aronowitz & Giroux, 1993). Such "actions (and inaction) by educators reflect and have implications for politics" (Ginsburg et al., 1995, p. 4) particularly in relation to power, interests, and the distribution of resources. In other words, "politics is about who gets what, when, and how" (Osborne, 1984, cited in Ginsburg et al., 1995, p. 6). Relatedly, then, politics in education is also about "who decides": whose needs get addressed and how they are defined (Fraser, 1989), as well as what type of knowledge gets transmitted and what kind of educational experience (intended or otherwise) gets provided, both overtly and through what Giroux (1988) and others refer to as the "hidden curriculum."

By casting Head Start as an educational institution, and by extension, the workers within it as educators, not only does it allow us to scrutinize the program regarding (among others) issues of authority, competency, accountability, resource incompatibility, professionalism, and ethics, it also allows us to view the program through a micropolitical lens. In other words, and to paraphrase Ball (1987), the future analyses of Head Start "must lie in the area of what we do not know . . . in particular in an understanding of the micropolitics" of life in Head Start: "what Hoyle (1982) calls the 'dark side of organizational life.'" I would argue, then, that to analyze Head Start in this way is not only a new and potentially fruitful way of looking at the program, it is also essentially a political act, for thus far in Head Start's history, the day-to-day reality of practice at the local program level has yet not "enjoyed" a micropolitical analysis. Yet, as the informants who shaped this work continually stressed to me, a critical investigation into the daily aspects of the program is needed in order to "analyze the distinction between what is, and what should be" (Giroux, 1983, pp. 8–9). Such distinctions are absolutely essential if the program is to be responsive to the needs of low-income families and to promote equity and justice in an era of increasing disparities between rich and poor.

As this work attests, the effort to fulfill curricular and policy demands in an environment marked by inadequate resources takes a toll on both the individual and collective lives of its informants. *Staff, Parents, and Politics in Head Start* provides an in-depth comparative case study of two Head Start centers and illuminates the micropolitics that exist within "schools" when staff and parents are confronted with inadequate resources, contradictory ideologies, and unequal mechanisms of power, privilege, and control; material and symbolic conditions that exist all too frequently in contemporary educational institutions.

The product of an ethnographic study of parent involvement at two comparative Head Start centers (Sissel, 1995), this work critically analyzes adult experience in Head Start in political terms. It frames the program as an interactive social system that is shaped by contested knowledge, conflicting expectations, and an ongoing struggle with the lack of resources, and it addresses the mechanisms of power and control in the allocation and distribution of such resources. This work also addresses the "hidden curriculum" that shapes programming for the parents and families it serves. In doing so, it critically analyzes the assumptions upon which the notion of parent participation in the program is founded and the way in which parent involvement is both interpreted and acted upon in day-to-day practice. Furthermore, it lays bare the dynamics of power and control that formed the foundation of the social relations between staff and parents and the way in which the material and symbolic resources in the program affected the conflicting interests, goals, and outcomes of involvement.

To make public this private world of Head Start is also a political act. Giroux (1983) has observed that an institution's "structural silences" and ideological messages construct and control the creation of knowledge that exists within and about them. Indeed, the lack of federal oversight of the parent involvement component and its attendant neglect at the local level (Zigler & Styfco, 1993; Washington & Oyemade, 1987; Washington & Bailey, 1995; Phillips & Cabrera, 1996), in combination with the lack of critical, scholarly attention that has been given to this issue, speaks to this silence. Thus, one objective of this book is to transform the "private" into the "public"; that is, to more fully explicate this link and to actively critique the potential, promises, pitfalls, and paradoxes of parent and staff involvement in Head Start.

The politics of exposing this private world and challenging this structured silence was made apparent to me when I presented a paper about this research (Sissel, 1994). Angered about both the substance of my findings and the corresponding critique, a professor in the audience approached me after the presentation to insist that I not make this research public, for in his view to challenge the myth that local Head Start programs always functioned effectively on behalf of families and consistently dealt with parents in empowering and respectful ways would endanger the positive view that the public had of the program, and could potentially compromise the very program itself. And yet, as I have discussed these findings at conferences around the country, and with colleagues who are knowledgeable of Head Start programming and policies, I was told time and again that my understanding and experience with the program was compatible with the experiences of others. While this congruency was gratifying, it was also troubling; for their affirmation not only validated my findings, but the silence that surrounded them as well.

ON RESEARCHER PERSPECTIVE, POWER, AND PRIVILEGE

In one sense this work on the microsocial politics of staff and parents in Head Start began in the early 1980s, when, as a new staff member at a shelter for battered women in Detroit, I was asked to serve on Head Start's Social Services Advisory Committee. From my work there I saw women — Head Start parents — actively engaged in meaningful work, in ways that I felt were empowering and authentic. Furthermore, I became alert to the fact that the policies of Head Start mandated programs to encourage and support the active participation and involvement of parents in both programmatic and policymaking functions. Because of this exposure, and my developing scholarly interest in the social processes of education for adults, as a doctoral candidate in Adult and Continuing Education at Rutgers University, I decided to frame my dissertation as a qualitative, ethnographic study of the Head Start setting as a place of learning (in the broadest sense) for adults. My intent was to characterize and analyze the structure and function of parent participation in this program, utilizing a holistic approach that incorporated administrative, staff, and parent perspectives.

As with any ethnographic research effort, it is the informants themselves who point to "what counts" (Wolcott, 1990), and who ultimately help the researcher focus the concepts, frameworks, and themes that emerge from the fieldwork setting. While I began with some very basic research objectives, such as to explain how parents are actually involved and how they learn in a Head Start program, to detail and describe the distinct types of learning activities in which parents engage, to discern the meanings that these activities may hold for parents involved in the program, and to describe the outcomes of those parent activities, I quickly found that the important findings were not centered in any particular individual parent's experience in the program (although each person's experience was certainly an essential part of the story). Rather, the central theme of the study that emerged was the way in which the structural and ideological factors of the program affected the sociopolitical dynamics of the setting, and how these in turn mediated issues such as resource distribution, access, information, parent participation, and staff interactions with parents.

The text that follows is representative of two frames of thought: first and foremost it is a chronicle of the experience of adults in Head Start from three perspectives: that of parents, staff, and my own as a participant-observer. As such, it documents the resource-poor environment in which the program functioned, and it reports the staffs' struggle to provide competent services under the constraints of inadequate funding, a lack of staff, and too little training and education. More than mere description however, this story of a year's experience at one particular Head Start places within a political framework the observable relations of power and privilege which mediated the transactions that took place among the staff, and between the staff and parents. In doing so, it juxtaposes Head Start's stated ideological promises of the empowerment of low-income adults in local communities with the hidden curriculum of disempowerment, which appeared to be the structural foundation of the reality of practice in this particular setting.

It is important to note that this work and the resulting analysis would not have been possible without the willingness and acceptance of the Head Start staff, and parents. They allowed me, as a participant-observer over the course of a full year, to step into the daily life of all aspects of the program. This included observing meetings of the Policy Council, parent groups, and staff meetings, and volunteering with and assisting staff, parents, and children wherever help was needed at the centers. While a regular schedule of activity was used to structure observations and interviews (for example, during the fall of the year I was a regular aide in one of the classrooms), I also tried to make myself available at all times, always ready to attend a meeting, to schedule an interview, to observe a parent in the classroom, or to help out with parent program activities. On some days, as little as an hour or two was spent at the field sites; on other days the hours stretched from morning to evening.

Along with my regular observations and participation in meetings and activities I also interviewed over forty staff members and fifty parents, many of them multiple times. While the majority of these individuals were parents and staff from the two targeted Head Start centers, a handful of individuals who were affiliated with different program sites were included at the urging of my other informants. Both staff and parents allowed me to constantly question them about their roles, continually offered me their input and opinions — often unsolicited — and alerted me to issues and concerns that they perceived as affecting their ability to carry out their roles as staff and parents in the program.

In addition to interviews and observations, also I asked the teachers, family service workers, and administrative staff for printed materials that related to the parent involvement component of the program. Staff members tried to be as helpful to me as possible in this regard, providing me with a mailbox at the Downtown Head Start center and supplying me with program manuals, handouts, letters, registration materials, activity sheets, calendars, meeting minutes, notices, program forms, brochures, staff reports, demographic summaries, performance plans, curriculum guides, and grant applications.

Gaining acceptance by the staff was not difficult. Two distinct groups of employees staffed the program: (1) the administrative, program-wide managers who supervised the staff, and (2) the center-level staff who provided the actual services. Interestingly, each group considered me to be like "one of them." The managers in the program perceived me to be much like themselves: an educated, skilled professional who had a measure of power and prestige. Because prior to and during this fieldwork I was acting as a consultant with community, human service, and education agencies with which they were familiar, I was viewed as being credible, capable, and connected to key players in the community.

On the other hand, it appeared my acceptance by the center-level staff was related to opposite reasons. While I had introduced myself as a "graduate student undertaking research," the term "graduate" had little meaning for them, and I was typically referred to as "the college student who was writing a paper for class." Thus, I was seen as someone with little formal power or status who was not only in need of information, but who was seeking to learn it from them. As a participant-observer who wanted to diminish the differences between myself and my informants, it was this role that I emphasized. And, while I recognized that as an educated white woman in this setting I held a privileged position, I drew upon my working-class roots and existing economic straits (at the time my husband and I were both minimally paid academics in training) to downplay any class or economic differences that existed between us. Furthermore, as I actively sought to "fit in" to the setting, I always dressed and spoke as casually and informally as did the employees (both administrative and center staff) and parents.

The parents in the program — almost all of whom were women — were also open and forthcoming. They, too, saw me as someone who was very similar to themselves; the mother of an infant who was trying to cope with the variety of demands with which they also had to cope: family, jobs, finances, schooling, and yes, the Head Start bureaucracy. That they considered me to be one of them was apparent every month when the federal food distribution program was held at the centers; parents consistently urged me to sign up to receive the commodities, lest my baby go without.

My role as a mother proved to be the best icebreaker with both parents and staff. I frequently brought my son with me to the centers; in fact, if I did not bring him, people expressed their disappointment in not seeing him. Other ethnographic researchers have also found that their real-life role of parent was valuable in gaining access to informants. Carol Stack, in her 1974 book entitled *All Our Kin: Strategies for Survival in a Black Community,* stressed the important role that her young son played in helping her develop trust. Indeed, in a similar way I credit to my son the development of my relationship with my informants; our shared experience of motherhood allowed me to step into their world in a way that

I might not otherwise have been able to do. The notion of motherhood also acted as a bridge that connected us despite differences of race, class, educational level, or culture. Having that shared experience of caring for a small baby and coping with a range of constraints helped me to empathize with these women, and they with me. Many, however, did not have the help of a spouse as I did. Being alone as single parents, these women expressed to me how good it felt to have someone to talk with about their personal concerns, and some welcomed our talks as a rare social occasion. As Bess told me, "Heck, I'm happy to have someone to talk to. There's never anybody to just listen to us sometimes, you know?"

Thus, as "the student" and "the mother," I quickly was seen as someone who was not threatening. That my informants felt safe around me was evident in that they had no qualms about expressing their opinions and concerns. For example, members of both groups of employees took me into their confidence and shared their complaints and concerns about the program and the staff. This was fortunate since it allowed me to garner a much greater range of the staff's perspectives than I could have otherwise. Parents, too, felt no compunction to hold back their thoughts and feelings about the program. The sensitive nature of their comments to me not only revealed their true concerns, but also their trust in me.

Becoming a part of program in this way allowed me to gain an accurate picture of the day-to-day life at Head Start. This was particularly important as I endeavored to discern the program's capacity for involving parents, the ways in which involvement and interaction of parents was promoted or discouraged, and the outcomes that occurred. Equally important, however, acting as a participant-observer helped me to foster a vital sense of credibility among the staff and parents, which in turn strengthened the validity of the study.

The validity of the findings were also enhanced by seeking feedback from the staff and parents. As the study progressed, I met often with both individuals and small groups of parents and staff to share my initial findings, and to ask them whether these findings seemed accurate and plausible. During these conversations they would frequently offer me additional insights or ideas that enriched my analysis and continued line of questioning.

In all of this probing and feedback, the protection of the informants' confidentiality was essential. In relation to this, several measures have been taken here, as well as in all published documents related to this research. First, I am using pseudonyms for all informants and for each Head Start center. Second, the actual location of those centers is not revealed, nor is that of the entire program. The name of the county where this research took place, while referred to here as "Morrison County," is not the county's actual name. Third, while this research was carried out in the 1990's, the actual year in which it took place is also not revealed here, in an effort to further protect and conceal the specific program and informants. Finally, while all informants agreed to participate in the study, there were some occasions when total anonymity of an individual was requested in relation to a particular comment. When this was the case the text attributes such comments to an anonymous source.

CONTENTS AND STRUCTURE OF THE BOOK

The book begins with an introductory chapter that "sets the tone" of the study and introduces the parent and staff informants who took part in it. It also begins to address the major analytical issues that are the focus of the book, such as the realities of the distribution of resources in the program, the typology and level of resources (material, informational, cultural, and interpersonal) found there, and their political import. As it is revealed that the program setting was typified by the inadequacy of resources, such as staff, materials, and facilities, the political nature of programmatic resource distribution and allocation begins to be illuminated. Chapter 2 then follows up on this introduction to the setting with an overview of Head Start's philosophy and framework, and an analysis of its ideology and promises in relation to the realities of practice. Beginning with a brief history of this federal program's purposes and aims, the chapter explores the contradictions that exist between the ideology of the program and its implementation.

Chapter 3 depicts the organizational culture of the Head Start sites included in the study, and focuses on the staffs' perceptions of their own and others' skill levels, the problems with accountability, coordination, and communication in the program, and the attendant infighting that was apparent in this setting. Clear differences in perspectives and qualifications resulted in each group (administration versus center-level staff) seeing the other as the source of the program's problems. These political realities, in combination with the program's resource-poor material conditions, lack of staff time, and little training, meant that staffs' levels of ability, interest, and willingness in working with parents was not great, and the result was that programming for parents had little priority. Hence, this section explores these broader issues and the way in which they affected staff and parent relations.

Parents, the majority of whom were women, were low-income but represented differing races, economic and family backgrounds, and education levels. Chapter 4 addresses the lives of these parents, and the way in which their material, informational, cultural, and interpersonal resources affected their interest and willingness to participate in the program. For example, men rarely participated, and higher socioeconomic-status (SES) women frequently did. Those who reported their own parents' support of education had higher expectations about involvement. This chapter also discusses the deficit perspective that functions in the program, and the way in which the staff viewed parents, their resources, needs, and demands, both as groups and as individuals. For example, the staff expressed expectations about parents in terms of their potential as human capital for the program. In effect, the way in which parents were spoken of and treated differentially was based upon the way staff perceived their attributes. Only those parents who were considered to be "worthy" and "like me" were encouraged by the staff to participate.

Informational resources also affected parents' interest and willingness to get involved. Chapter 5 addresses the contradictory messages that were provided to parents about the importance of their involvement in the program, about the structure and intent of the program, the way they as parents could play a role, and the possible benefits to themselves and children. Parents were in fact given very little meaningful information, and rarely was it offered in a comprehensive, cohesive manner. Therefore, this section also focuses on the ways in which the staff communicated with parents, what it was that parents knew about the program, the types of expectations that parents had as a result of this presence or absence of information, and the way in which communication among staff and parents affected the political dynamics between them. Clearly, when parents' high expectations about how they and their child should be served, communicated with, and welcomed into the center were not met, the frequent result was distrust. This then promoted division between those parents who wanted to meaningfully participate and those staff members who resisted parents' full inclusion as partners in the program.

The control of communication with and among parents was one way in which staff exerted their power and authority. Chapter 6 addresses this as a form of control, and describes other ways that staff wielded power over parents. These included concepts of "appropriate involvement," uses of authority, and the limitation of choice. This chapter also addresses the structural basis of the staffs' power. While stemming from the cultural meanings that both parents and staff held about the authority and expertise of schools and educators, the authority that the staff obtained from their ascribed roles was not legitimated by their knowledge, expertise, and/or experience. In order to conceal their deficits and support their role as authority, the staff distanced themselves from parents by speaking of them in a negative way, ignoring them, or limiting their participation.

As a result of the control that staff exerted over them, parents responded in various ways. Chapter 7 addresses the forms of resistance and accommodation located in the program and evinced by both staff and parents. Some parents accommodated the political structure by becoming a part of the system; others gave in to the political dynamics and "learned when to quit" after trying to make change or remedy problems without result. Likewise, their resistance also took various forms, ranging from passive nonparticipation to active organization; and as parents schemed against the staff, and in particular, the administrators, they negotiated the politics of unequal power inherent in the program.

The final chapter addresses the way in which staff and parent politics intersected and affected the implementation of program plans and outcomes. The very real differences in programming that were resultant of these interpersonal and programmatic politics are depicted in scenarios of the highly charged and emotion-laden final days of the program year. The book concludes with an analysis of the ways in which issues of power, control, and collaboration are manifested as "successes" and "failures" in programming. Implications of the study's findings, questions for reflection, directions for further research, and closing comments complete the chapter, and the book.

CONCLUSION

What follows is a chronicle of my year-long experience as a participant-observer among staff, parents, and children at two Head Start centers. As such, it is a depiction of the struggles over power and the contradictions between ideologies and actions that were an inherent part of this environment. It is also an explanation of the way in which hegemonic staff and parent relations based on domination and control were reproduced, resisted, and influenced by broader issues of gender, class, race, and ability. Ultimately, it is an analysis of the way in which staff and parent interactions are affected by the politics of the program, its personnel, and the politics of personal privilege.

It is my hope that the multiple levels of discourse found within these pages offer a much-needed and long-overdue analysis of adult involvement in Head Start. The story that is presented here is offered in the spirit of advocacy for those whom the program was designed to serve: needy children and families. It will, at times, be angering, for what is illustrated here raises serious concerns about the capacity of the program to meet the needs of families in Head Start. Furthermore, it also raises questions about some of the most foundational principles on which the program functions.

Yet because this work is the result of an in-depth, comparative study of two specific Head Start centers, it is important to note that not all Head Start programs will fit the description that is found here. Therefore, these findings may not be universal to all programs. This document, however, has been written in such a way as to provide readers with a "thick description" (Geertz, 1973) from which they can make comparisons to other parent involvement or adult education initiatives in Head Start or school settings.

Taken as a whole this investigation has important programming, practice, and policy implications for the Head Start program, its sponsoring agencies, and the individuals and communities it is supposed to serve. Moreover, it provides a critical, analytical framework that contributes to new ways of thinking about the political nature of resources and relationships in a variety of "school" settings. As an analysis of the symbiotic relationship that exists between resources, staffing, and program implementation in relation to parents and families, this book provides an intriguing case study of the politics of programmatic and personal resource allocation and its relationship to resistance and accommodation of power and control in educational settings. Because of this, it is my hope that this work will be instructive to the wide variety of students, practitioners, scholars, and policy-makers who are interested in the meaning, process, and potential outcomes of engaging parents in the educational process of their children, and in upgrading and transforming the quality of education in this country. This includes those in Head Start and in the field of early childhood education, K–12 educators, and professionals in educational administration, leadership, and policy studies. Furthermore, as a study in the dynamics of participation of disadvantaged adults in social welfare, compensatory, and volunteer programs, this book also provides a much-needed, new approach to analysis of that phenomenon and is appropriate for the fields of adult and continuing education, sociology of education, social work, public administration, and public policy.

Ultimately, what follows offers a venue from which we can begin overdue discussions about Head Start and its relationship to the individual and collective lives of the adults in the program and their community. As such, it reinforces the need to uncover the hidden mechanisms that shape our assumptions, our actions, and our power as educators, it encourages reflection regarding the ethics of programming that promises something different than it delivers, and provides an impetus to develop a new collective call to action based on principals of justice for the marginalized, the poor, and the silenced.

NOTES

[1] Washington and Bailey (1995) note that research, demonstration, and evaluation (RDE) funding as percentage of the overall Head Start budget was reduced from 2.5% of budget in 1974 ($10,097,500) to 0.11% of budget in 1989 ($1,358,500). In FY 1996 and 1997, Head Start allotted $12,000,000 each year for RDE, or 0.35% and 0.31% of the total budget, respectively (Head Start Bureau, 1997).

[2] For an excellent discussion of the politics that influenced this decision, see Zigler & Valentine (1979) and Zigler & Muenchow (1992).

CHAPTER 1

In the War Zone

Head Start's Facilities and Funding

In the broadest sense, the politics of resource distribution and it's connection to programmatic inadequacies in Head Start has long been recognized. For example, while over 16 million children and their families have been enrolled in the program in the past thirty-four years, because of funding constraints only 20 percent of all children eligible for the program have been able to be served in a typical year (Zigler & Styfco, 1993). Since 1985, federal funding levels have increased from $1 billion to $3.9 billion in FY 1997 (U.S. Department of Health and Human Services, 1998), thereby allowing enrollment of additional eligible families, but even with the recent expansion in the 1990s, the program still only serves 40 percent of all eligible children (U.S. Department of Health and Human Services, 1994). Furthermore, the 1,440 local grantees and the 16,636 Head Start centers that are the recipient of these monies struggle with the material realities of inadequate facilities, low pay scales, and a chronic lack of staff (U.S. General Accounting Office, 1994). According to this GAO report, in 1994 up to 90 percent of Head Start programs reported having insufficient staff to provide needed services.

This chapter puts these figures into context and addresses the way in which the lack of such resources sets the tone for the entire program, shapes the attitudes of the staff, and ultimately influences the program's invitation to parents and the caliber of service delivery provided to children. Through descriptive narrative and informant quotes, this introduction centers on this program's chronic lack of material resources and foreshadows the ongoing struggle over them that will be depicted in subsequent chapters. Because material resources and material relations were both the real and the figurative foundation for the culture of the organization and the climate of each center, they affected the tenor of the social relations that occurred between members of the Head Start staff, as well as those between parents and Head Start staff. Furthermore, the resource inadequacies present in the setting acted as a de facto catalyst that shaped what day-to-day tasks were to be accomplished, whose needs were to be served, and what the overall programmatic priorities were to be.

Blase (1987) has noted that the "tactical use of power to retain or obtain control of real or symbolic resources" (p. 288) is at the heart of the micropolitics of educational institutions. Clearly, conflicts are inevitable in situations where space is a problem, and where there are too few resources with which to do the job. When priorities compete in organizations, struggles ensue and something must give way (Bolman & Deal, 1991). This research indicated that sometimes this "something" is the inability to fulfill programmatic mandates spelled out in Head Start policy guidelines. At other times it will be shown that a lack of material resources results in a disregard for the welfare of the children or respect for parents and families, and at still other times what occurs is the debunking of the myth of the "big happy family" that is often spoken of in relation to Head Start (National Head Start Association, 1989).

In this context, then, being "in the war zone" is representative of more than the ever-increasing violence that plagues the neighborhoods of many urban Head Start centers (Phillips & Cabrera, 1996), although this is an important contributor to the ecology of many school settings. Rather it is a metaphor for the way in which decrepit or otherwise inadequate facilities can temper the social interactions that occur there.

Relatedly, as this chapter details the lack of material resources available in Head Start settings, we are reminded that the physical entities described are more than objects. They are also symbolic measures of value and importance, and instrumental signs of meanings about the world (Richmond & McCroskey, 1995). Just as the attainment of the corner office is one symbol of the successful business executive (Monk, 1994; Knapp & Hall, 1997) and the deterioration of urban school buildings reflects the lack of consideration that society has for minority, inner-city youth (Kozol, 1972, 1991), the lack of adequate resources for Head Start programs *may also be* indicative of greater meaning, since as Giroux (1983) has pointed out, the relations of agency to structure can be seen in material conditions. Thus, as we begin to explore the private world of Head Start centers that will unfold here, we must not only pause to reflect on the way in which the lack of material resources affects service provision to children and families, but we are also forced to ask a question that is fundamental to the very values of the program, and indeed, to our society. To paraphrase Valerie Polakow (1993, p. 102), we must ask ourselves, "Do poor families matter? Are poor families cheap?"

SETTING THE TONE

In the past year the neighborhood had gone from bad to worse, and in the last few months the staff at the Downtown Center had become especially alarmed by the increasing crime wave in the area. Now, because of their concern for safety, the door to the building was kept locked after the children had arrived for the morning. Visitors to the building, or others like myself who did not have keys, had to be let in by someone inside. So, on a bitter March morning , I found myself standing in the cold, banging on the main door of the Downtown Head Start Center in order to get someone's attention. Having run into this problem several days earlier, Lillian, the nurse at this center, had told me

> You have to be careful. The neighborhood around here is bad, so you have to watch yourself. We're keeping the door closed these days; anybody could come into the building. (Lillian, nurse, Downtown Center)

Her comment stemmed from the fact that there had been five nighttime break-ins at the center so far that year, and once a thief had entered the building during school hours and stolen some of the purses from employees' desks. Drug dealers and prostitutes were common in the neighborhood, now, and drive-by shootings had recently become a regularity. The staff were feeling extremely anxious and leaving the door open during the day did not seem reasonable to them anymore. Even though locking it was inconvenient for parents or others who came to visit, the doors were locked at 9:00 each morning.

Some staff members now felt so threatened that they wanted to be transferred to another center. They felt particularly unsafe at night, and hated having to return in the evening to attend occasional parent meetings. One young Black woman, a teacher's aide, had admitted her concern to me one day after one of the center's break-ins.

> I hope I don't get placed here next year. I don't mind working with Carla, but if it's here, I quit. It's too dangerous here, in this neighborhood. The shootings, the drugs. Forget it. I won't be back. (Penny, teacher's aide, Downtown Center)

The Downtown Center was the largest Head Start center in Morrison county. It had eight classrooms that served 192 children, some in full-day sessions, and some in half-day sessions. The staff at the Downtown Center included one full-time (Harriet) and one part-time (Fran) family service worker who were responsible for parent programming, one full-time nurse, eight teachers and eight teachers aides, and six bus drivers and three kitchen staff. Also located at the Downtown Center — but in a separate office space up on the second floor — were the offices of the county-wide administrative staff, including the Director and all six of the department coordinators.

At this hour the building's parking lot was filled with cars. The parking area was flanked on three sides by red-brick buildings. The Head Start center was the largest of these; it was a huge, two-story building on the south end of the parking lot. It consisted of classrooms, offices, a cafeteria, a gymnasium, and an auditorium, and had originally been a Catholic school. Rising crime and civil-rights protests in the early 1970s resulted in "white flight," and when middle-class families moved out of the downtown area and into surrounding parts of the county, the school closed. The large brick convent that stood adjacent to it on the west edge of the lot was also abandoned. The other two buildings on the lot were still used by the diocese. One of these was the massive St. John's church, which stood directly across the northwest corner of the parking lot; the other was the parish rectory, connected to the church by a covered walkway. Both the church and rectory were still used, and although struggling financially, the church had a small but active congregation.

This square block of church buildings was a much-needed "bright spot" in the neighborhood. To the north and west, and stretching for blocks, was a part of the city known as the "war zone." Drug-related shootings were not uncommon, and illicit drug sales could be found only a block away. To the east of the center ran a main street that provided a business corridor for the local residents. Bodegas, run-down clubs, an occasional restaurant, and liquor stores — all with bars on their windows — were interspersed with vacant lots and empty buildings with broken and boarded-up windows. Many were painted with gang symbols and graffiti.

Farther east stood one of the city's housing projects. I could easily see its fifteen stories stretching into the sky. Constantly in the news, Parkview Homes was notorious for the rapes and the shootings that took place there, as well as for the political squabbles that were a constant source of tension between the residents and the city. Because of its infamous reputation, most of the staff at the Downtown Head Start Center refused to go there, regardless of the mandatory policy of making home visits to Head Start families living there.

The view south from the building was both greener and cleaner. That side of the school faced Market Avenue, which served as an informal demarcation line in the neighborhood. South of Market Avenue, the "war zone" gradually ended, and the streets were cleaner and safer. This part of the neighborhood was a tree-lined area where one had to be cautious at night, but it was considered safe during the day. A local university dominated the area. The college campus was a favorite of the teachers at the center; during warm weather the teachers and their students would take short walking trips to campus and back, and sometimes the children had the opportunity to visit the museums and libraries there.

Standing on the back steps in the cold, I again knocked loudly, and then peeked into the window of the Family Service office, which was located on the first floor near the entrance of the building. This window overlooked the parking lot and if you stood on the doorstep and leaned over far enough, you could see into that office. Neither Harriet nor Fran, the two family service workers,[1] were at their desks, so I banged on the door again, this time hoping that perhaps Lillian, the nurse, or one of the teachers would hear me. The nurse's office was only a few doors down on the same floor; across from that were two classrooms. I knocked again, loudly enough that someone should have been able to hear me. Whether anyone would interrupt their work to investigate the noise, was another question, however, for the locked door also inconvenienced the staff. They hated having to answer the door, and avoided it if they could, preferring to let someone else handle it.

Finally, after about fifteen minutes (which, unfortunately was not an unusual amount of time) Harriet came down the hall and noticed me standing at the door. She let me in the building, and together we stepped into the family service office. The family service office was a long narrow room approximately six by twelve feet. Squeezed into this space were two desks with chairs, two file cabinets, a typing table, and an extra chair. Harriet's coworker, Fran, was not at this center on Thursdays, so I took a seat behind her desk, being careful not to bump the broken desk drawer that perpetually threatened to spill its contents onto one's lap.

As usual, the office was a mess. Two Styrofoam cups, half-filled with coffee, were sitting on Fran's desk. Both had been sitting there for days and spots of mold now floated on top of the greasy film. A note I had left for Fran three weeks earlier still sat in the same place, ringed with coffee stains. Next to me, by the window, was Harriet's desk. Stacks of supposedly confidential files were lying out in the open, interspersed with a disorganized array of meeting notices, class rosters, notebooks, fund-raising literature, and referral forms. Next to the desk by the wall was a typing table that held an old broken typewriter. It, too was covered with piles and piles of papers, as was the radiator near the window. On the floor in between these two desks a telephone lay disconnected in a mangled heap of wires. It had not worked properly the entire time I had been at the center, and finally, after repeated requests to the administration to get it fixed, Harriet and Fran had simply thrown it down, out of the way.

This small office with its clutter and dirt was often the first thing that parents and other members of the public saw as they came into the Downtown Head Start center. Its condition was a sore point with some of the managers in the program.

> Oh, that office down there. It's the first thing that people see when they come in and it's disgraceful. Now granted, the rest of this place isn't great, but that is a shambles. It's embarrassing, and it sets the tone for what people think of us. (Elizabeth, special needs coordinator)

"One Extreme or the Other"

The building that housed the center was charming in many ways. The high ceilings were paneled with the decorative tin plates of eras gone by. Heavy oak moldings lined the doorways and windows, and the tiled floors were laid out in a parquet design. The windows, which reached nearly to the ceiling, let in lots of sun. The new coat of semigloss yellow paint that the landlord applied to the walls every fall gave the place a glow of possibility and hope.

The staff cared little for these aesthetics, however, for this old building was in need of major repairs — problems that an occasional coat of paint did nothing to fix. The building's ancient, crumbling bathrooms, the worn-out heating system, doors that jammed, and electrical outlets that did not work were a major source of complaints among the staff. There was no air conditioning in the building, and the heating system was inadequate and sometimes nonexistent. In August the building was a virtual furnace and in the winter people froze. As Barrie, the health coordinator, said, "I hate the heat and the cold here. It's either one extreme or the other. Some days, I actually think it makes me sick."

The administrative offices for the county Head Start program were housed on the second floor of the building. The director used the old principal's office, but the health coordinator, the family service coordinator, the transportation coordinator, the nutrition coordinator, the education specialist, and the special needs coordinator shared space in two classrooms, partitioned with room dividers and book cases. There was a chronic lack of cabinets, tables, bookshelves, and general organizing space. Consequently, stacks of papers and boxes sat in piles on desks and floors in much the same way as they did in the family service office.

By contrast, the classrooms were tidy and usually well equipped. Keeping them that way was a struggle, however.

> The centers and classrooms are fairly well equipped, although budgets used to be high for supplies and no longer are. Our budget keeps getting cut and toys and equipment are getting higher all the time. I have to work within a strict budget, and we need a range of materials to meet the varied developmental needs of children. . . . It takes approximately $10,000 to start a new classroom. Replacing equipment and toys can be expensive too, because of wear and tear, and theft, which happens sometimes. I try to make people accountable. I try to get donations, but it's tough. (Candice, education specialist)

While having a range of toys for the children was required by Head Start, the cleanliness of the classrooms was required by state daycare regulations. The people responsible for keeping them clean were the teachers and their assistants, yet because the center was typically in short supply of cleaning materials, they were kept locked up. To use them, teachers had to make requests to the center manager. The staff hated the bureaucratic annoyance of having to ask permission for items such as paper towels, detergent, and window cleaner. After struggling with the situation for most of the year, and having no luck in getting the policy changed, the teachers simply began buying the supplies themselves.

While the classrooms were kept clean, the common areas of the building were not cared for as conscientiously. In previous years the center did not have a janitor and the building suffered from the neglect. Even though there was a custodian this year, food, napkins, and milk spills often remained on the cafeteria tables and floor after breakfast and lunch, and often remained there into the next day. The bathrooms were typically dirty, and they sometimes lacked tissues, soap, or towels. The plumbing system was antiquated, and toilets were often not usable as filth spilled from them. As a result of having too few functioning commodes, the lines of youngsters waiting to use the bathroom always stretched down the hallways after breakfast and lunch. The teachers constantly complained about the wasted time that occurred because of the lack of usable toilet facilities, as well as the overall condition of the building. As one teacher noted: "This building is awful. You know, the physical facility is important to teaching and class management."

"If We Only Had a Better Space"

The Harbor Street Center was the comparative site for this study. Like the Downtown Center, Harbor Street was located in a church building. Unlike Downtown, the building was small and tidy, and it was situated on the main street of a small working-class community on the outer suburban/rural edges of Morrison County. Approximately thirty minutes' distance by car from the Downtown Center, getting to the Harbor Street Center entailed traversing past retail strip malls and fast-food restaurants, then past light industrial parks, chemical plants, and a landfill. Largely populated by descendants of turn-of-the-century Irish and Italian immigrants, the area also had a growing group of recent Latino immigrants. While this community was somewhat more financially advantaged than the downtown area, it still struggled. In the Harbor Street area the families typically depended on low-wage retail jobs, or mid-wage seasonal manufacturing that offered no guarantees of consistent work.

The Harbor Street Head Start center served sixty-eight children in two classrooms, each of which held a morning and an afternoon class. The Protestant church that housed the center was a small, two-story structure attached to the main body of the church. A kitchen and dining room were located on the first floor, and two classrooms and an office were on the second floor. A basement meeting room was also a part of the facility. Two teachers, two teacher aides, a cook, a part-time janitor, a part-time nurse, a part-time family service worker, and two bus drivers staffed the center.

While the Harbor Street Center staff did not have the same concerns about the building that the Downtown Center staff had in terms of heating, electricity, and plumbing, the availability of physical space did present a problem, particularly as it related to parent activities. For example, though required in the Head Start performance standards, the parents at the Harbor Street Center did not have a parent room they could use for meetings and classes. As Debbie, the family service worker explained:

> Last year was horrendous, trying to line up meetings. This year is a little better. There are many night meetings at the church, not only us, but

> AA, NA, and other groups.[2] So we are always competing with others for space to have meetings.

Instead of having access to an appropriate meeting room, the year that I was there the parents were forced to meet in a small office area on the second floor. And yet, meeting in that cramped office was sometimes a problem as well. Although the Head Start staff had full use of it by day, they had to have permission from the church to use it in the evening. One night during a parent meeting, the parent chairperson, Bobbie, was pulled out of the meeting by the minister's wife. A few minutes later Bobbie came back into the room looking upset, but proceeded with the meeting. The next day she told me what had taken place.

> Supposedly the room wasn't booked, and the minister yelled. . . . She tried to tell me we weren't supposed to be there, that Rhonda [the center manager] hadn't gotten the room reserved. Rhonda knows the rules, so I don't buy any of it. I just think it is pretty funny. [It's like] they pulled me out to make an example of me.

Space and layout constraints were also found at the Downtown Center. One example of this was related to the two classrooms on the second floor. Because the children were given breakfast, lunch, and snack each day down in the basement cafeteria, this meant that the children had to go up and down two long flights of stairs three times a day. The two teachers in these rooms, Miss Carla and Miss Diane,[3] complained that this meant that a huge part of their day consisted of this climb up and down, rather than time spent in the class. Furthermore, Miss Carla had a mild heart condition that sometimes made her feel dizzy when she took stairs. Rather than being given one of the two classrooms on the first floor, or one of the four that were in the basement, she told me that her pleas for a change were ignored.

The lack of space for required program activities such as registration, parent meetings, and school programs was also problematic. While the old school had large rooms such as an auditorium (the "big room"), a gym with a basketball court, and a cafeteria, the employees had been ordered not to use these unless special approval from both the Head Start administration and the church officials had been given. This was due to the fact that while the Head Start program leased the classroom and office areas from the church, technically they did not lease the entire building. Consequently, Head Start did not have full access, and if these rooms were needed, Head Start had to pay the church $25 to $35 dollars each time. This policy was new to this school year and staff were displeased with it, as there was little additional money available in the budget, and given the fact that the program was already paying a level of rent that it could barely afford. This extra-fee policy especially affected the family service staff, since it had an impact on their programming abilities with parents.

> We really struggle with lack of space here. Head Start must pay for each room we use and they cannot afford more. Even the gym may be hard to get for the parent orientation. We may have to hold parent meetings in the classrooms this year. (Lorna, family service coordinator)

Despite the policy, the staff would still use the gym in the basement from time to time, sneaking the children in on inclement days for short bursts of play. This type of informal use became increasingly difficult as the year progressed, however, for the church began turning off the electricity in these rooms.

This was a problem even when they wanted to pay the usage fee. For example, one rainy day in October the family service staff had hastily organized a late-registration day. Fifteen children had relocated or dropped out, so they had arranged for families on the waiting list to come in to enroll. Harriet asked me if I would help them, since all teaching staff would be busy in class that day. When I arrived to work at the "welcome table" the big room was very cold and dark, there was no heat, no electricity, and there was barely enough light to read the forms that I was handing to parents. Throughout the morning Harriet repeatedly left the room to request that the electricity be turned on, but to no avail. After two hours, Fran, Harriet, and I were chilled to the bone. Fran made a point of telling me: "See why I keep telling you that you really have to love this place to work here?" I found it interesting, however, that neither wanted to give up on the room to seek the warm, well-lit environment of the hallway just outside. Rather, because "they had always used the big room for registration," they were determined to stay put, despite the cold, the dark, and the fact that fewer than half of the potential families had shown up. It would be much later in the year before I would realize how metaphorical this setting was in relation to the way in which the program typically kept parents in the dark and out in the cold.

It became apparent as the year progressed that the Downtown Center did not want to pay the extra fees for any type of room use. Nor, did it seem, were they willing to champion the facility needs of the parents. Yet, according to the Head Start program guidelines each center was supposed to have a "parent room" where meetings, programs, and workshops could be held, and where parents could relax and interact together.

As with the Harbor Street Center, the Downtown center did not have such a room, and what little space they were occasionally using was quickly taken from them. For example, in December the church notified Head Start that the cafeteria space was to be for Head Start's use *during the day only;* the parent group would not be allowed access to it at night. From then on, Jinny, a teacher who was especially supportive of parents, allowed the parent group to use her classroom on meeting nights.

Problems with the lack of space were a topic of discussion with the staff throughout the year, as facility problems had direct ramifications on programmatic and personal outcomes.

> In my view, a parent room would make all of the difference. If we only had a better space where they could get together anytime they wanted, they could come in and hang out, get to know each other, develop trust, you know? If I had a room, just one room, I could do so much. It would be a great place for parents to come and just get out of the house, 'cause you know that they don't have no money to do that, to go someplace. (Harriet, family service worker, Downtown Center)

Within several weeks of this conversation, the Head Start Policy Council voted to allocate money for a parent room in the Downtown Center. I asked Harriet about this, thinking that she would be excited. Her skepticism took me by surprise as she told me the following:

> I'm not gonna get my hopes up. I've seen space come and go. For right now, it is just an idea, and just cause it got brought up doesn't mean that it will happen. Until it's committed, I'm not gonna get excited. Just cause you plan this year doesn't mean that you can do it next. . . . And, I don't even know if I'll be here next year, the way they bump us around sometimes."

"Father James Wants Us Out"

While getting full access to the space within the buildings that housed these two Head Start centers was problematic, often just having the proper facilities to house the program was difficult.[4] Problems with landlords were a recurring theme. At the Downtown Center, the program's relationship with its landlord was especially tense and it didn't take long before the staff began to get the message that the church no longer wanted them as tenants.

By winter the church's intentions seemed clear. One night in December as I arrived for a parent meeting, I found everyone, parents and staff members alike, sitting and shivering in their cars, unable to get into the building. Finally, at 7:00 o'clock, a police car drove into the parking lot. Harriet got out of her car to greet the officer, and the two conferred for a moment. Then he unlocked the door.

When I asked Harriet about it, she said that when she arrived her key would not work and she could not get the door open to let everyone in for the meeting. Thinking that the church would have a key that she could use, she and one of the parents went to the rectory and rang the bell. No one would come to the door, however. Instead, someone inside shouted for them to go away, saying that they were going to call the police. Harriet yelled back and forth with them, and told them to go ahead, call the police. At least that way they could get into the building, she reasoned, since the police also kept a key that they used to check the building when the burglar alarm went off. While the building was opened in time for the meeting, Harriet was still angry. She felt that in turning her away, the church people had not acted "very Christian."

By the end of the year, rumors were circulating at the Downtown Center that the church was raising the rent again in an effort to make Head Start leave. According to Barrie, the health coordinator:

> Yes, the church is raising the rent. Father James wants us out, plain and simple. Money is the bottom line. If he can get us out, he can get another tenant in who will give him more money, like the county day care program. . . . I've heard that Desmond was looking around for a new place now and that they might move this site to a new building, closer to downtown. Whatever they decide though, for sure the staff will be the last to know. We never get to give any input into decisions like this.

Barrie's suspicion was confirmed later that same week as I talked about Head Start with a young Black community organizer I knew who was running for city council. He shared with me what he knew about the Downtown Center:

> There are a lot of rumors about Head Start going around, and about how they don't pay their fair share of rent at St. John's. A lot of people

> are upset about St. John's relationship with Head Start. People don't think they are paying enough rent, and taking advantage of the church. One group from there approached me and asked me to deal with it. They contributed to my campaign, and then said that they wanted me to take on this issue. I told them that I saw it as a county issue, and a problem between agencies. No way could I get involved with their contract, that's up to them to re-negotiate the rent. So, I gave the money back. They weren't very happy about it. (Byron White, candidate for city council, downtown district)

The other Head Start centers in the county had also experienced problems with their facilities. Because the Head Start budget allocations allowed for only a certain level of rent payment, programs were often hard-pressed to find suitable spaces that fit within their budget. While the Morrison County program had negotiated the rent with the church, the church now wanted more. In fact, because of this kind of situation, entire centers were uprooted periodically, kicked out of their buildings to make room for better-paying tenants. This was tragic in some cases, for it seemed that once a center had established itself as a part of a community, they were often asked to move out. As I probed this issue, I heard many references to "the old North Branch center." It had been a great facility, but after years of being subsidized by the local school district (the rent had only been $1.00 per year), the Head Start program was kicked out.

According to Fran, "in the old days," the $1.00 lease was quite common, as communities actively sought a Head Start center in their area. Now, as she explained it, with the rising cost of utilities and insurance, few churches or schools could afford the cost or the risk of having a center in their building. Because of this, some of the centers in Morrison County had been forced to move two or three times in the space of a few years.

Similar scenarios are played out each year across the nation. The GAO reports that while churches and schools have in the past traditionally offered space in their buildings to Head Start programs, many are now "reclaiming previously donated space, forcing many Head Start programs to look for alternative space in the community" (U.S. General Accounting Office, 1994, np). In fact, nationally the mean lease length for a Head Start center is between one and three years, and according to the National Head Start Association (NHSA), half of all programs had vacated at least one center in the past three years. As with Head Start in Morrison County, the most common reason that programs cited for leaving a facility was due to the landlord's request for increased rent (Collins, 1992).

Finding new or replacement sites is not easy for programs, and NHSA reports indicate that it sometimes takes up to two years to locate adequate space, resulting in the inability to provide services to children and families (National Head Start Association, 1992; U.S. General Accounting Office, 1994). Nationally, two-thirds of Head Start directors report difficulties due to lack of suitable facilities in their area, or high renovation costs that would be required if the programs were to meet day-care licensing requirements (U.S. General Accounting Office, 1994). Because few buildings in high poverty areas meet standards of sufficient space, lighting, ventilation, and heat, and offer environments free of hazards such as lead paint and asbestos, Head Start spends from $20 to $30 million each year on renovations — improvements that yield the program nothing when the center is forced to leave the building. Relatedly, NHSA estimates that Head Start spent $13 million between 1987 and 1990 to renovate buildings that Head Start no longer uses, and only one program out of ten had lease agreements that allowed for reimbursement for such capital improvements. Thus, private owners of real estate get their buildings improved at government, and poor families', expense. Recent legislation that allows programs to purchase their own facilities promises to curb some of this waste, yet few programs are in the position to fund major capital expenditures.

Meanwhile, the majority of directors polled in the NHSA survey viewed their present facilities as being adequate, but at least one-third of all centers and their classrooms were deemed substandard. Space needs, playground concerns, plumbing, roofs, kitchen facilities, flooring, and heat were listed as serious problems (Collins, 1992). The decrepit facilities, the lack of space, and the political struggles that marked the relationships of the centers with their landlords were not the only thing that constrained the program. The problems with other aspects of the program's budget were major concerns as well.

PROGRAMMATIC RESOURCES AND THE POLITICS OF FUNDING

Head Start programming in Morrison County consisted of seven separate Head Start centers that served nearly six hundred low-income children and their families. Waiting lists at each of the Head Start centers were common, and, in fact, only 25 percent of those eligible for the program in the county were served during any one program year. Like typical Head Start agencies around the country, the countywide Head Start program in

Morrison County was to provide a spectrum of services to children and families, including health screening, nutrition, education, and advocacy and assistance. These services were administered with a budget of approximately $2.5 million, $2 million of which was received from federal allocations. The additional $500,000 came from matching contributions from the local communities in Morrison County and from the large contracting community action program (CAP) that had managed the Head Start services since this federal initiative was begun in 1965 (Head Start Needs Assessment, Morrison County).

Staff in the Head Start program included both administrative employees and center-level workers. Management positions included the education specialist (Candice), the health coordinator (Barrie), the special needs coordinator (Elizabeth), and the family services or parent involvement coordinator (Lorna). Each of these coordinators were supervised by the director of the Head Start program (Valerie), who in turn reported to the executive director of the Morrison County Community Action Program (Desmond). Center-level workers included teachers, teachers aides, bus drivers, family service workers, and nurses. Supporting their efforts on a contractual basis were occasional family therapists and speech therapists. In all, a total of seventy individuals (administrative and center-level staff) worked to provide services in nineteen Head Start classrooms around the county.

Money problems were a continuing theme throughout my year at Head Start, and trying to get straight answers about the program's $2.5 million budget was difficult. Neither the staff nor the parents on the program-level Policy Council (who were supposed to be in charge of the program's finances) seemed to understand the budget, and the Head Start director avoided direct questions about money when they were posed to her. One thing was clear, however: nothing was clear. This lack of clarity resulted in frustration as staff and parents alike were given murky reasons as to why open positions were not filled, why basic supplies could not be purchased, and why dollars that were supposed to be in the budget were not there.

During my year there a county-level "shortfall" of $200,000 was reported, and while one supervisor described the situation as being related to "debt reduction," parents were incensed and felt that it somehow had just disappeared. Whether out of my naiveté or lack of privilege in the setting, I was never able to ascertain what had occurred. Regardless, it wasn't important that I understand the real situation with the money; rather the salient point was that the parents on the Head Start Policy

Council,[5] who were supposed to be partners in the management of the program, also didn't know what the true financial situation was. As Bobbie, the parent chair of the Harbor Street Center, put it: "How do you not find $200,000?"

Furthermore, because there was never enough money to provide the services that were supposed to be offered, the result was continual maneuvering of funds, the putting off of hiring needed staff, and trying to find any money possible to put into the program's coffers. The following section details some of the ways in which problems with finances were manifested in the program.

Never Enough Money

While the lack of adequate fiscal resources had an impact on the program's ability to lease and maintain adequate facilities, financial problems also affected the program's ability to acquire needed materials for all programming purposes. Even the basics were often not available when needed.

An example occurred early in the year as the program set up the required confidential files for each child and their family. As a volunteer in the family services office, I was asked by Fran, one of the family service workers, to make up files for each enrolled child. I dutifully began the task of writing each child's name (by hand, since the typewriter in their office was broken) on labels that would be transferred onto manila folders. Three-quarters of the way through I ran out of file folders. When I requested more from Fran, she said to me, "be realistic, there's never enough money, and they'll just tell us to go without." The needed supplies never appeared while I was helping in the office that fall, and the leftover paperwork eventually got shoved into a large box and was stuck into a file cabinet.

Another example of the extreme lack of cash available to the program could be seen in the political maneuvering that occurred one night during the Morrison County Head Start Policy Council meeting The Downtown Center parent group had recently held a very successful fund-raiser which would allow them to buy gifts for the children for the Christmas holiday. Yet, rather than let the parent committee of that center have access to their earnings, Desmond and Valerie announced at this meeting that since the Downtown Center had been very successful at their fall fund-raiser, they were making an administrative decision to move $1,000 out of that Parent Fund and put it into the general operating budget of the program.

The parents were furious. They perceived it as typical of the way in which administration treated them — without much recognition that their activities and participation were important. Not only was this unfair, they argued, it was wrong; the administrators were not allowed to do this. After much heated exchange between the parents and the administrators, Desmond and Valerie finally backed down when Francine, the parent chair of the Downtown Center, had pointed out their error out at the meeting. Afterwards, she explained to me that what the administrators had tried to do was penalizing them for being successful:

> They took it from the Downtown account. They took it with the rationale that our fund-raisers were so successful that we didn't need it. We showed them how wrong it was to do this to us. We were being penalized for doing something successfully. (Francine, parent, Downtown Center)

This kind of behind-the-scenes budget maneuvering was often reported, and many staff and parents alike expressed great frustration. This frustration turned explosive on more than one occasion and their anger was especially apparent when the paucity of resources directly affected the welfare of the children.

Spoons and Milk

The depth of the anger and frustration that the staff felt regarding the lack of material resources was evident one morning as I was helping Miss Carla with the children's breakfast. While cereal and milk were on the menu, there were no spoons to be found; all were being used by other classes. It meant that we had to wait until another class finished eating, then collect and wash the spoons, and then finally, feed the children. Our day would start at least a half hour late. Carla tried to be lighthearted, but I could tell that she was angry, and she commented that several times in the past she had purchased utensils for the center because of this very problem.

When it finally came time for our turn with the spoons, we discovered that there was no skim milk. Children in the program typically drank whole milk, but a few, such as Alicia and Kiri, had a note from their doctor and required skim milk. When I asked the cooks in the kitchen why there was no skim milk, they shrugged and explained that the milk delivery had been "short" that morning. Their solution was to "add water to some regular whole milk." This made Carla furious, for while the fat level in the milk would be diluted, so would the nutritional content.

I assumed that by lunchtime the situation would be solved, and that someone would have called for more milk, or gone out and purchased it. Not seeing it on the serving table, I once again requested it from the cooks. They looked at me like I was being outrageous. "We're not allowed to go out and buy a couple of half gallons!" they said. So once again the girls got watered-down milk.

In the same way that the lack of milk cheated children and the lack of spoons kept entire classes waiting, the disrepair of phones, typewriters, and copiers also wasted a lot of time and kept the efficiency, effectiveness, and the capabilities of the staff and their services to parents and families to a minimum. For example, if the photocopier was broken (as was often the case), the staff would leave the building to make copies. The closest copier they could use was miles away at the CAP agency, so making copies turned into an afternoon event whereby staff were out of the office — and unavailable to families. In addition, it was ironic that the lack of money for repairs resulted in unneeded additional expenditures of money for local travel.

Employees at all levels had the same complaints: their jobs would be much easier, they could get more work done, and they could do a better job if they had the right resources. Yet this lack of supplies, food, and equipment were not the only resource problems that staff encountered. Employees and the services that they were supposed provide were also often missing.

Lack of Staff

The lack of staff in Head Start programs is a national problem. When surveyed, over 86 percent of Head Start directors reported that they have insufficient qualified staff. Mental health and disabilities services, parent involvement, and social services programming are areas that were indicated as especially lacking. Lack of staff leads to large caseloads for those who are in place (U. S. General Accounting Office, 1994). According to the GAO, over half of all Head Start programs report caseloads for family service workers at over 100:1, which is three times the recommended level.

In line with national reports of inadequate staffing levels, the lack of staff also appeared to be a chronic problem at the Head Start program in

Morrison County. Not only was the program understaffed in some areas because no additional positions would fit within the constraints of the budget, but when funded positions did become open they were often left unfilled for months. This was true for both county administrative and center staff positions. For example, in the administrative area the program had gone without a special needs coordinator for over two years, did not have an education coordinator on staff, and during my year there the family services coordinator job had been left open for several months.

Problems at the center level were just as acute. Teaching positions remained open, bus driver jobs went unfilled, and family service positions were left empty for months at a time. Sometimes an entire year passed without the required center-level staff in place. One center in Morrison County went without a teacher all year long (the Morrow Street Center). This situation concerned people such as Marlene, the branch manager of the Downtown Center. She noted that it was difficult enough for a trained teacher to work with twenty children in a class, each of whom needed extra attention. When bus drivers with no training in working with young children ran the classes because teaching positions went unfilled, it was a source of anger for both staff and parents.

For instance, at Harbor Street one of the teachers was out ill for the last several months of that school year. Days without proper staff became regular occurrences, and the parents began getting angry that their children did not have "real teachers" in the classroom.

> The other centers been out without a teacher all year too. There should be a substitute. . . . And the more the parents do it, the less they'll get a substitute. Somebody said, well, Rhonda said they was gettin' us one. I said, what makes you think that they'll get us a substitute before they get Morrow Street a real teacher? You know? (Bobbie, parent, Harbor Street Center)

The perception among the staff was that positions went unfilled in order to save money. As staff members commented:

> They'll fill in with other staff until they decide if they want to spend the money on hiring someone new. That was a joke, you know . . . ha, ha. . . . but it is really true, they'll put off hiring someone as long as they can, if they can get by with it and save money. (Fran, family service worker, Downtown Center)

> They try to save money so that they can reduce this stupid debt,[6] and they end up jeopardizing people because of it. They do this all the time. They are just too cheap to fill the positions that are needed. (Elizabeth, special needs coordinator)

One service area neglected during that year was speech therapy. While many children in the program had speech problems, speech-therapy services were not available to them because Elizabeth, the special needs coordinator, had not been given approval from the administration to contract with the needed therapists.

> The administration is dragging its feet on approving contracts, probably to save money. It's very unfair though, since the teachers feel like they have no backup. In the priority meetings, when a child is brought up, the teachers feel like they might as well not highlight an issue since there won't be any help for them. (Candice, education specialist)

> Although there is supposed to be, they have no speech therapists this year yet. So even if a problem is noted in a child and they report it to Elizabeth [the special needs coordinator], teachers are left up to their own. (Marlene, teacher, Downtown Center)

Staff "Benefits": Still in Poverty. Even when open positions were approved for hiring, finding appropriate, qualified staff who would work for the low wages Head Start paid was sometimes difficult. According to the U. S. General Accounting Office (1994), low salaries impede the ability of local Head Start programs to hire staff who have appropriate skills and training. This is especially true regarding teachers. The 1994 GAO study found that the highest-paid teachers (those with the longest tenure) averaged $15,039 per year and new teachers were typically paid only $12,077. Other data indicate similarly low salaries for other positions; for example, the national average for teacher aides was $9,500 yearly (Phillips & Cabrera, 1996).

Wages at the Morrison County Head Start program were no different. Family service workers made the most of those employed at the centers, about $15,000; teachers earned about $12,000, and bus drivers, bus and teacher aides, and cooks earned the least, approximately $8,600.

While one goal of the Head Start program was to employ parents in the program as a means of lifting them out of poverty, some parents told me that while they eventually wanted a job with the program, they could not afford to take one. For example, Carmen was currently receiving welfare, food stamps, and WIC, which just barely covered her rent and other expenses. If she were to get off welfare and take a job with Head Start, Carmen told me that she would not be able to make it on what the program paid. "Head Start had a job open for a bus aide, but they only make six dollars an hour, and I need at least seven or eight dollars an hour to make it."

At these levels, if a staff member had dependents and no income-producing partner, it often meant that employees were still at or below the poverty level. According to the U.S. Census Bureau, in 1995 the poverty-level threshold was around $10,000 for a family of two and $12,000 for a family of three, and for a family of four (three of whom were children) that figure was $15,719. On the first day that the "Commodity Day" was held at the centers I discovered that almost half of the staff at the Downtown Center were below the poverty threshold and qualified for this free federal food program. Thus, rather than lifting families out of poverty, Head Start appears to be keeping them there, in low-skilled jobs with little hope for significant improvement.

According to the GAO (1994), reasons for the low wages included the fact that Head Start teachers and other staff typically do not have the same educational backgrounds and qualifications of those providing similar services in other settings. Because they are less qualified, the rationale has been that Head Start workers could be paid less. And while the 1994 GAO report indicated that during 1992–93 nearly all Head Start programs received funds for the purpose of quality improvement, since wages had been low for so long, directors also reported that even with significant pay increases, parity with other providers was unlikely to happen anytime soon.

Head Start directors in this study also reported using new monies to increase or to begin to provide fringe benefits. While data are not available indicating the number of programs nationally that do or do not provide fringe benefits or retirement plans, the lack of benefits was a problem in Morrison County. Due to their personal circumstances, some of the staff (e.g., Lorna) felt this reality more keenly than others.

When I began my fieldwork, Lorna was employed as the family service coordinator, and had been with the program since its inception in 1965, when she had begun as a board member of the community action agency that sponsored Head Start. While she had been the family service coordinator for many years, she told me that she had little savings and no pension beyond Social Security. In her late fifties now, she had been ill quite some time and wanted to quit, but was afraid of being thrown into financial straits. A few months after I met her, Lorna's condition became acute, and she was finally forced to quit, penniless and pensionless.

MATERIAL RESOURCES AND THE EFFECT ON STAFF MORALE

Trying to do a job without adequate facilities and materials, with little pay and not enough staff, was stressful. Staff's negative attitudes about the resource problems pervaded their jobs, and a reference about it was brought up to me nearly every day. While data do not exist that indicate whether staff morale is a chronic problem in Head Start programs across the country, research indicates that increases in pay can lead to increased feelings of satisfaction in some circumstances (Lawler, 1981). In fact, the GAO (1994) has anecdotal reports that when directors of Head Start programs have used their recently acquired Quality Improvement Funds for improving wages and benefits, they also perceived increased levels of staff morale at their programs.

Research on schools indicates that resource issues do indeed affect the attitude of school employees. For example, research on teacher morale indicates that it is related to teachers' beliefs that resources are available to them that will allow them to implement the strategies, programs, and policies that are required of them (Corbett, Dawson, & Firestone, 1984; Boyd, 1992).

The physical working conditions of the school, one aspect of its ecology (Snyder & Anderson, 1986), have also been found to be essential to the overall climate of the school. The physical and material environment are thought to reflect an institution's outlook on learning (Kleberg, 1993), and include the physical size and layout of the setting, material conditions or accessibility to resources, standards of cleanliness and the quality of maintenance, and related factors such as safety concerns, comfort level, and policies (Boyd, 1992; Kleberg, 1993).

At times the remarks of the Head Start employees served as striking indicators of the frustration, exasperation, and anger they felt about the circumstances of their working conditions. One morning as I sat in the family service office, making up labels for nonexistent file folders, a Head Start nurse from one of the other centers stopped into the office. As she and I chatted about my research, Melba had this advice to share with me:

> Honey, when you finish your studies, don't work for one of these poverty programs. Go for the money. Go some place where you know

> your paycheck will be on time, and they give you the materials you need to work with.

Melba's disgruntled attitude was echoed by others as well. The manager of the Downtown Center summed it up best when she noted how the staff reacted to the paucity of resources:

> Many teachers just feel, why should they even bring up a problem, since nothing will be done about it. It makes for bad staff morale. (Marlene, center manager)

Yet, while their complaints filled my notes, many of the staff sought to serve their clients well despite the reality of working in a continual state of shortage. Many of the staff were quite dedicated to the program and so had worked under these conditions for years; they had become used to "making do," "getting by," or "putting up with" the problems. And while some employees were more vocal about this atmosphere of scarcity and brought up problems with the administration from time to time, most seemed resigned to this less-than-desirable situation, and reported giving up after getting no response or seeing little or no result. Some, like Charlotte, who was told by her superiors that she should stop bringing up problems, gave up after threats of being dismissed.

> I've tried to make changes, to voice complaints and be an advocate for the kids, in everything from the meals to the filthy bathrooms. I was told, though, that I had better stop complaining, and that if I didn't, I might be let go, regardless of how good I was with the kids. (Charlotte, teacher, Downtown Center)

Thus, despite the fact that this antipoverty program was supposed to advocate for the needs of the poor and seek change with them and for them, acceptance of the impoverished material conditions in the program was the expected norm. Yet, as Ginsburg and his colleagues (1995) remind us, educators not only reproduce and accommodate their material conditions, they also resist and contest unequal distribution of resources. As shall be seen in the following chapters, however, sometimes these acts of resistance, while creative, actually functioned to reinforce the legitimacy of an unequal and unjust system. Thus, despite Head Start's professed goal of support and empowerment, in some cases what happened instead was the fostering of injustice against the very families for which Head Start was designed.

NOTES

[1] Also called Family Support Specialists.

[2] Alcoholics Anonymous, Narcotics Anonymous, Boy Scouts, Girl Scouts, and other groups met regularly at this site.

[3] It should be noted that the title "Miss" was the common term used for teachers and teacher aides in this setting. Children, parents, and other staff typically referred to those staff in this way, and they with each other.

[4] In the early days of Head Start, acquiring facilities to house programs was not a problem as communities actively encouraged the establishment of Head Start centers. In fact, it was not uncommon for a program to use a facility in a church or school virtually for free.

[5] Federal Head Start Performance Standards require that each Head Start grantee have a "board of directors" made up of at least 50% of parents of Head Start children. This body, called the Policy Council, which is supposed to assist in decision making about all aspects of the program, is discussed in depth in Chapter 2.

[6] This comment is related to the missing $200,000 in the budget that was referred to in a previous section.

CHAPTER 2

Head Start's Philosophy and Framework

An Overview of Ideology, Politics, and Promises

When President Lyndon B. Johnson announced the beginnings of Project Head Start during a ceremony at the White House Rose Garden in 1965, Head Start was promoted as a family-focused preschool program that would provide social and educational activities to both children and their parents, with the promise of individual support and collective empowerment. While it began as a short-term, experimental, summer enrichment program for four- and five-year-olds, the program's administrative placement in the Office of Economic Opportunity (OEO) was indicative of an even broader, more lofty mission: the eradication of poverty (Washington & Oyemade, 1987; Gillette, 1996).

Through the dual mechanisms of compensatory education for children and collective community action and jobs creation for their parents, the program's two-generation focus was designed to provide the one-two punch that was needed in order for the War on Poverty to succeed. It was also considered to be good public relations for the OEO,[1] which had been handling controversy connected to its Community Action Program (CAP) emphasis (Zigler, Styfco, & Gilman, 1993). Because, as one observer put it at the time, the program promised important, and politically palatable "educational, health, and guidance services to children.... who through accident of birth into poor families would enter the competitive struggle in the world's richest society terribly handicapped before they reached the first grade of school" (Donovan, 1967, p. 82),[2] such enthusiasm was generated among policy-makers that a lightning-speed expansion of Head Start occurred "almost overnight" (Donovan, 1967). In just a few months, Head Start had gone from an eight-week, prekindergarten summer session to a full-scale program stretching across a full academic year (Zigler & Valentine, 1979; Gillette, 1996).

Indeed, by August 31 of that summer in 1965, when President Johnson had pronounced that Head Start had been "battle tested and proven worthy" (Johnson, 1965, in Zarefsky, 1986, p. 137), $70 million had been expended to establish 11,068 Head Start centers in 2,700 poor communities across the nation (Washington & Oyemade, 1987; Shriver, in Gillette, 1996). Unprecedented for its capacity to mobilize, in such little time, a program that served 561,359 children over a summer in a unique, multifaceted health, education, and human services setting (Zigler, Styfco, & Gilman, 1993), its visible and vocal supporters included a diverse array of public and private citizens such as community organizers, teachers, clergy, social scientists, physicians, congressional wives, and the First Lady (Gillette, 1996). Thus, in a heady rush of enthusiasm, generosity, and excitement, Head Start was embraced as "an ideal symbol for the new war on poverty" (Williams & Evans, 1969) and it was perceived to be an "instant success" (Zigler, Styfco, & Gilman, 1993; Gillette, 1996).

Interestingly, despite President Johnson's glowing assessment of the program, little evaluative data beyond enrollment figures backed up the perception of the program as an unqualified success. In fact, no planned agenda of research or program evaluation that would guide Head Start's administration and implementation was developed during the program's inception (Steiner, 1976; Washington & Oyemade, 1987). Rather, as Steiner (1976) points out, "child development experts moved from experiment to institution without a wide-ranging debate about likely costs, benefits, or alternatives" (p. 29). Instead, and in tune with the Community Action Program emphasis of the OEO, program designers promoted the importance of local autonomy, based on the belief that each community would know what kind of programming low-income children and families needed most (Zarefsky, 1986). Thus, grantees were invited to create programs that attended to what they perceived to be the most salient local needs. President Johnson himself (in Zarefsky, 1986) set the tone for this focus on autonomy in his message to Congress on March 16, 1964, wherein he argued that "each community knows best and should not have plans imposed on it from Washington." Picking up on this perspective, Sargent Shriver noted in a speech in May of that year:

> what will work in Cleveland will not work in Los Angeles, and a program that Chicago might use to fight urban slum poverty will not take

> root in the rocky soil of Appalachia. That is why the heart of poverty legislation is local community action and voluntary participation. (Shriver, in Zarefsky, 1986)

In some cases this perspective proved to be a strength of Head Start as heroic efforts emerged and high-quality programs developed. James Gaither, staff assistant to President Johnson from 1966 to 1969, recalled this era of optimism and experimentation:

> If you read the original OEO act, it is an unbelievable piece of legislation, because it basically just said: "here is a big pot of money, and you can spend it to alleviate the problems of the poor." They just launched these programs without worrying too much about being able to account for every last penny, feeling it was more important to start addressing the problem, start training people, to start getting kids in school, start giving them their first dental checkup, their first health exam, getting parents involved in early childhood education. All of those things they first got started, and the controls came later. (in Gillette, 1996, p. 152)

In many instances, however, as programs have been left to define "good practice" for themselves, quality has suffered (Zigler, in Kramer, 1994, p. 43). While the goal of developing quality services has been a value consistently communicated at the federal level (Richmond, in Gillette, 1996) as additional programming mandates and performance standards were written into law over the years, the view of the need for quality also went hand in hand with the early, optimistic belief that "good intentions" counted the most, and that providing something, anything, for children and families in low-income communities was better than doing nothing.

So, while the mission of Head Start and the attendant standards of performance provided each local program with ideological foundations and programmatic directives, meaningful oversight mechanisms that kept local programs accountable to the original promise that was made to families — regarding assistance, education, empowerment, and economic gain — have all too frequently been traded for idiosyncratic "interpretations of needs" (Fraser, 1989). Without a rigorous program evaluation component (Zigler, Styfco, & Gilman, 1993; Sugarman, in Gillette, 1996) that both guides practice and consistently assesses the way in which policy is operationalized, local interpretations are oftentimes grounded in prejudice and manifested in unequal privilege, power, and politics. Thus, without careful attendance to the tenor of the social relations that exist in programs, and the firm commitment to the ideology of authentic empowerment, the promise of what Head Start could be for communities becomes deferred, and the hope for families, diminished.

This chapter reviews and critiques several aspects of the mission, ideology, and promise of Head Start. The original premise of Head Start will be considered in relation to key programmatic concepts such as empowerment, "maximum feasible participation," local autonomy, policy enforcement, and quality. Each of these issues will be addressed in relation to the promises that are made to parents, particularly regarding support to their families, participation with their children, and the development of meaningful leadership and partnership regarding decision making and administration of the program.

By viewing the policies of the program from a grounded, critical perspective that uses as a framework the social reality of staff and parents in the program, I will explore the question of how policy is perceived, interpreted, and attended to by Head Start staff and parents, and the way in which this policy is then negotiated and translated into practice. As will be illustrated, in this particular program (and in the two centers affiliated with that program that are examined here) the philosophy and mission of the Head Start program was largely not understood, attended to, nor even discussed by the employees. Furthermore, the micropolitics of the setting appear to be influenced by a range of differences that include race, class, ability, experience, and beliefs, in addition to the world of difference that often exists between our behavior and the ideologies we draw upon to interpret and evaluate our experiences.

The scenario that follows illustrates the difficulties that often occur when policy becomes muddied by human interests and the politics of practice. For as Michael Apple (1982) has observed:

> just as the school is caught in contradictions that may be very difficult for it to resolve, so too are ideologies filled with contradictions. . . . Lived meanings, practices and social relations are often internally inconsistent. They have elements within themselves that see through to the heart of the unequal benefits of a society and at one and the same time tend to reproduce the ideological relations and meanings that maintain the hegemony of the dominant classes. (p.15)

MAXIMUM FEASIBLE PARTICIPATION: A BIG DEAL?

The sun and the temperature had both dropped. Despite the early March chill, the man speaking to the group of parents in the crowded preschool classroom was sweating profusely. Clearly uncomfortable, now and then he mopped his brow uneasily with one of the cheap paper napkins from the refreshment table. Seeing his distress, one of the family service workers near him poured him some soda. As she handed it to him the Styrofoam cup shook in his hand and the liquid spilled onto one of the empty chairs, forming a puddle on a stack of papers that the parents had prepared for the meeting. Ignoring the mess, "Mr. Executive Director" proceeded on with the rather windy speech he was delivering.

Seated at the back of the small classroom with my infant son asleep beside me, it was easy to observe what was happening. The executive director of the Morrison County Community Action Program seemed to be nervously reaching for just the right words, while trying to maintain a self-important stance of authority. In response, many of the parents were eyeing him with looks of doubt. Some were whispering to each other. Others simply sat quietly with their arms crossed, listening.

The topic of this meeting, and what the parents were waiting to hear, was whether they would be allowed to organize a graduation ceremony in June for the Head Start preschoolers who would be moving on to kindergarten. In previous years, other centers in the county had ended the year this way, and the parents at the Downtown Center also wanted a graduation complete with miniature caps and gowns, and a visit by Big Bird, who would distribute certificates to the children.

The parents had first approached the Head Start director, Valerie, about their idea. Their request was promptly denied, but with no rationale given. Determined to press the issue, the parents had invited her and her boss (the executive director, Desmond) to discuss the issue at tonight's meeting. They wanted to hear why their proposal had been denied, and they wanted it to be reconsidered.

Although it was often difficult to induce parents to attend evening meetings, parents felt strongly about this issue, and tonight the room was filled with African American and Hispanic parents from the neighborhood surrounding the center. Most of the adults present were mothers, although a few men were also in the audience. Two of the mothers, Francine and Marilyn, had rallied the group for a fight, and as Harriet, one of the center's family service workers had predicted the morning before the meeting, the place was tense:

> It is going to be a pretty heavy meeting. There is going to be a lot of yelling and shouting. Desmond and Valerie are going to be there to talk to parents about this cap-and-gown thing for graduation. Valerie doesn't want to do it and so Marilyn has asked them to come and discuss it.

That same morning Harriet had also told me that she felt that the parents should be able to organize a graduation if they truly wanted to do it, and were willing to work for it.

> Isn't that the whole point of this program, to get parents involved and care about what happens to their kids? Well, they are, and their opinion is being ignored. Administration doesn't really support parents, but sees them as a pain.

Harriet's assessment of the administration's view of parents appeared correct, for at noon that day Valerie had announced that she would not be attending the meeting: she simply refused to discuss a graduation. When that was announced at the beginning of the meeting the parents were indignant, but the group's defiant demeanor had slowly simmered down to a "wait and see" attitude. There had been no guarantee that Desmond, the executive director, would show up either, and after almost ninety minutes of waiting, the group was becoming pretty glum. While they were waiting, Marilyn, a parent who had been a major force behind planning the graduation and mobilizing parents to attend tonight's meeting, stood up and read the letter that she had sent to Valerie. Marilyn then distributed copies of the letter.

> Dear Ms. Browning;
>
> I, Marilyn Tidwell, am writing on behalf of the parents of the children at the Downtown Head Start. . . . In graduating in caps and gowns we believe that the children would gain a sense of achievement . . . and know what it means when they see their older siblings graduate in caps and gowns.
>
> They would know that they have achieved another plateau in their educational climb. . . . What better way to impress upon them that they are learning, growing, achieving and being successful. . . . We know that we are privileged to have Head Start in our community. Let us show that we appreciate what it has done for our children. Let our children walk proud.

> We the parents realize that this is a government funded program, so we are willing to do whatever it takes to see our children graduate in caps and gowns in a closing exercise. We would like your support in helping us to help our children achieve this goal.

As Marilyn read her letter, many heads around the room had nodded in affirmation. They, like many other low-income parents who want to confer hopeful symbols of success onto their children (Kozol, 1991), felt that a graduation ceremony would be positive for their children, and they did not understand why the request had been denied. After Marilyn finished, the group discussed Valerie's decision, and together they speculated on why she had stayed away from tonight's meeting. They also questioned whether Desmond would be coming. Harriet and Fran, the two staff members present, looked quite uncomfortable with the parents' questions and admitted that they did not have any answers for them.

Desmond finally arrived. Bursting into the room without any explanation for his tardiness, or even a friendly hello, he began by scolding the parents for imposing on his time.

> I was not intending to come tonight to speak to you, but I began getting beeped at 6:00 o'clock and so I felt compelled to come. . . . This is taking time away from my family and my important work, which means that now I will be up until midnight at least, completing it.

No one in the room seemed one bit distressed at the possibility that they might have disrupted his night. In fact, just having to be there to plead their case was disrupting their night, and now he was keeping their children up late. As he complained about his own personal problems, the look on their faces could best be summed up as, "who cares?"

After this harsh admonishment, Desmond then abruptly changed his tone. Despite having just told them that they had no business imposing on his time, he now complimented them for "getting involved" in the graduation effort.

> Learning about the ways to interact with the system and change it is key, and is one of the main points of the program. I'm proud to see parents challenging the system, as this is what a community action agency is all about. . . .
>
> I am a parent myself, so I know what it is like to challenge schools for my child's good. I believe that parents know what is best for their child, since they are their first teachers. But, you must remember that

> parents are not educators either. They need input from teachers and educators.

On and on he went, lecturing them about how pleased he was that they were taking an interest in their children, and about the importance of "maximum feasible participation" of parents to the overall mission of Head Start. Yet, by 9:00, thirty minutes into his visit, he had not yet responded to the issue at hand. As his talk stretched on parents began to shift uncomfortably in the toddler-sized chairs, and people began to get up, ducking past him and leaving the room to have a cigarette, check on the children playing in the next room, or to stretch their legs. Some eventually wandered back in, but many ended up standing in the hallway, chatting among themselves. Those in the room rolled their eyes, and looked at the carpet and at each other, as if to say, "enough already!"

Finally, one of the parents interrupted the executive director and pointedly asked him whether there were any written Head Start policies that prohibited graduation ceremonies. He conceded that there were not.

A wave of relief swept over the parents, followed by a barrage of questions. If it was not written policy, then why did Valerie say no? Desmond chose not to respond to this direct question. Rather, he took the middle ground and remarked: "I want you to know that I back the director 150 percent, but I have told her that I didn't consider this to be a big deal, so I want to incorporate parents into the process." As I listened to his answer I pondered its irony: would he have come to meet with the parents if the issue had been "a big deal?" Furthermore, are parents invited to participate only when very minor matters are addressed, and not when the issues are important ones?

Desmond then informed the parents that he had made a decision: a committee made up of parent representatives from each Head Start center in the county would be developed to discuss the matter of a graduation. As a wave of cheers went through the room, I wondered how Valerie would feel about this, since it appeared that he was overturning her decision. Having made that announcement, he readied to leave, but not before circling the room like a true politician, working the crowd and shaking each parent's hand.

I eagerly awaited his approach to me, for while it was mid-year into the program, Desmond and I had not met. Although Valerie had informed him of my research, my phone calls to him had gone unanswered. Thus, I hadn't had the opportunity to speak with him yet. Anticipating that I would now have the chance to introduce myself, I extended my hand as he approached. But, before I could say "Hi, I'm . . .," he brushed quickly by. As I stood there, mouth open in surprise, holding my son in my arms, I began to notice that I was not the only one who was not afforded the chance to speak: no one got to say anything to him. As he quickly moved on to the other parents and then out the door, I realized that he had taken me as just one more parent and treated me accordingly.

When he was gone, Francine quickly ended the meeting. Although it was late, the parents talked excitedly among themselves around the refreshment table. Marilyn and the other parents absolutely glowed from the coup that they felt they had just made, despite the fact that all they were promised was another meeting to discuss it. After helping to clean up the classroom in preparation for the next day's class, I left the building with the family service workers, Harriet and Fran, and Francine, the parent chair.

Talking over coffee the next morning, Harriet told me how Valerie had put her off yesterday, and wouldn't even consider coming to last night's meeting. She also revealed that it was she who had paged Desmond last night, and that at first he too had refused to come talk with the parents. She also told me the tactic she had used to urge him to come.

> I was really upset that neither of them [Valerie or Desmond] was going to come, even though they had been invited. I called him and told him that he really should come to the meeting. . . . I told him about the importance of parent involvement, and why he should come and talk to the group. . . .
>
> I told him that our job is to get obstacles out of parents' way so that they can get active, work with their children, change their lives. So many times they hit dead ends. Things don't work out the way they want them to. . . . As I see it, it's our job to help them learn the channels and procedures that it takes to work within the system. If we don't even let parents have their say, then what are we doing?
>
> What is important to the staff or parents may not be the same, but the process of involving parents is always needed. We may not agree on everything, but don't stop the process of discussing it just because of that. That is all the more reason to involve parents. You gotta let 'em grow. Some of their ideas are kind of kooky, and I may not agree with them, but I think you have to be supportive of what they want, and help them see it through.

While throughout the fall and winter I had become aware of aspects of the program that were less than helpful for parents, up to this point I had wanted to believe that the situation was due to either a lack of resources, benign neglect, or unplanned ineptness. Now, however, with this incident my perceptions of the program were becoming crystallized. In Desmond's response to parents lay the tangible evidence of the hypocritical messages and programmatic contradictions that were inherent in the program. In fact, this contradictory message was apparent in most aspects of the Head Start program in Morrison County. That message was this: "Take an interest in your children, even though we are not really interested in you. And be involved in some small way, but do not bother us, because although the rhetoric of Head Start states that parents are a vital part of the program, they are not really important enough to warrant an investment of our time and energy." Thus, while administrators spoke of ideals of empowerment and emancipation, they treated parents with manipulation and disregard.

THE PARENT INVOLVEMENT MISSION OF HEAD START

From the very first conception of Head Start the rhetoric of parent involvement was accorded an importance not previously seen in educational programming (Zigler & Valentine, 1979). Developed out of the Office of Economic Opportunity and with clear links to that office's Community Action Program, this pioneering emphasis on parent involvement was focused on empowerment of the poor through decision making in the program, and the development of economic self-sufficiency through job placement at the Head Start centers.

By working towards "maximum feasible participation" of poor adults in programs designed to provide needed services and create change in communities, the premise was that "the system" would become more responsive to the needs of the poor. Yet, Zarefsky (1986), among other scholars and historians of the period (e.g., Gillette, 1996), notes that this term, and that of "community action itself, was an ambiguous term that was inherently vague, for legislation did not specify the nature, extent, level, goals, consequences, or standards of participation" (p. 45). In fact, various interpretations of what was by "community action" and "maximum fèasible participation" abounded among policymakers and program planners.

In the introduction of his oral history of the War on Poverty, Gillette (1996) summarily defined it by stating that "involving the poor was considered central to the idea of community action," as a way to "energize impoverished neighborhoods to combat poverty" (p. xix). Yet, disparate views and ways of defining and operationalizing these concepts are reflected in the oral histories that he documents. For example, Frederick O'R. Hayes, former assistant director and then deputy director of the Community Action Program, noted that "the intention was not a radical shift of authority to the poor"; rather, "the school and social services needed to improve what business would call 'customer relations' by doing a better job of listening to, responding to, and communicating with their clients" (in Gillette, 1996, p. 74). Adam Yarmolinsky, chief of staff for the War on Poverty Task Force, concurred, noting that maximum feasible participation "meant that you involved poor people in the process, not that you put them in charge" (in Gillette, 1996, p. 77). Similarly, Kermit Gordon, former director of the Bureau of the Budget noted: "I'm sure all of us at that time thought of community action as organized, controlled, and managed in a sense by elite groups — by the city government, by business groups, by churches, by labor unions, by nonprofit social organizations, welfare bodies, etc." (in Gillette, 1996, p. 78).

Daniel Patrick Moynihan (1969) points out that the phrase "maximum feasible participation" and the entire language of the Economic Opportunity Act that spelled out the functions of the Community Action Programs referred to service provision to the poor rather than their actual empowerment. As he explains, the community-action legislation was worded so as "to ensure that those persons excluded from the political process in the South and elsewhere would nonetheless participate in the benefits of the community action programs of the new legislation" (p. 87). Hence, the purpose of "maximum feasible participation of the residents of the areas and members of the groups involved in the local programs" really related to making certain that service delivery focused on the needs of the poor and not other groups with better political connections. Furthermore, the idea of service delivery was key, not that the poor should truly participate in defining and managing the program. "It was taken as a matter beneath notice that such programs would be dominated by the local political structure," Moynihan asserts.

However, William Cannon, assistant chief of the Office of Legislative Reference in the Bureau of the Budget and who helped craft the OEO legislation, disputed this perspective, noting that:

> maximum feasible participation and community action was supposed to be a method of organizing local political action, community action. It was just that. It was not a delivery system. (in Gillette, 1996, p. 80)

Frank Mankiewicz, director of the Peace Corps and colleague to Shriver, also argued that the intent was to challenge the existing power structures through collective action and remake them with input by the poor.

> Moynihan is wrong when he says that this concept of community action as an essentially revolutionary activity was not understood by the people who drafted it or by the OEO. It was pretty clearly understood by us. (in Gillette, 1996, p. 86)

While it was true that some factions of the administration and the participants in the field believed they were given the green light to foment real, sustaining change (Greenberg, 1969, 1998), this was clearly not a perspective shared by all policy-makers. And, some like Herbert J. Kramer, OEO's Director of Public Affairs, readily admitted: "I don't think anybody fully had an understanding of what community action was" (in Gillette, 1996, p. 192). In actuality, the ambiguity of the term was perceived to be a benefit by some. Harold Horowitz, associate general counsel for HEW, who was assigned to the War on Poverty Task Force, put it this way:

> That's the glorious thing about statutory drafting or writing contracts or things like that. You can fall back on words like "maximum" or "reasonable" and "feasible" and what have you, and fend off questions about what that means specifically. (in Gillette, 1996, p. 81)

Hugh Heclo (1986), in his analysis of federal antipoverty policy, addresses what resulted when policy language was ambiguous, confusing, and ultimately contested.[3]

> On the one hand, community action programs sought to mobilize and empower the poor as a new political force challenging local power centers. On the other hand, community action sought to elicit a coordinated response from local social agencies that were heavily dependent on established political structures. . . . The result was an even more rapid erosion of political support than had greeted similar New Deal aspirations for the rural poor. (p. 322)

In response to the lack of political support for real systemic change, President Johnson's message to Congress on March 16, 1967, laid the groundwork for the dismantling of any true groundswell of grassroots citizen action that might have resulted from antipoverty programming. In that address, Johnson noted that "there should be a requirement for representation of local public agencies on Community Action Boards as well as representation for the neighborhood groups to be served" (in Donovan, 1967, p.137). Reporting on that speech, *The New Republic* summed up this implementation of antipoverty policy by pronouncing that the entire effort had "degenerated into a joke."

> The President officially bid farewell to the original poverty program last week by asking Congress to tie local community action to city hall. . . . The President's latest proposals would turn the whole program into a handy patronage device. . . . What began as an attempt at fundamental change has degenerated into a joke. (*The New Republic*, March 25, 1967, in Donovan, 1967, p. 137)

As is apparent, then, such confusing and contradictory aspects of the War on Poverty left the various programs created during that time without "a clear sense of mission, without a vision of how their goals might be achieved, and without a workable rhetoric" (Zarefsky, 1986, p. xiii). While a radical, social change perspective that stressed social and political empowerment of the poor through collective action and education about the structural inequalities of society and needs of their communities had been envisioned by some of the policy-makers overseeing the development of the program, "controversy . . . ultimately engulf[ed] the community action approach . . . as empowerment of the poor trigger[ed] local power struggles" (Gillette, 1996, p. xvii). Thus, the more radical goals of the antipoverty programming became defused and diluted, and even though the original language of empowerment and emancipation remained intact, the less politically challenging perspective of promoting individual growth and change won out in programs as the years progressed (Valentine & Stark, 1979).

In the place of a social-change approach, the result was politically palatable programming that stressed the need to change individuals, rather than systems. This deficit perspective of parents, children, and families will be addressed more fully in Chapter 4, but in essence programs focused on individual betterment and personal development of parents through therapeutic approaches and the acquisition of resources and skills (such programmatic initiatives will be addressed in Chapters 5 and 6). This view emphasized that individual change, rather than social change, would be the focus of these programs (Valentine & Stark, 1979; Greenberg, 1998; Ames & Ellsworth, 1997).

Head Start's mixed bag of policy and practice imperatives has gone largely without explicit definitions and standards of good practice, particularly as it relates to parents. Therefore, the people whose lives are affected by such lack of clarity in policy are left to the whim of "administrative caprice" (Fraser, 1989, p. 152) as understanding or misunderstanding of policy affects the social relations of power and privilege that exist between program administrators and staff, and between staff and parents.

This is because policy as symbolically reflects social relations and it acts as a mediator of social relations in several ways. First, as Freire and Macedo (1987) explore in their book, *Literacy: Reading the Word and the World*, policy as rhetoric is a form of communication that recreates and reinterprets reality through the act of putting the world into words. Second, while policy and programming imperatives have the potential to be emancipatory when the disenfranchised are partners in its creation (Cervero & Wilson, 1994, 1996), policy in most instances reifies the power and legitimates the authority of its creators (Fraser, 1989). This stage of policy creation and the issue of who is involved in defining what the needs are and who is deemed needy sets the stage for all further interpretations and actions regarding program creation and implementation.

Third, when policy is linked to expert knowledge and professionalism it is difficult to read and understand by those outside the inner circle of policy development. As such, a gatekeeper or interpreter (the "helping" professional) is needed to help others (the needy client) understand how reality is constructed and how it should be interpreted (Mickelson & Klenz, 1998).

Finally, policy is not only related to symbolic power; it also gets translated into dollars, and thus, not only intersects with social relations, but functions to define the material conditions of individuals and groups. Therefore, in the day-to-day process of program implementation, the kind of practice that is offered in programs is negotiated within the parameters of the policy and in response and in relation to the material conditions, human interests, diversity of goals, perceptions of power, and ethics (Ball, 1987) that those very policies have circumscribed. In a similar way, policy affects evaluation functions, whether they occur, how they are carried out and by whom, and to what end the information is used. Thus, social relations affect, and are affected by, the development of policy and all that ensues as a result of its creation: the interpretation of programmatic mission and goals, the development of rationale for appropriation and allocation of funding, the selection of methods and techniques for administration and implementation of programming, and the assessment of programmatic outcomes.

In Head Start, while parents were always an integral part of the program design, their actual role, while symbolically intact, has been somewhat ambiguous, contested, and subject to interpretation by practitioners in programs. Involvement of parents in the governance of the program was first written into law in 1967 (P.L. 90-222, Sec. 222 [a][1][b]; Head Start Bureau, 1967), and then formalized in 1970 in the Head Start document known as "70.2." Included as Part B of the *Head Start Policy Manual*, the document that provided local programs with information about the overall mission of Head Start and the performance standards and objectives of each service component, the 70.2 document outlined in detail specific roles and functions for parents in the program. The language in this document provides a glimpse of the worthy goals and idyllic aspirations upon which the program was founded:

> Head Start believes that the gains made by the child in Head Start must be understood and built upon by the family and the community. To achieve this goal, Head Start provides for the involvement of the child's parents and other members of the family. . . . Every Head Start Program is obligated to provide the channels through which such participation and involvement can be provided for and enriched. Unless this happens, the goals of Head Start will not be achieved and the program itself will remain a creative experience for the preschool child in a setting that is not reinforced by needed changes in social systems into which the child will move after his (or her) Head Start experience. . . . This involvement begins when a Head Start program begins and should gain vigor and vitality as planning and activities go forward. . . . Project Head Start must continue to discover new ways for parents to become deeply involved in decision-making about the program and in the development of activities that they deem helpful and important in meeting their particular needs and conditions . . . (Appendix B, Head Start Policy Manual — The Parents, I-30-2 (a) Introduction, *OCD-HS Head Start Policy Manual: Head Start Program Performance Standards*, 1970)

Having served as a guide to programs for twenty-seven years, the *Head Start Performance Standards* were recently revised and new standards went into effect in January, 1998 (Federal Register, 61: 214, Tuesday, November 5, 1996, *Head Start Performance Standards*). Although in 1970 the guidelines stipulating what types of information and education should be provided and what parent participation should look like (in areas such as education, health, nutrition, parent activities, and program management) were presented with emphatic clarity, this new document, according to the Federal Register, "*simplifies and reorganizes the standards in an effort towards increasing programs' understanding of their obligations* [emphasis mine], and to encourage the integration of the range of service activities that programs are to provide" (Federal Register, 61: 214, Tuesday, November 5, 1996, *Head Start Performance Standards*). This statement suggests that Head Start staff members must have lacked an understanding of these policies. Indeed, this research indicates that orientation and training regarding the policies, and then subsequent enforcement and adherence to the policy of parent involvement is a very real issue that goes beyond problems with clarity. In other words, while all staff may not understand the policies, those who do understand them still may not be supporting or following them for other reasons.[5]

Nevertheless, in both the original and revised documents, the important role that parents play in a child's life continues to be recognized, and each Head Start program and center is required to have a plan to involve parents in all areas of the program. Furthermore, the new proposed standards not only retain the range of emphases on parent involvement, but also add required programmatic initiatives. Thus, the new *Head Start Performance Standards* are designed to strengthen the policy of parent involvement, reminding programs that efforts with parents should be defined as "working in partnership with them." Areas with partnership potential include opportunities such as volunteering in a variety of program areas, educational programming, access to family services and assistance, and leadership development. For example, programs are to promote parent involvement through participation in home visits and parent/teacher conferences; by organizing committees and fund-raisers; assisting in the classroom and on field trips; and through the development of parent-initiated activities, workshops, and conferences (Adams, 1976; Abt Associates, 1978; Andrews, 1981; Washington, 1985; Copeland, 1987; Office of Child Development, 1970; 1996).

While parents cannot be mandated to participate in any of these activities, the guidelines state that programs are required to offer them to parents. Furthermore, programs are to have in place an effective system of communication that ensures that all parents receive information about both the availability of and the range of opportunities open to them.

In the Head Start guidelines (both 1970 and 1996), it is required that programs provide parents with a physical space in which to meet and participate in activities. They must be allowed to have access to the building at all times and always be "welcomed as visitors and encouraged to observe children and participate in group activities." Programs are mandated to offer training workshops for parents in topics such as parenting, nutrition, health, and first aid, and the new policy also now requires that programs offer parents adult literacy services, either on site, or by referral. Furthermore, parents must be provided the opportunity and support to "work together, and with other community members, on activities that they have helped develop and in which they have expressed an interest" (*Head Start Program Performance Standards*, 1996, Subpart C: Family and Community Partnerships, [g]2).

Family support and assistance with needs has always been an emphasis in the policies as well. While "family needs assessments" have been required upon enrollment from the beginning of Head Start, the new guidelines stipulate that parents now be active partners in this effort, and be given the "opportunity to create, in conjunction with the Head Start staff, an individualized *Family Partnership Agreement* that articulates each family's responsibilities and goals, as well as the timetables and strategies they will use for meeting those goals." Relatedly, so that parents can act on the fulfillment of their parental responsibilities as provider, guardian, and first teacher, programs are required to regularly provide parents with updated listings of social service resources. While not stated as such, it is presumed that if requested, families will be assisted with services, referrals, and resources as they go about the implementation of their goal-related strategies. Also notably absent in this policy are suggestions for parent and program advocacy in relation to the development or enhancement of services that might not be available for families, although needed.

As a means of helping parents to achieve self-sufficiency, provisions for the creation of jobs for parents in the program have been emphasized in both 1970 and 1996 policies. The policies state that "current and former parents must receive preference for employment vacancies for which they are qualified" (*Head Start Program Performance Standards*, 1996, Subpart D, 1304.52, [b]3). However, because no paid employees (or any member of their immediate family) are allowed to serve on any policy or parent committees, if parents should become employed with the program during the year in which their child is enrolled, they are required to relinquish any active roles with these bodies that they may have been assuming. While parents may continue to attend parent functions and work with committees in perfunctory ways, by agreeing to employment they give up the right to vote on any matters.

The leadership roles for parents and the importance of the parental partnership function as it relates to the management of the program are also spelled out in the *Head Start Performance Standards*. Parents are to have input into programmatic areas such as the "development of the program's curriculum" and "planning, implementing, and evaluating the program's nutrition services." Opportunities through which parents can participate in such "shared governance" (including policy- and decision-making with the program) exist at two levels: the center level, where they can serve as officers for each of the Head Start center's parent committees, and the county or program level, where they can be involved on Policy Council and other Head Start committees.

The mandate of active involvement of parents on "Policy Council" addresses the fundamental principle upon which Head Start was founded. This aspect of the program, more so than any other, was to serve the function of developing community-based leaders and to train and empower parents in ways that they could be advocates for their children. This partnering of parents with management was pioneering in its premise, as was the mandate that this "board of directors" must be made up of at least 51 percent of parents whose children were enrolled in Head Start. Yet, how much input parents actually have on these boards remains a question.

TAKING A BACK SEAT IN MORRISON COUNTY: THE CHARADE OF PARENT INVOLVEMENT

At the Morrison County Head Start program, sixteen people were on the Policy Council; ten of these were parent representatives. Parent representatives are elected by the parents from each center, with the number of elected representatives differing depending on the size of the center they serve. For example, in Morrison County the large Downtown Center had three parent representatives, while the smaller Harbor Street Center had only one parent representative.

The Policy Council's function is to both oversee and participate in the entire administrative functioning of the program, including collaboratively making decisions regarding grant and program development, fiscal oversight, program evaluation, curriculum development, employment and personnel practices, including hiring, parent involvement, and program communication, among other responsibilities. In carrying out these responsibilities, Head Start's paid administrators are supposed to work closely with their Policy Council. Recognizing that shared power and empowerment of parents must be goals in the program, the following admonition to administrators was stated in the 1970 program policies.

> It may not be easy for Head Start Directors and professional staff to share responsibility when decisions must be made . . . [but] the Head Start staff must take care to avoid dominating meetings. . . ." (*Head Start Program Performance Standards*, 1970, Appendix B, The Parents, Head Start Policy Council)

In fact, parents in the Morrison County Head Start had very little power in most of their stipulated program roles, a point that will be more fully addressed in Chapter 6. In the following situation, however, their lack of power in the management of the program is illustrated. In this section it can be seen how Desmond, the executive director of Head Start's sponsoring Community Action Program, controlled the parents' input in virtually every area of the program.

The month was June, and the last Policy Council meeting of the year was scheduled to begin. Nearly everyone had assembled, but Raymond, the elected chairperson and a parent representative from the Morrow Street Center, was not yet there. Rather than wait for him to arrive, however, Desmond took the lead and began to conduct the meeting: "Since we have a lot of business to do tonight, I want the regular meeting suspended. Let's just clean up the issues [the proposed agenda items] for the year and proceed with the issue of next year's enrollment. . . ."

He then instructed Francine to make a motion that tonight's agenda, except for the selection of next year's Head Start families, be canceled. It was surprising to me that she did just that, and without hesitation. Another parent seconded the motion. A vote was then taken and the motion passed. There was no discussion regarding the items of business on the agenda, nor about whether Desmond had any authority to take this sweeping action.

Shortly thereafter Raymond arrived. As Raymond, who had a somewhat severe disability, limped into the room, Desmond greeted him in a loud, jocular tone. "Raymond, we did you a big favor tonight! We suspended your whole agenda!"

In response, Raymond frowned and looked puzzled. But instead of saying anything, he looked down at the floor, and then around the room, trying to locate an empty seat. They had all been taken. No one, it seemed, had saved a chair for the Chairman.

Finally, after a moment of uncomfortable silence as those in the room looked uneasily around — and anywhere but at Raymond — Harriet, a family service worker at the Downtown Center, offered him her seat. It was way off in the corner, however, not at the head of the table where the chairman of the Policy Council should sit, and where Desmond now stood. As he slowly limped over to the corner, his head down and shoulders stooped, Raymond's disability seemed especially pronounced, and in a metaphor made manifest he slowly, silently, settled into the only place offered him: a "back seat" in Head Start.

Francine, the parent chair at the Downtown Head Start, had regularly shared with me her views that Raymond was powerless. In fact, she derided him, noting that "he does whatever Desmond and Valerie want him to do." While critical of his lack of power, in this incident she didn't see her complicity in his disempowerment. When I asked her about her motion to suspend the agenda, she explained that it was the excitement of having the opportunity to "really make decisions about the program . . . and to choose next year's families" that had motivated her into complying. In fact, the "decision making" that took place that night regarding the selection of families was ceremonial only, for the family service workers merely presented a presorted list of applications that parents then perfunctorily reviewed. This power of the pen, the act of placing their signature on the application form indicating that they had approved this family's selection, was a seductive form of pseudo-power that other researchers have also seen in Head Start (Ames & Ellsworth, 1997).

Another incident, this one also involving Francine and her signatory role, provides another example of how the administration was successful in, as Francine called it, "shutting up" parents. This situation regarded the annual evaluation process of the program that, under law, the Policy Council was responsible for undertaking in conjunction with the administration and other members of the community. This process of self-review was one of the few regular oversight mechanisms that the Federal government used to monitor programs. Programs were to assess their effectiveness and progress in meeting program goals, and in following federal regulations.

Referred to here as the "SAVI," the Morrison County Head Start had not been using this survey-like instrument on a yearly basis as a means of assessing any shortcomings that might exist in the program. This year, parents were upset and frustrated about a number of aspects of the program, particularly the parent involvement and leadership aspects of the program. In response, Francine had made the motion in Policy Council requesting that the SAVI be undertaken. Despite the fact that the guidelines were clear that the process was to be collaborative and open, and that programs were obligated to report any shortcomings to the federal government, along with plans for improvement, in this year at least, it appeared as if the administrators did not want the evaluation completed in a truthful and forthright manner. Harriet related how events in this situation had transpired.

> Francine had requested that they do this self-assessment, the SAVI. Well, they did all the components but ours, social services and parental involvement. They told Francine, and us, that we could do nothing with it, that it had to all be done at the main office. But, they told her that [before they could do this section] she had to sign off on it. At first she signed the paper, but then she realized that they would be able to write in anything that they wanted, and have it look like she approved of it. So, she wrote an official letter and told them she wanted her name taken off of it.

By the end of the program year in June, an angry and frustrated Francine still had not gotten any response from Desmond or Valerie. In fact, no one could get any firm answers about the evaluation, including myself. Eventually she resigned herself to accepting the fact that she had acted too hastily, and vowed that she would "know better next time."

LOCAL AUTONOMY, COMPLIANCE, AND QUALITY: A CONTRADICTION IN TERMS

Harriet had more to say about the way in which the honor-code system of self-assessment and program evaluation worked, and how administrators could "make the program look good."

> We may look good on paper, be in compliance and everything, but a lot of times that is just because of the way they put it. . . . Like, well, on the books, since the paperwork is done, it looks as if the home visit was made, like we know what everybody's home situation is like. Well, that's not the case, but they sure aren't going to tell regional [supervisors] that.

According to the *Head Start Performance Standards*, programs that do not provide for each of the specified program areas, including the requirements regarding parent involvement, are considered "out of compliance." The original Head Start policy document outlined what needed to be in place regarding parents if a program is to be considered "in compliance":

> The content of the program *should* [emphasis theirs] include:
>
> Training in all program components, in a way which allows parents to understand the Head Start program as an interrelated whole and to facilitate parent participation in the preparation of the work plan and budget.
>
> [Training regarding] ways in which parents can assist staff in setting the goals of the local program and the goals of other community institutions concerned with children and families, in a way which allows parents and staff to see these goals as an interrelated system. . . .
>
> Training that occurs in a planned and continuous fashion, beginning with and continuing through the grantee's funding cycle, with adequate parental input in the design and evaluation of the program. (Subpart E, Section 1304.5-5, Parent Involvement Plan Content: Parents, Area Residents, and the Program, (1-3) pp. 61-62, *OCD-HS Head Start Policy Manual: Head Start Program Performance Standards*)

Valerie, Head Start director in Morrison County, explained that she did not like having to interact with the parents in the program. She often found it to be "irritating to have to deal with the parents in the program," so in previous years she had delegated her role to the family services coordinator. After reporting this to the Head Start officials, however, she now had to do the job herself, so the program would be in compliance.

> Most years it is okay, it is usually a fairly structured thing. But honestly, between you and me, I hate it. Policy Council has always been a pain, but this year it's even worse. It's my job, so I have to do it. Lorna used to do it, but then we were viewed as out of compliance and I had to take it on.

As Valerie described, programs were to adhere to the honor code that accompanied this autonomous system of evaluation, and were required to report any and all problems. Programs deemed out of compliance are required to produce a "quality improvement plan," that details how the particular problem will be resolved. Programs that report severe problems are considered "deficient," and must adhere to an improvement plan designed, not by themselves, but by the Head Start officials. Those who do not correct these faults "within the prescribed time period" are subject to losing their funding, and being shut down.

Despite such policies, there is very little oversight of the management in programs to ensure that what is being noted on the forms is in fact real, or even agreed to by all parties. In reality, very little paperwork and reporting has been required of programs. As Julius Richmond, the first national director of Head Start, noted during the program's formative years: "we tried to set up reporting systems that would assure accountability," but there was difficulty "in getting people to fill out forms when they were in the midst of caring for children" (in Gillette, 1996, p. 296). This laissez-faire attitude set the tone for the development of a constellation of factors that have impeded program oversight and evaluation. For example, allocations for research, demonstration, and evaluation (RDE) have typically been minimal. Washington and Bailey (1995) report that in 1974 only 2.5 percent of the overall Head Start budget was earmarked for research and evaluation. By 1989, this percentage had dropped to about one tenth of one percent (.11 percent) of the total budget. While overall appropriations for Head Start have increased during the 1990s, along with increases in the RDE budget, 1997 appropriations for this category remained at only one third of one percent (.34) of total allocations (U. S. Department of Health and Human Services, 1997).

Reductions in training and technical assistance were cited by the National Head Start Association (in Washington & Bailey, 1995, p. 122) as a key programmatic concern during the 1980s, as program visits and monitoring capabilities were decreased. In today's allocations, program monitoring and review make up approximately one quarter of one percent (.27) of overall budget (U.S. Department of Health and Human Services, 1997).

In fact, Head Start has historically placed little emphasis on program quality, evaluation, or oversight (Chafel, 1992). For example, few or no standards have regulated the qualifications of nonteaching staff (Omewake, 1979; U. S. General Accounting Office, 1994) in the past, and Edward Zigler, one of Head Start's founders and a staunch advocate, estimated that only 40 percent of Head Start programs have been thought to be providing quality services, and 30 percent should be shut down (in Kramer, 1993). Yet, as Zigler and Styfco (1993) have observed, with little meaningful oversight of programs being undertaken, Head Start grantees rarely lose their funding.

Too often in the past, when the program's budget was expanded, the emphasis was only on opening more spaces for more children. As Zigler (1994) has observed:

> quality problems have actually plagued Head Start since its hasty beginnings. In a matter of a few months, the program was transformed from an idea before the planning committee to a national summer preschool serving over one-half million children. Quality controls were left behind, and the program has been playing catch up ever since. (p. 38)

Thus, while it is laudable that Head Start expanded enrollment 67 percent from 1989 to 1995 (Powell, 1996), as Zigler (1994) notes, "simply throwing money at the program is not the way to help Head Start grow" (p. 44). While the passing of the Head Start Expansion and Improvement Act of 1990 was designed to begin to remedy the past lack of emphasis on quality, the result has been growth that has been "frenzied, and not well planned" (Zigler, 1994, p. 39). Indeed, according to the General Accounting Office (1994), programs were given more money to enroll more children but the attendant required resources of additional staff, adequate facilities, and appropriate and effective training initiatives were often not readily available. So, while the 1990 legislation provided major increases in funding and provisions for quality improvement, including improved oversight, as a national program, Head Start continues to play "catch up." Even with the disbursement of quality improvement moneys, the fiscal reality is somber at best: the $523 million granted to programs specifically for "quality improvement" between 1991 and 1995 computes to a yearly average of only $715 per staff member, or $2,461 per Head Start classroom (U.S. Department of Health and Human Services, 1997).

In the meantime, as low levels of programmatic oversight and too few quality initiatives have predominated over the years, the problems and concerns of the families and communities that the program is designed to serve have become more complex. Head Start staff are now confronted with problems that they are likely to be unprepared for and unskilled to deal with (Zigler & Styfco, 1993); child abuse and domestic violence, drug abuse and gangs, teen pregnancy, single parenthood, homelessness, and AIDS (to name only a few) make the job of providing services more complex and demanding. Indeed, the world of service needs and service provision in the 1990s is different than that of the mid-1960s and 1970s when the program was designed (Zigler, 1994). And yet, while the problems of children and families have become more intractable, requiring greater levels of expertise, empathy, and vision, the capacity of the program to meet their needs is questionable. This situation is made more problematic when the mission of the program is vague, not consensually shared among Head Start staff members, and without clear and direct practical implications for practice.

THE MISSION OF HEAD START IN MORRISON COUNTY

The Head Start program in Morrison County struggled with a lack of material resources. And, in the same way that this Head Start had fiscal problems and its facilities were not fully functional, the mission of the program as it related to parent involvement was also not fully realized, despite the policies of Head Start that spelled out the ways in which parents were to be involved and what kinds of activities were to be offered to them. Hence, as will be illustrated throughout this book, practice at this Head Start corresponded very little with what the policies indicated it should be.[5] Such an outcome is not surprising when Head Start staff not only had divergent views of the mission, but also did not discuss with each other what those views were. Furthermore, some staff members admitted that they had no clear view of the mission, since they had not thought much about it. Lillian, the nurse at the Downtown Center, expressed confusion regarding the goal of parent involvement:

> I don't know really. I guess to get them to come in and help us. We need them just to help out, to answer phones, to get the door, help in the classrooms, things like that. (Lillian, nurse, Downtown Center)

Those staff who were able to articulate their perspective of the mission of Head Start had a range of differing perceptions. These perspectives were often related to their role in the program. Their responses regarding the mission of parent involvement could be grouped into five areas: an exclusive child-centered perspective of the mission; a behavioristic focus emphasizing a deficit perspective of parents; a humanistic mission of personal support to parents; a social service orientation focusing on helping parents learn to interact with human service systems; and a more radical emphasis of empowering parents to challenge the systems that serve their families.

The child-centered approach to parent involvement was expressed by teachers in the program. To these women, the key purpose of parent participation was to ensure that the children achieved success, rather than a primary focus on any adult-centered outcomes. Examples of these kinds of comments include the following: "to get them involved, for their children's sake" (Miss Billie, teacher aide, Downtown Center) and "to help the children, to get them ready" (Miss Anita, Cedar Heights Center).

The deficit perspective of parents and the concomitant idea of "fixing" behavioral flaws in individual parents was frequently expressed by staff members whose job it was to provide services to families.

> I see the mission as giving parents direction. A lot don't have the proper idea of what being a parent is. They didn't have structure in their own lives growing up, and don't see what they need to be to be a good parent. They also need to learn how to follow through on things, like taking their child to the doctor or dentist, getting their immunizations. Many don't understand that health status can affect their child's learning ability. (Sally, nurse, Harbor Street Center)

> One thing that is so important is to help them get organization in their lives . . . so that they can get their problems on focus and then act towards fixing them. (Joyce, family service worker, Harbor Street Center)

Some staff, particularly those who had been former parents with the program, stressed the idea of personal support, and the comforting role that they believed Head Start was to provide to parents.

> Many of these parents have low self-esteem, like I did, and seeing their children progress gives them a positive outlook. (Miss Carla, Downtown Center)

> To reach people that really need to be reached. There are a lot of needy people out there. A lot of them are under tremendous pressure, financially, personally. Head Start should be helping these parents out of poverty. It should be a social thing for them too. (Miss Charlotte, Downtown Center)

Other staff, such as administrators, emphasized the idea of "learning how to interact" with the systems that serve their child. This concept of interaction was related to helping parents develop understanding of how the system worked, and how to fit into it, not how to challenge it. This idea of "appropriate involvement" is addressed fully in Chapter 6.

> Besides the social service work with parents, the goal here should be to help parents learn how to interact positively with school personnel. (Valerie, Head Start director)

> Our job is to help parents learn how to appropriately interact with the institutions that serve their children. (Elizabeth, special needs coordinator)

Only a few staff, those who had been former parents and those with a long tenure in the program, expressed the view that the mission of parent involvement was one of empowerment with the goal of challenging, much less having a hand in *shaping* the system.

> We need to help parents learn how not to let people intimidate them, that their opinions count. . . . (Fran, family service worker, Downtown Center)

> So many times they [parents] hit dead ends, things don't work out the way they want them to. We're supposed to be there to guide them, but often times we're the ones [Head Start] who put those walls against them. The staff get mad at me when I say that sometimes, but it's true. As I see it, it's our job to help them learn the channels and procedures that it takes to work with the system. . . . I tell 'em [parents], if you see a problem, address it! Don't take nothing from administration just 'cause they say so. (Harriet, family service worker, Downtown Center)

Although each of the concepts that staff expressed were consistent with the various themes within the Head Start program goals, the staff realized that they were not agreeing on the purpose of parent involvement and the role that parents should be taking in the program, nor were they discussing their views with each other. Marlene, the manager of the Downtown Center, was one of many who admitted that she had never talked about this issue with the family service workers or any of the other staff.

> We never discussed it. I really don't know what they stress or what they tell parents about the program. (Miss Marlene, teacher, Downtown Center)

Valerie, the Head Start director, recognized that there were diverging views among the staff, as well as a lack of discussion regarding the mission of parent involvement. She also appeared resigned to that fact.

> I don't think we have one [a mission], not a clear one anyway. What we expect for parents, and from parents, is muddled. There's a lack of clarity on the part of staff. The family service workers think it's fund-raisers for toys, and the other staff disagree. But getting them to talk about it is another thing entirely. (Valerie, Head Start director)

Barrie, the health coordinator, spoke extensively about the problem in communication, and the need for a common mission in the program.

> There's no common mission about what to do with parents and why. This is true among family service workers, nurses, teachers, the branch managers, and even the administration. They should all work together in this regard, and they don't . . . But it's elemental . . . everyone has to be on the same wavelength. Communicating with others, knowing how to work with and talk to parents is also essential. What we need is a theme for the year, have a clear mission, and some goals to meet. We need a training about this, with all staff, at all levels, to come to a consensus, and then do it. But there's no vision, from the top on down. We need to come to a consensus on a mission, or, come up with a clear directive, and then ask those who don't buy into it to leave. Instead, there's just a lot of bad feelings among the staff, and no one, not the parents, the children, or the staff wins.

Others on staff concurred with her view, and were quite discouraged.

> A lot of times it's just really discouraging . . . But it's hard to do what you want to do for parents when staff don't work together to make it successful. I just think that it's important that everybody work together with parents. (Miss Anita, former parent and teacher, Cedar Heights Center)

In these comments it is evident that when the mission of a program is not consensually shared at all levels, the various interpretations can result in contradictions, constraints, and conflicts, thus affecting subsequent policies, programming, and outcomes. In fact, because they were not communicating about the role of parents, staff members were often working at cross-purposes. For example, while the teachers were supposed to encourage parents to help in classrooms and on field trips, and family services workers reported that parents were always needed for these events, Marlene had a very different perspective on the issue:

> No, we really don't need the parents to help. We'll have a teacher, an aide, a bus driver and a bus aide, so we don't need parents. Sometimes they'll express an interest and just come, but we don't ask them. (Miss Marlene, teacher, Downtown Center)

HUMAN CAPITAL AND CAPITAL CREATION: GOOD FOR SOMETHING

Curiously, however, parents were seen as being needed in one regard, or "good for something." The myopic focus on fund-raising that was found in this program[6] (and that, relatedly, is also a cornerstone of parent involvement efforts in preschool and K–12 settings around the country), for example, indicates how the various approaches to parent involvement in Head Start have shifted from radical, to humanistic, to capitalistic philosophies. Parents are now seen as human capital — individuals who produce funds for the program. Their role as entrepreneurs, marketers, and creators of capital for the program is structural in origin, because of the lack of adequate fiscal resources made available to the program.

Yet, it is ironic that this human-capital perspective is lacking in other areas of the program. While the intent of the parent involvement component was to help children and families achieve economic self-sufficiency, historically little or no effort ever went beyond placing parents into low-paying jobs in the program. In a pointed critique of the contradictions within this aspect of the program, Cahn and Passett (1971) assert that

> while job placement has been a component of citizen participation, it is a fallacy to assume that such efforts can in any way make meaningful change when the job is so low-skilled and low-waged that people remain in poverty, when the job offers no meaningful training and advancement opportunities, when acceptance of the job disenfranchises them from providing any meaningful input into the workplace or program, and when the workplace is antagonistic to the formation of unions which would allow employees to develop a collective voice. (p. 39)

So, although both President Johnson and Sargent Shriver stressed that the mission of the OEO was "a hand up, not a hand out," and was intended to "stimulate self-help rather than welfare dependence" (p. xv), little initiative in this regard occurred. While Zigler and Muenchow (1992) report that the Head Start Supplementary Training Program resulted in 12,000 Head Start staff receiving some college credits by 1973, and that at least 1,000 individuals acquired either their A.A. or B.A. degree through this support, many others did not participate in this program. Furthermore, while the Child Development Associate (CDA) program, which was developed under the leadership of Edward Zigler in 1972, was very innovative in that it made available community college–level training to some Head Start staff, few employees proportionate to the actual numbers of staff actually received this training.[7] Furthermore, with this program's focus only on child care and employment in child-care settings (although vitally needed), it provided a training mechanism for only those parents and staff who wanted to pursue that line of work, which was then, and remains today, gender segregated, low status, and grossly underpaid regardless of the importance of the work involved — that of caring for our children.

KEEPING THE PROMISE TO PARENTS AND FAMILIES: AN ETHICAL IMPERATIVE

The political reality of near silence in the program regarding the mission of parent involvement, in combination with the program's poor material conditions, was the unstable foundation upon which staffs' ability, interest, and willingness in working with parents was based. The result was that programming for and with parents had little priority, despite the fact that written policies of Head Start stressed that parents should be considered integral, active partners in the program. As Harriet commented to me:

> The teachers forget that this program is not just for kids. It's for the whole family, and we are supposed to be working together. The teachers just don't see the whole picture. (Harriet, family service worker, Downtown Center)

The disjuncture that existed between the intentions of written policy and the realities of practice in this program thus reminds us that policy, and thus power, has moral and ethical implications. Foucault (1980) identified two sets of concerns in this realm: the political relations of power (what goes on between people) and the ethical (one's actions in relation to the institution). Because these actions and relations may shift, and the kinds of daily practice decisions that one makes may be the result of, or in spite of, one's role in the system, we must affix moral responsibilities to policies and to our actions (Cervero & Wilson, 1994).

Indeed, the promises that schools, human services, and programs like Head Start make to parents and families when they suggest that involvement, empowerment, and education are possible, have ethical and moral implications. As Larry Kennedy (1991, pp. 7, 25), a nonprofit human service consultant, has stated:

> when a client arrives at the doors . . . he or she may be carrying a huge personal burden well beyond the scope of the services offered by the volunteers and staff. It is essential, therefore, that the nonprofit [organization] promise only what it can deliver, and that it deliver on its promises. . . . [thus] when measuring the quality of your services, the goodness of your mission pales by comparison with the soundness of doing things right.

Put another way, it is ethically imperative that both individuals and organizations constantly question their actions in relation to their mission (Knauft, Berger, & Gray, 1991), and link, as Kennedy (1991, p. 7) has suggested, the mission of the organization with "personal character, organizational honesty, and competence."

Related to this ethical imperative of honest, competent programming is the fact that as Head Start programming became more individualized and less politicized, the mission and goals of the program focused more on personal problems of families than on collective needs of families in low-income communities. In doing so, the irony of changing from a community action emphasis to individual skills development cannot be overstated, for even while shifting to this approach the emphasis on hiring grassroots members of the community — primarily parents in the program — remained. Yet, such vastly different approaches to programming require very different skills, levels of training, and experience of the staff who are responsible for carrying out these functions. And when differences in programming occur without significant changes in the requisite skills of the staff, it not only compromises the potential well-being of the families in the program, but that of the staff in the program who are made to feel unsupported, inadequate, and ill-equipped. In other words, it is not only an ethical issue, but one of justice as well. As we will explore in the following chapter, when staff, who may be highly dedicated but provided with few resources (material, informational, etc.), are asked to tackle difficult and intractable problems that they may have little knowledge of, then it compromises them as well — their feelings of efficacy, their sense of self, and their view of what is possible. And in a program that is supposed to empower, not degrade, this is a grave contradiction. In essence then, with no career path that builds staff as skillful employees of the program and that matches their needs, the needs of the program, and the needs of the families, Head Start can be seen simply as a holding zone — not a real head start.

In conclusion, along many lines, in spite of the rhetoric about its importance, the Head Start leadership at the national level has done little to support parent participation and programming. Commenting on the watered-down meaning of *maximum feasible participation of parents* as early as the 1970s, Cahn and Passett (1971, p. 39) noted that "citizen participation does not mean the illusion of involvement, the opportunity to speak without being heard, and the receipt of token benefit." In fact, I would suggest that the historical absence of better funding of the entire program (child-centered and adult programming), which would include necessary fiscal resources for parent involvement personnel, training, and research in this area, indicates that this tokenism has proceeded unchecked, and despite its stated ideology, parent involvement is nothing more than a shallow promise. In fact, it seems that within both the mindset of policy-makers and the actual practice of Head Start program personnel, the idea of parents as important partners has shifted from "the zone of deviance and moral suspicion" (Polakow, 1993) to a "zone of indifference" (Bolman & Deal, 1991, p. 198).

Furthermore, the neglect of a focus on parental participation at the national level legitimates the limited emphasis and energy about issues of parent involvement at the local level. Indeed, with too few resources, a lack of a clear moral imperative, and virtually no oversight, the Morrison County parent programming efforts were not only downplayed to perfunctory levels, but authentic efforts at actively involving parents as meaningful programmatic partners were actively resisted. Therefore, the reality of parent involvement as a component of Head Start is revealed for its inconsistencies: rather than being integral, central, and imperative, it has been made marginal. In the course of dissipating this mission, low-income parents themselves have also been marginalized and disempowered, and the hope of enfranchising them, as authentic leaders and contributors to the program has been largely lost.

And yet, as will be seen in the following chapter, most of the staff themselves were largely disempowered, silenced, excluded from input. The social relations of the program and the reasons for the silence among them is the focus of Chapter 3. As will be illustrated, a host of programmatic problems afflicted the program, in addition to its lack of material resources and shared vision of the scope and purpose of parent involvement. These programmatic problems include issues such as staff preparation, education and experience, programmatic orientation and training, coordination, supervision, and accountability. Each of these factors affected staff relations, access to resources, and levels of power. These micropolitics of the staff in turn influenced the absence of dialogue that existed about the mission of parent involvement.

NOTES

[1] The Community Action Program within the Office of Economic Opportunity had emphasized collective action and the mobilization of the poor as a means of challenging existing social and political conditions that kept them marginalized, disenfranchised, and underemployed. Officials in local communities who participated in OEO programs thus were obliged to support their own downfall, so to speak. Gillette's (1996) fascinating oral history of the War on Poverty provides local reactions to such federal policies.

[2] This quote is an excellent example of the deficit view of low-income families that pervaded the program and the stigma that is connected to being low-income in this society, then and now.

[3] Note that even this language treats the poor as a target of mobilization, rather than seeing them as capable of mobilizing themselves through the vehicle of such programs.

[4] Chapters 4 through 8 explore the numerous non-training or clarity-related reasons why the staff may not be adhering to the *Head Start Performance Standards* regarding parental involvement.

[5] While this study focuses on this particular Head Start, data on caseload levels of family service/parent involvement staff indicate that significant numbers of programs have also not fully implemented parent involvement programming according to policy guidelines. See Ames & Ellsworth (1997) and Payne et al. (1973).

[6] See Chapter 7 for a full discussion on the contradictions regarding fundraising in the program.

[7] According to Zigler & Muenchow (1992), as a result of the creation of the CDA in 1972, over the course of a twenty-year period 30,000 Head Start teachers have participated in this employee development program. Yet, while successful as an innovation, these numbers should be significantly higher, as last year alone Head Start had 85,000 teachers and teacher aides in 42,500 classrooms. Due to efforts at increasing quality, as of 1994 (Zigler, Styfco, & Gilman, 1993) at least one staff member in each classroom was required to hold the CDA; thus, those numbers should have gone up significantly between 1994 and 1999. Further-

more, the new Head Start Performance Standards that went into effect in January of 1998 eventually require classroom teachers to hold an A.A. or B.A., and staff in supervisory roles must have B.A.s. Chapter 3 goes in-depth into the training and qualifications of Head Start personnel. Part of the problem in low participation rates lies in the fact that Head Start has only in some years provided tuition assistance to employees. And with chronically low pay scales (see Chapter 3), Head Start employees can little afford the cost of even a community college.

CHAPTER 3

A House Divided

The Micropolitics of Head Start Staff

In the *Micropolitics of the School*, Steven Ball (1987) calls our attention to the notion that the micropolitics of educational organizations cannot be understood without some comprehension of the external environment in which they function. Blase (1991a) takes this position further, citing empirical evidence of the way macro-level social, political, and cultural factors influence the micropolitics of schools. Jorde-Bloom's (1988; Jorde-Bloom & Sheerer, 1992) social system perspective further links factors in the external environment to the working conditions, social processes, and outcomes of child-care programs.

The links between policy and practice issues cannot be underestimated. Fiscal constraints are particularly important; as Bolman and Deal (1991) have observed, politics are more salient, intense, and divisive in difficult times, and when resources are scarce or inadequate, conflict is inevitable.

This theme of scarcity and the siege mentality that separated the staff into different groups of "us" and "them" is the focus of this chapter. Because the employees were the key resource in the program, and the caliber of the human resources in an organization is directly linked to its outcomes (Kennedy, 1991), their quality and competency also functioned as a resource that affected the micropolitics of the program. As will be illustrated, the program's poor material conditions, in combination with problematic human resource issues, had a synergistic affect in promoting the dysfunctional social relations within the organization. As Bolman and Deal (1991) have noted, in any organization, factors that affect social relations include issues of difference, interdependence, and power. At this Head Start, difference among the staff was expressed in terms of role and status in the program, education level, and class. Because of conflicts around these differences, interdependence and collaboration was made problematic. This lack of collaboration promoted power struggles and micropolitical activities of accommodation and resistance.

This chapter opens with a brief overview of the organizational structure of the program (see Figure 3.1), followed by an introduction to each staff position at Head Start. Brief profiles of the individual employees in this program who were particularly pertinent to the study are included in this section. Their views of their role in the program are presented, followed by a discussion that explores how these individuals also perceived the role and function of their co-workers. In doing so, a range of politically charged issues that were present within the program are explicated, and the way in which these issues affected the working environment and the culture of the organization is revealed.

STAFFING AT THE MORRISON COUNTY HEAD START: AN OVERVIEW

The Head Start program in Morrison County was sponsored by the Morrison County Community Action Program (CAP), a community-based, antipoverty program that had been the recipient of the Head Start contract in that county since the program's inception in 1965. The Head Start program ran seven separate Head Start centers in the county. Programming at these centers was administered by the Head Start director and six component coordinators. These middle-management positions supervised their respective center-level workers. For example, the education specialist was charged with coordinating all teachers and teachers' aides, the health coordinator provided direction and oversight to nurses, and so on. Branch managers acted as the head teacher and manager of each center, and were responsible for making sure that all center-level program services were carried out in a competent, integrated manner, since every job within a Head Start center is in some way related to providing services to children and their parents. Education, nutrition, health, transportation, and family support and advocacy are all essential components of Head Start, and in a similar way, each type of employee is vital to the overall mission of the program.

Figure 3.1 illustrates the organizational structure of Head Start, while specifically highlighting the two centers selected for this study:

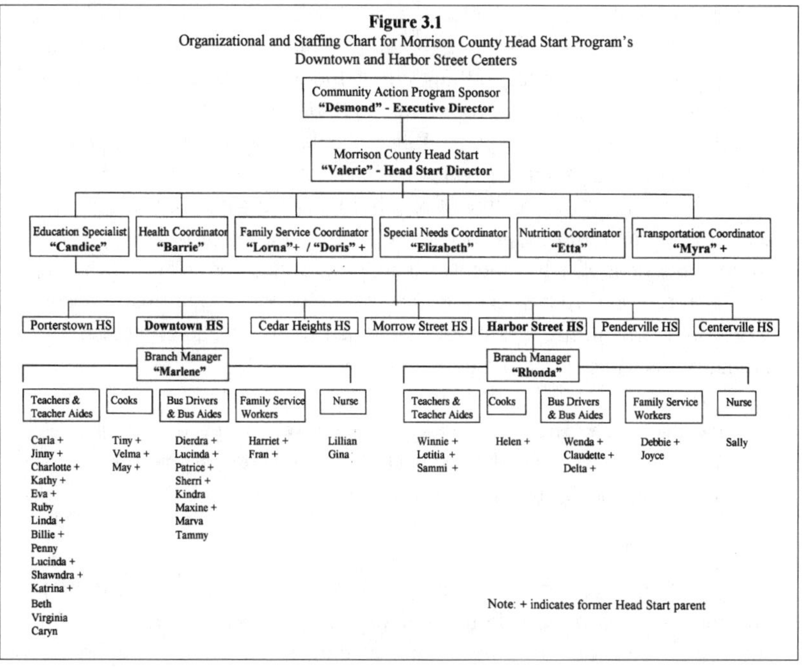

Figure 3.1
Organizational and Staffing Chart for Morrison County Head Start Program's Downtown and Harbor Street Centers

Downtown and Harbor Street. This chart provides information regarding the number of staff (not all were full-time employees), and the roles and respective names (actually pseudonyms) of those at these two Head Start sites. As previously noted, the Downtown Center was the largest center in the county with almost two hundred children enrolled and thirty employees. Harbor Street was one of the smallest Head Start centers, with ten staff serving sixty-five children and their families. Hence, it is the difference in size that accounts for the differing amount of staff for each of these centers. Note, too, that the staffing details of the other five centers in the county are not displayed.

TEACHERS AND TEACHER AIDES

The duties of the teachers in the classroom lay in directing activities in four primary areas. The first duty involved carrying out the required curriculum, which emphasized fine- and gross-motor–skills development as well as verbal skills and social skills. These were to be accomplished through painting, drawing, and cutting; music and dance; the manipulation of puzzles, blocks, and beads; playing matching and board games; arts and crafts; listening to and looking at books; discussing the weather and the calendar; talking about foods and experimenting with cooking; and going on field trips and neighborhood walks.

The second area of responsibility was related to maintaining a clean, organized classroom that provided a variety of materials for the children to use. The third duty was that of regularly assessing each child's growth and development through periodic monitoring and recordkeeping. These three functions, which related to managing a classroom of eighteen to twenty three- and four-year-olds who typically had a great many needs, were time-consuming tasks that demanded creativity, intelligence, and empathy. As Miss Jinny[1] put it:

> It's a holistic experience. We work on cognitive, social and emotional skills, and believe me, these kids need all that here. They need self-help skills too. They just need me. (Miss Jinny, teacher, Downtown Center)

The final aspect of thc teacher's job was to communicate with parents, sending information home regarding ways to work with their child, informing them of upcoming parent meetings and events, telephoning them about special needs or progress of their child, arranging parent-teacher conferences, and planning and carrying out home visits with each family at least twice each year. Central within all these forms of communication, teachers were to encourage parents to volunteer with and for their children in the classroom, on field trips, and in other areas such as assisting with the preparation of instructional materials.

The teacher aides assisted with all of these duties as needed, and with the general care and instruction of the children. In particular, they were to provide the teacher with support with the setup and cleanup of classroom activities. When the teacher was not present, the teacher aide was in charge of the class, and was typically assisted by available bus drivers or bus aides.

Eight teachers and an equal number of teacher aides staffed the eight classrooms at the Downtown Center. Of the teachers at the Downtown Center, all were women; three were white, and five were African-American. Their corresponding classroom aides were also women, six of whom were African-American; the other two were white.

The much smaller Harbor Street Center, with only two classrooms, had a teacher and a teacher aide for each room. Similar to the Downtown

Center, all teachers and teacher aides were women; there was one white teacher, one African-American teacher, and one white aide and one African-American aide.

The ages of all these women ranged from early twenties to approximately fifty. All were high-school graduates; two teachers (both of whom were the branch managers) had college degrees. While no particular level of education was required for either of these jobs at the time of the study, the national Head Start program encouraged teachers and aides to obtain the Child Development Associate (CDA) credential, and of the eighteen non–college educated teachers and teacher aides, four teachers had acquired this training, and one aide was in the process of its completion.

NURSES

Another key position at the center level was the nurse. Nurses in Head Start were required to hold a minimum of a Licensed Practical Nurse (LPN) credential. Nurses were to teach health information in classrooms, do health assessments, care for sick children and staff at the centers, dispense medications, and keep each child's record up to date regarding physicals and immunizations. They were also required to schedule the necessary appointments with the appropriate health providers for the children's dental exams, hearing and vision tests, and screenings for lead poisoning. Nurses were also responsible for working with the parents, following up on the child's status after scheduled health appointments, and educating and counseling parents about health issues. This was easier said than done, and in actuality, quite time-consuming; as Lillian noted, "It's hard to get parents to return permission slips. They hate doctors and dentists so they avoid it for their kids too. So, it seems like we're always playing catch-up."

One of the first opportunities for parent contact was during the registration process when the nurse interviewed parents about the child's health and well-being. Utilizing a questionnaire, she probed issues of the child's general health, his or her language and socialization skills, sleeping habits, dietary restrictions, and information about the mother's health during pregnancy. She also asked about the discipline techniques used in the home. She then measured and recorded each child's height and weight.

Each center had a nurse assigned to it; smaller centers like Harbor Street had a nurse available only on a part-time basis. Lillian had been the full-time nurse at the Downtown Center. A white woman near retirement, her duties were made more demanding by the fact that the center, and hence, her caseload, was so large: she was responsible for providing care and follow-up to 196 children. Despite Lillian's long history of commitment to Head Start, she had quit in September of that year, shortly after I began my fieldwork. She told me that she was simply worn out, fed up, and so felt the need to finally quit. She was briefly replaced by Gina, a young African-American woman who was bitter about the fact that the workload was so heavy she had to take work home with her to "catch up." At one point she had told me, "as long as I realize the [the job will never get done] I won't get upset about it." Still, this rationalization of the job didn't help ease the stress of it, and she quit within two months.[2]

COOKS

Each center also had at least one cook. The cooks checked in food deliveries, prepared meals and snacks, and were responsible for cleanup. The job did not require special certification or skills in cooking, for the food preparation that was done could really be quite minimal. It involved work such as heating soup, chopping vegetables for salads, making sandwiches, or heating food in the oven. The responsibility for menu planning did not fall upon the cooks; rather, the menus were prepared by the Head Start nutritionist, who also had the duty of ordering the necessary food.

The quality of the food and the atmosphere of the breakfast, lunch, and snack periods was established in large measure by the cooks. Some cooks went beyond the perfunctory role of food preparer and participated as full members of the Head Start center. For example, Della's kitchen at the Penderville Center was filled with song and smiles and words of encouragement for the little ones as they filed past. Mavis's kitchen at the Morrow Street center was homey and ripe with the good, sugary smells of ham and sweet potatoes baking, and pungent greens boiling on the stove. Others, like Tiny at the Downtown Center and Helen at Harbor Street, were matter-of-fact kitchen managers who had little to say to anyone other than the other cooks. Neither provided any special touches for either the food or the other folks at the center, big or small.

Many of the cooks at the Morrison County Head Start had been there twenty years or more. All of the cooks, except one, were African-American women. Because of its large size, the Downtown Center had three cooks; Harbor Street had one, the only white woman. Most had had children in the program, and had gained the job as parent hires. The cooks typically expressed the view that their job was something that was convenient, steady work. As Helen, at the Harbor Street Center indicated: "I didn't want to be a cook, and I wouldn't do it anywhere else, but it's okay for now." None of the cooks I interviewed indicated any ambition to move on to something else. Some expressed the lack of desire to move on because they were content; others had no idea of what they might otherwise do.

BUS DRIVERS AND BUS AIDES

In the same way that the children had to be fed, mended, and taught, those who did not live close enough to walk with a parent also had to be transported to and from the center. Filling this role were the bus drivers, who were responsible for getting children to and from school, as well as to Head Start–sponsored activities like dental appointments and field trips. They were responsible for maintaining and cleaning the buses, keeping them safe and in good order. Bus drivers were required, by state law, to have a special driver's license that allowed them to drive buses. Each driver was supposed to have a bus aide to assist them, although this was not always the case at either the Downtown or the Harbor Street centers. The Downtown Center had four bus drivers and four aides, all of whom were African-American women. The Harbor Street Center had two drivers, each of whom were white women, and for most of the year that center had only one aide, an African-American woman.

In addition to basic transportation duties, bus drivers were also responsible for acting as a main communication conduit for the program, as they handed parents the notes from teachers and announcements about activities at the Head Start center. Also, because they were the staff members who saw the parents twice each day, as parents dropped their children off and picked them up from the bus, the drivers were required to update each family's emergency telephone numbers. Therefore, their role was not only critical to the welfare of the children, but was very important to the smooth running of many aspects of the program.

FAMILY SERVICE WORKERS

Fran, one of the family service workers at the Downtown Center, first became employed in Head Start as a bus driver. Now, as a family service worker, she was responsible for duties in three distinct areas: recruiting and enrolling children and families, assisting families with a range of needs, and coordinating the program's parent activities. In her role as an advocate for families, she and the other family service workers were to provide a range of social and educational services, including making social service referrals, arranging educational programming for parents, and training leaders. Fran, who split her time between Downtown and another smaller center in the county (the Penderville Center), worked with Harriet, the center's only full-time family service worker. Both were white women in their forties who had initially become affiliated with the program as parents of enrolled Head Start children. Neither had any schooling beyond high school. Harriet was feisty, determined, and cynical, while Fran was gentle and easy-going.

Debbie provided services to the other site of this study, the Harbor Street Center. Debbie was a high school–educated white woman in her early forties who also had responsibility for programming at the Morrow Street Center. She left the program in November, and was replaced by Joyce in February. Joyce was an African-American woman in her thirties with a B.A. degree. Unlike Debbie, who was bubbly and friendly, Joyce was perceived by me — and others — to be curt and argumentative.

Two other family service workers also worked in this county-wide Head Start program during my year there: Consuelo and Doris. Consuelo was a college-educated Latina woman in her mid-fifties, who worked full-time at a large, urban center in a primarily Hispanic community. Doris, a white woman, split her time between the remaining small Head Start sites — Cedar Heights and Centerville.

Each of these five women had a caseload of about 120 families. While each worker viewed their role somewhat differently, the theme of support, assistance, and meeting a family's needs was consistent. So was the enormity of the job, and the inability to "do it all."

> I see my role as a liaison between the parents and the agency, and as an advocate for the parents in the community. I help parents learn how to access services, how to get what they need, and how to be assertive. (Debbie, family service worker, Harbor Street Center)

> [My job is] making home visits, assisting parents with needs and problems, coordinating parent activities at the centers, and coordinating the registration of the children and families. The family service and parent involvement is separate, you know. That is two full-time

> jobs, if you ask me. It's too much. . . . [But] sometimes I think the staff thinks I just sit in here and talk all day. There are days I get so fed up, I could just walk away. (Harriet, family service worker, Downtown Center)

THE ADMINISTRATION

Managing these personnel were the administrators of the program. At the center level, a head teacher or "branch manager" supervised that center's activities and staff. As a teacher, the branch manager reported to the education coordinator. Other coordinators at this level of management were those who had responsibility for managing the various administrative departments or "components." These coordinators included the nutrition coordinator, the transportation coordinator, the health coordinator, the education coordinator, the special needs coordinator, and the family service coordinator. Coordinators answered directly to the Head Start director, who was ultimately responsible for the fiscal, programmatic, and personnel management. Her boss was the executive director of the community-action agency that sponsored Head Start.

The Branch Manager

The branch manager for each center was both a classroom teacher and a manager. The branch manager organized the center activities, and suggested and approved field trips. She held biweekly staff meetings, and in conjunction with the education specialist, observed and supervised teachers. She did these extra duties with no assigned office space, no clerical help, and no extra time set aside in her day. While this was not much of a problem at small centers, at large centers with many employees, such as the Downtown Center, the job was often time-consuming.

Marlene, the branch manager at the Downtown Center, was a college-educated African-American woman in her late thirties. Conscientious in her duties, and with eight classrooms to supervise in the building, this meant that Marlene's own class was often managed by her teacher aide, Beth. Marlene depicted her job as being the administrative link between the center and the administration, and a "troubleshooter" with staff when parents had complaints, problems, or particular needs.

Rhonda was the branch manager of the Harbor Street Center. She was a white woman, also college-educated and in her thirties. At such a small center, Rhonda's supervisory duties over staff were not as demanding as Marlene's. Instead, as she explains here, she stressed the importance of her role as a program liaison to parents.

> Well, I have two roles, one as branch manager, and the other as teacher. As branch manager I have to be the one that they [parents] feel they can come to if there is a problem with things like transportation, nutrition, or anything, really. As branch manager I sit in on parent meetings to offer suggestions. I can't vote, but can give input about what is appropriate for the kids. I educate them by giving my advice at the meetings about what they could or should do with the kids.

The Education Specialist

Candice was the educational specialist for the program. She was a white woman in her thirties, with a bachelor's degree in early childhood education. Candice had stressed to me that she was the "education specialist," and not the "education coordinator," a job designation that commanded more pay. She was doing both jobs temporarily, as the education coordinator had left at the end of the previous school year and had not yet been replaced.

Candice supervised all teaching activities, and as such was in charge of all the teachers (including branch managers) and teacher aides in the program. She assisted the branch managers in their planning at the center level, and worked jointly in observing and evaluating the other teachers and aides. She was responsible for overseeing and developing the curriculum, integrating educational ideas into the program, and advising the teaching staff about methods of instruction. Along with supervising the teaching staff, she also had to order equipment and evaluate each classroom to ensure that it had the required materials.

Candice also acted as the liaison with the state child-care certification agency, and compiled statistics for local, state, and regional agencies, held curriculum meetings with teaching staff on a monthly basis as a means of helping them understand the teaching/learning goals and objectives for the upcoming month, and was also responsible for establishing a program-wide Educational Advisory Committee made up of parents, community members, and staff, which was required (by the *Head Start Performance Standards*) to meet periodically and provide input into curricular issues. In addition, Candice was also required to produced a monthly calendar for parents that corresponded with the curriculum objectives for the month containing suggested educational activities they could do at home with their children. It was a heavy workload, and as the year progressed she became rankled by the fact that she was doing both jobs but only getting paid for the lesser position.

The Family Service Coordinator

The Family Service Coordinator supervised all family service workers in the program. As manager of the program component, she was responsible for all matters of enrollment, assistance, and involvement of families it was her job to ensure that the social services provided to families and the educational programming required for parents were carried out according to the *Head Start Performance Standards,* and in a competent, effective manner. This entailed ensuring that confidential information about children and parents would be handled correctly, that parents had appropriate educational activities available to them at each center, and that parent committees at each center were in place and actively functioning.

As required in the original *Head Start Performance Standards*, each year she was to organize a Social Service Advisory Committee made up of parents and others, who were to make recommendations concerning the need for and level of social services in the community. Furthermore, she was responsible for developing annual, detailed plans about the provision of social services, the incorporation of parents into the program, and the ways that the program would be promoted in the community. Finally, she was to maintain regular reports of the activities of the family service workers, and to keep demographic statistics of the enrolled families.

Lorna had been the family services coordinator for the program almost since its inception in 1965. She had begun as a board member of the community-action agency that sponsored Head Start, and then moved into this paid position. Years earlier, she had a child in the program, and now had a grandchild enrolled in one of the county Head Start centers. Due to a prolonged illness, she left the program a few months after I met her.

After Lorna left, her position remained open for five months. Rather than hiring a replacement staff person right away, Valerie, the Head Start director, finally decided that Lorna's duties should be temporarily given to Doris, one of the family service workers. Consequently, for the remainder of the school year, Doris was responsible for all of the duties of her own job, as well as those of Lorna's.

Doris was not quite sure that she wanted this job. She had begun as a bus driver at Head Start and had no experience in managing people. And, like Candice, while she had her hands full trying to do both this job and her own, she was not being compensated for the extra duties.

The Special Needs Coordinator

In 1973 the federal government mandated that Head Start must begin to accept children with disabilities, and each local program was to have in place policies, procedures, services, and referral systems for special needs children that adhered to national guidelines. The staff person who coordinated these services at this program was Elizabeth. Her work involved doing developmental assessments (physical, cognitive, and speech) on each child, and then referring them to services as needed. She also communicated regularly with local school districts that had school-based programs for handicapped preschool children, in an effort to ensure the proper placement of children according to their needs. For example, children with extremely severe disabilities attended school-based, specialized programs in the county instead of Head Start. She explained the process of how such children might be assigned to a special program:

> If he or she is considered to be environmentally deprived, resulting in speech, motor, or intellectual lags, then the child stays in Head Start. If it is something else, organic or congenital, then the staff recommends that the child go through the school system, perhaps doing half days at each program.

This meant that Head Start focused on the less severely impaired children. Nevertheless, of the nearly six hundred children in the program, approximately 20 percent had what Elizabeth described as some type of "learning disability."

Elizabeth was a college-educated, fortyish white woman who effused a sense of order and organization, as well as a comforting motherliness, particularly toward the children. She was friendly, but always busy and brusque. During my year there, she was the only person staffing that area, although in the previous year she had had two full-time workers who specialized in learning disabilities. This year, however, one of the staff positions had been cut from her budget and the remaining staffer was out on maternity leave, and had not been replaced. Furthermore, the contractual speech and occupational therapists whom she relied on did not become available to her until the very end of the year. As a result, when trying to provide services to six hundred children, Elizabeth was at her wits end.

This was only Elizabeth's second year with the program, but she knew Head Start well, for she had moved to the area from another state where she had been the family service coordinator at a Head Start program. Her former job had taken a toll on her, however, so when she relocated she had chosen not to work for an entire year. Then Valerie, the Head Start director, contacted her and begged her to take the job, despite the fact that Elizabeth knew virtually nothing about disabilities or special needs. Out of dedication to the program, she agreed. After all, as she put it, "they needed me, and no one had been in the position for over two years."

The Health Coordinator

The health coordinator acted as a liaison with health providers in the community, supervised the nurses, ordered supplies, and oversaw the entire health component. The person in this position was responsible for organizing and coordinating all the dental and health referrals and services, supervising all the health screenings that were provided for children, and acting as the representative for Head Start when the state undertook their health-records audit of preschool programs. This person was also responsible for organizing the mandatory Health Advisory Committee for the program that was made up of health-care providers and parents.[3]

Barrie, the health coordinator for this Head Start, was the most educated and prepared of all the coordinators. A businesslike white woman in her early forties, she came to the position with a master's degree in Health Administration. She also had a lengthy background in health services programming prior to Head Start, where she had been for two years. Like her peers nationally, Barrie faced a difficult job in locating health-care providers who would serve the children for the typically low rates that Medicaid paid for dental and medical care for Head Start kids (U. S. General Accounting Office, 1994).

Barrie also ended up performing the duties of nurse at the Downtown Center when Lillian left early in the school year. For two months Barrie had to do her own job and act as a nurse before she could find a replacement for Lillian. Then, Gina, the new nurse, left and she had to do the nurse's job again. Luckily, in the midst of this staffing crisis, Barrie was able to convince Lillian to come back for the remainder of the year, and so finally, Barrie was able to concentrate on the demands of the health coordinator position alone.

The Nutrition Coordinator

Each Head Start program was required to enlist the services of a certified nutritionist who planned the breakfast, lunch, and snack menus for all of its Head Start centers. At this program, Etta filled that role. A middle-aged, college-educated white woman, her duties were to arrange the menus according to daily food requirements, order the food, and hire and supervise the cooks. I rarely saw Etta, who worked only on a part-time basis. Although several nutrition-related educational objectives were stated in the *Head Start Performance Standards* regarding both children and parents, none of the staff in the program, including Etta, saw her role as being related in any way with parents. Citing this reason, she opted not to be interviewed during the course of the study.

The Transportation Coordinator

Myra, who shared office space (and the same desk) with Etta, was the transportation coordinator. Also part-time, Myra's role was to hire and supervise the bus drivers and bus aides for the program. A middle-aged, African-American woman with a high-school degree, she had become affiliated with Head Start as a parent of an enrolled child. Myra, who was very shy, also indicated that she saw no reason to be interviewed, and declined.

The Head Start Director

Supervising all of these staff was the Head Start director, Valerie. A white woman with a Master's Degree in early childhood education, she was in her late forties. She was considered to be a knowledgeable professional and was well respected by the human service community in the area. An employee of Head Start for years, she had started with the program as educational coordinator and worked up to the job of director. However, after several years in this role, she had left, claiming that she was burned out and needed a change. According to her and several other staff members, when she left she was replaced by an administrator who was "an incompetent." The result was programmatic disaster and fiscal mismanagement.

Valerie was then asked to come back as the director of Head Start, and she reluctantly agreed to take on this challenging task, in order "to save the program." While she was skilled, motivated, and seemingly quite dedicated to Head Start, she had also shared with me that the morass of problems "were overwhelming." She found the program's financial resource and personnel deficits to be a major headache; so whenever I saw Valerie, she appeared tired and cynical. And yet, it seemed that Valerie did indeed believe in Head Start's potential to make a difference in the lives of low-income families. Her anger and frustration appeared to stem from the fact that she felt the program deserved much more. Furthermore, she had to deal with a controlling boss.

The Executive Director

Desmond was the executive director of the Community Action Program (CAP) which was the sponsoring agency for Head Start in Morrison County. A middle-aged, African-American man, he had been in his position for several years. His reputation in the broader community was somewhat controversial. Different segments of the community, including influential corporate vice presidents and CEOs, city managers, and non-profit development-agency directors, while being supportive of Head Start, felt that as Executive Director of its sponsoring agency, Desmond was not providing essential leadership around issues of quality and fiscal responsibility. Some community members even held the opinion that he was detrimental to the program.[4]

One such leader was a man I will call Grant. Grant's job was to assess social services needs and monitor program services in the community, and in this capacity he and Desmond had had several very public disagreements regarding approaches to community problems, program development, and accountability issues. Grant described Desmond as "manipulative and controlling" of both budgets and people. Grant and others also characterized him as not being straightforward about the way in which federal dollars were spent and programs were carried out. Because he resisted open cooperation in terms of sharing information and planning with other providers, the programs that Desmond administered were open to suspicion, and some perceived him to be mismanaging scarce resources.

Valerie had told me of the tension that existed between herself and Desmond and she described him as being "difficult to work with." I could concur with this view, for in an effort to interview him I had called him several times throughout the year, yet he never returned my calls. Frustrated, I even went to his office to try to meet with him. Still he would not see me, since, according to the secretary, he "was in a meeting." My low status as "the student" may have explained his lack of responsiveness to me; yet others, such as parents and staff, also had similar experiences of having their phone calls ignored.

While Valerie never admitted this directly to me, human-service professionals in the community and various Head Start employees had told me that Valerie had been wishing to change jobs for some time because of the situation with Desmond.

The Head Start staff also had strong opinions about Desmond, and expressed their frustrations about a range of problems, from what they described as his hollow promises to the fact that he often hired friends and family with few qualifications. One staff member, who asked to remain anonymous, shared these feelings:

> He tries to control the entire program. His wife is a bus driver in Harborville, and people say that he put her there to spy on the program. That way he could get direct info [information]. It's all political. . . . I guess everyone hoped that with Valerie [back on staff] things would change, but he controls it all. By the way, only believe three-fourths of what he says. . . . (Head Start staff member)

"IT'S ALL POLITICAL": DIFFERENCE, INTERDEPENDENCE, AND POWER INEQUITIES AMONG THE STAFF

As that anonymous staff member observed, many on the Head Start staff recognized that the social setting of the program had political dimensions inherent within it. In this comment, the phrase "it's all political" summed up the reality of the unequal social relations extant between the staff, and the struggles over power, information, ideology, and resources that were present in the setting despite the program's participatory, egalitarian rhetoric of empowerment and "maximum feasible participation."[5] While these feelings of frustration were voiced regarding the program's problematic material resources, the typical work overload, and the lack of preparedness for themselves, the staff also expressed their concerns about each other as resources. Complaints abounded in relation to issues of training, supervision, coordination, and accountability, and there were frequent disagreements about the types of skills, knowledge, and experience that were considered necessary within the setting and in relation to specific job duties.

Opinions about these issues differed, and splits in opinion could be seen, for example, between those with college educations and those without these credentials, and those with middle-class backgrounds versus those with low-income backgrounds. Furthermore, different duties and job functions in the program, as well as whether or not they had previous experience as a parent in the program, also influenced employees' perspectives.

Distinctions were found along the following dichotomous lines: professional versus grassroots staff (who were typically the college-educated versus high school–educated employees), and administration versus staff, although a staff member's identification with these groups was sometimes fluid and shifting, depending on the circumstance. The differing and sometimes very divisive opinions that existed between these groups were compounded by the unequal levels of training and skills present within the staff, and the program's inadequate levels of resources for providing such training to upgrade their skills.

Bolman and Deal (1991) have observed that politics and political behavior[6] is "more visible and dominant under conditions of diversity than of homogeneity" (p. 188). In fact, the issue of difference was central to the way that organizational politics were played out in this program, and the way in which the staff resisted collaboration with others for the good of the program, the children, and the parents whom they were entrusted to serve.

NONPROFESSIONALS VERSUS PROFESSIONALS

A major factor that shaped the program's staff politics was related to issues of education. The staff divided themselves into two camps: the professional staff (those with bachelor or graduate degrees), and the nonprofessional staff (those who held only high school diplomas).[7] Each of these groups, the professionals and nonprofessionals, felt that the other did not understand the importance or significance of their jobs. Hence, staff relations within the program were tense, and it was typical that staff felt unsupported by each other, and unappreciated in their work.[8]

Since the program was staffed primarily with grassroots nonprofessionals who had little prior formal education pertinent to their positions, the more educated staff felt that the ability to deliver critical program services suffered. For example, the professionals felt that many of the nonprofessional staff were clearly ill-equipped and misguided in most aspects of their jobs. Once, when Elizabeth (the special needs coordinator) was complaining about Lorna (the family service coordinator) she made a point of minimizing the level of education Lorna had, commenting: "Heck, we don't even know whether or not she even has a high school diploma." And, as Candice, the education specialist, once complained: "We ask people to take on more than they can do here, because we have set up a professional program, but we don't staff it with professionals!"

This "professional" versus "grassroots" dichotomy regarding staffing emerged in several arenas. From the perspective of the nonprofessionals, the problem lay with the professionals in the program who were not "grassroots." For example, Harriet, a family service worker who began her tenure with Head Start as a parent and who did not have a college degree, complained that although the policy guidelines stated that Head Start jobs should be offered to parents first, some new staff were not former parents. Because of this, she reasoned, they did not understand the population they were attempting to serve.[9] Furthermore, she and others without college training felt that the education that the professionals had was basically meaningless; it only served as a status symbol, demarcating them from the other staff who did not have degrees and making the educated/credentialled staff think that they were superior.

Harriet felt the college-educated staff looked down on the other staff, typically those who were former parents. Furthermore, she and the other nonprofessional staff felt that they "got no credit" for what they knew.

> Just 'cause they have a college education, it doesn't mean anything. And besides, some people with degrees aren't even trained in the area that they work in. Elizabeth doesn't have a degree in special ed. . . . And Barrie isn't even a nurse. . . . I'm sick of how they think they are better than us. We go to training sessions, but they never give us any credit for what we learn there. (Harriet, family service worker, Downtown Center)

Candice, among others, concurred that a division existed between those with a college degree and those without one.

> There is a major philosophical difference between those who are educated here, those with degrees, and those who don't have them. There is a lot of jealousy and resentment. When Marlene, the branch manager who has a BA, was hired, people [the teachers and teacher aides] were angry that she was above them. . . . Many staff don't see the relevance of further education, and they think that they should all be considered equals. (Candice, education specialist)

An example of the divergent "professional" and "grassroots" perspectives that existed between the more formally educated, managerial employees and the lower-level, center-based employees was evident as it related to the meaning and importance of confidentiality. There were essentially three perspectives on the matter. The first perspective was found in entry-level Head Start employees such as cooks, bus drivers, bus aides, janitors, and teacher aides who had had little or no training in the provision of education, health or human services. As such, many also had no understanding of the need for confidentiality. As Fran described it, [some employees] "don't even understand the meaning of the word [confidentiality]." One critical incident involving confidentiality took place when a bus driver found out that someone connected with the program had HIV/AIDS. Upon learning this, the bus driver made a point of making sure that all the staff, parents, and children with whom she came in contact were aware of this fact.

Directly opposite this type of (mis)understanding was the perspective of confidentiality that was held by the family service workers in the program. Also nonprofessionals, their concept of confidentiality was extremely rigid, and it allowed for no sharing of information whatsoever, with anyone, regardless of the situation. As a result, they would not share any information with their other colleagues within the program, despite the fact that the various service components of the program were to work in an integrated, collaborative fashion.

The professionals expressed yet a third view of confidentiality. To them, both the indiscriminate and the inflexible way of handling information was irresponsible and inexcusable. They believed that when working together to serve families, information must be shared with each other. When these last two ideas of confidentiality (rigid versus "need-to know") conflicted, it resulted in the following types of scenarios.

The first involved a child who had been abused at home. In such situations this information was supposed to be shared with the nurses, teachers, and coordinators at "priority meetings" so that the child's best interest would be addressed and a course of action could be followed by all. Yet the family service worker who was aware of this problem had kept the information from the others on staff, including the other family service workers. In sharing this scenario with me, the coordinator, who eventually discovered the abuse herself, told me that she had confronted the family service worker, who had explained that she did not reveal the abuse to anyone at all, since it was "confidential."

Candice and Barrie felt that this family service worker's view of confidentiality was not only uneducated and naive, but dangerous as well.

> How can they refer a family to the therapy team and not even tell them they are an abuse case? The problem is that they are not trained professionals, they are not social workers. (Candice, education specialist)

> If the family service workers know about [something], they won't tell, 'cause they have this screwy view that if they are told something, they aren't supposed to tell anyone. We all agree that it's 'cause of their lack of education and training. They just don't get the picture. They just don't understand the importance of the information. And since they

> keep it to themselves, believing that they can handle it, they don't bounce off the situation on others, and talk about how to deal with it. They don't even share the information without the names. (Barrie, health coordinator)

The second situation that depicted this rigid view of confidentiality involved a parent volunteer who had offered to help the nurse at the Downtown Center. Gina and this parent had been recording each child's height, weight, and blood pressure onto various required forms. When Harriet, the family service worker, saw what the volunteer was doing with Gina, she demanded that they stop immediately, since they were violating "confidential information." Both Gina and the parent were shocked, for neither felt that they were doing anything improper with such basic health information. Gina became angry because she needed the volunteer's help, and the parent got upset because the family service workers had been stressing the need for volunteers in the program, and she had offered her help. During the ensuing argument between Gina and Harriet, the woman volunteer finally walked out, disgusted by the situation.

While the professional staff felt that this skewed view of confidentiality was related to a lack of training, Barrie also thought it had to do with the fact that the family service workers identified too closely with those families that they served. As she saw it, because they had been parents with the program, they were protective of all types of information, no matter how trivial.

> They try to do it all, and they think they can do it, but they don't have the ability. [So, while it's from] the lack of training, it's also the family service workers' protective feelings for the parents, since they all used to be in that position. (Barrie, health coordinator)

FORMER PARENTS AS STAFF

Barrie's comment about staff as former parents was a pertinent one; since Head Start placed an emphasis on the placement of parents into jobs within the program, many of the employees had begun their involvement in the program as parents. The intent of this policy was to help them develop skills, increase their income, get them off welfare, and eventually out of poverty. Interestingly, while the rationale for hiring parents was to lift them out of poverty, many remained in this state due to low wages once employed in the program (see Chapter 1).

Of the thirty staff at the Downtown Center, twenty had been former parents with the program. Other centers around the country have similar proportions of parent/employees (U. S. General Accounting Office, 1994). Because I considered these particular staff to be an important resource for the study, I interviewed many of them at the other five centers in the county in addition to those at the Downtown and Harbor Street centers. They shared their experiences with me as parents in the Head Start program, as well as how they now saw their roles as staff.

Staff typically spoke positively of their experience as parents in the program, and they embraced the opportunity to reminisce with me about how they got involved as a parent in Head Start and how and why they subsequently moved into a job there. Many expressed gratitude at being given a chance to work there, since for most it was their first job outside the home, and often times, the only job they had ever held. Some spoke of their work merely as jobs, something that paid a little and was convenient; others discussed the way becoming employed with the program gave them a sense of direction and changed their lives; still others revealed the deep, continuing commitment they felt to the program, and the desire to make a difference for other children and families in poverty.

While the parents viewed their transition from parent to staff as highly positive, the hiring of parents was sometimes thought to be problematic. The professional staff worried that many were not skilled enough to do their jobs. Candice noted that parents' disadvantaged backgrounds were often reflected in their poor reading skills, and she doubted whether some were literate enough to read and complete the program's paperwork correctly, despite being written at a sixth-grade level.

> The family service workers never think that a parent has a problem with reading. I think it's because they don't understand the difference between being partially and fully literate.

I, too, sometimes wondered about the staff's literacy skills. For example, one day as I was looking for Miss Carla, the teacher aide in her class told me that Carla was downstairs helping a parent with a bicycle that one of the children had won in a fund-raising contest. Not wanting the children to overhear, she carefully spelled out her version of the word *bike*: "B I C K."

Because of the teaching staff's lack of skills, Candice also complained that she had to make detailed, weekly plans for the teachers. Many had moved from their role as parent into jobs as teacher's aides, or even as cooks or bus drivers, and then into a position as a teacher. While some had obtained their CDA (Child Development Associate Certification) at the community college, the level of instruction this training provided was extremely basic, and many still needed explicit directions in order to do their jobs. Despite their lack of education, some resisted the idea that they needed to have more training and development.

> Teachers have problems discussing problems they see in the children, or even ideas about education of the child in general. They are just not trained. . . . You have to get to their level, understand where they are coming from, and that they are not as educated as they should be in such areas as child development and teaching technique. . . . On the other hand though, some think that they know everything, and can learn no more. (Candice, education specialist)

Furthermore, she added, with little developmental background, these staff had difficulty monitoring and assessing the children's development:

> It's a lot of work for them, and sometimes it's difficult to make good notes since they do it in class and at meals, and they must remember to write it down accurately. They're not trained in observation, so that adds another difficulty. But, they manage. (Candice, education specialist)

Yet, former parents could — and did — make excellent employees. Miss Jinny and Miss Billie were highly respected, and Miss Charlotte was considered to be one of the best teachers in the program.

Programs were lucky when former parents like these three stayed with the program despite the material conditions and work overload. For women like this, the emotional connection and dedication to the program kept them in their jobs, year after year. Others, however, stayed because they thought that there was no other job they could do, or no other options for them. When Debbie, the family service worker at Harbor Street, left to take a higher paying job with Child Protective Services, Bobbie, the parent chair at Harbor Street, told me how proud she was that Debbie could finally get out of the system:

> I was sad to see Debbie go, but glad that she got a better job, 'cause people at Head Start told her that she could never get another job since she didn't have a college degree. They treated her really mean, and she worked for practically nothing. Do you know that year after year, new

> aides would be hired in, and they all made more money than Debbie, who had been here for twenty years.

So, while Head Start did provide parents with employment, as indicated in Chapter 1, they were jobs that kept them in poverty. Furthermore, Head Start offered little training to them once on the job. Clearly, without an opportunity to upgrade their skills through continuous, meaningful training and development, the possibility of developing the "career path" that had been envisioned by two of the initial developers of Head Start (Julius Richmond and Jules Sugarman, in Gillette, 1996), to help the parents move up and on to better paid positions, was rarely realized.

"NO ONE GETS TRAINED PROPERLY"

The skill levels of Head Start staff and the need for requirements and set qualifications have been a topic of debate on the national scene, particularly as it relates to the health-care and family/social services staff (U.S. General Accounting Office, 1994). Yet the desire to increase formal educational qualifications comes into conflict with the goal of providing parents with jobs. It has been argued that having minimum educational qualifications would put in jeopardy the program's explicit policy of providing parents with employment (U.S. General Accounting Office, 1994). Yet the fact that Head Start may be asking them to do a job they are not fully equipped for is not only ironic, it is unjust — to the parent who is hired, their co-workers, and to the children and adults whom she or he is supposed to serve.

Former parents were not the only ones who were ill-prepared for their jobs. Skilled, effective staff were needed in all areas of the program, yet Valerie, the Head Start director, sometimes joked to me about how poorly trained her staff was. For example, when the special needs coordinator came into the job she had no skills related to testing and assessment, and no knowledge of disabilities or special education. She also had no guidance in gaining that expertise, and had to learn what she could on her own.

The director was not the only one who noted the staff's inadequacies; they were highly critical of each other, and repeatedly pointed out the problems to me. For example, teachers complained about family service workers, and vice versa; and the professional, administrative staff complained about almost everybody. Yet, such discussions did not solely consist of finger-pointing. Many also spoke of the fact that they themselves lacked the skills and preparation needed to do their jobs well. For, while staff came to their positions equipped with good intentions, such goodwill did little to make up for their critical lack of information and education in programming areas of health, education, and human services.

The staff was in complete consensus regarding the lack of information that was provided to them about Head Start and about their specific jobs and roles in the program prior to beginning their work in the program. All agreed that they had been given little orientation, and as a result, many felt unclear about their jobs and inadequately prepared. As Marge, a nurse at the Porterstown Center, explained: "I think they just presume that you know what you are doing. You are really left on your own." Others shared similar views:

> I only had two days of orientation. They just assumed that I knew how to do a job like this. If we had better training and orientation, we could be more aware of what each section is doing. It's so new to me, that sometimes I have to go to other people to find out what I am supposed to do. (Joyce, family service worker, Harbor Street Center)

> Candice helped me by gathering up all the stuff for me to read, but figuring out how to apply it and what was needed happened as I went along. (Rhonda, branch manager, Harbor Street Center)

> Every component is the same, no component has an orientation. Everyone tries to help each other 'cause no one gets trained properly. (Sally, nurse, Harbor Street Center)

While some training opportunities were made available for the staff, such as an occasional workshop on domestic violence or drugs, most staff did not attend these sessions. The rationale was often that there was not enough money in the budget to send the staff, or the training did not fit into the needs of their job.[10] Sometimes the administration made seemingly irrational decisions about training opportunities. For example, as health coordinator, Barrie had wanted to attend a statewide Head Start conference on AIDS. While she had been told the program could not afford it, Lorna was allowed to go, even though she was retiring within the next month and would not be utilizing the information and skills in the future.

Those who did attend workshops were supposed to bring the information back to the other staff. Harriet, family service worker at the Downtown Center, saw this as an unrealistic expectation: "We can go to a workshop, but the teachers or the bus drivers don't get to, so they don't know about the stuff we do. They can't get it just from us reporting about it at a staff meeting." This was true. From my own observations I knew that Harriet had minimal presentation skills and could not provide information in a logical and coherent manner. Her manner of "reporting about it" to the others in staff meeting was to note that it was "really good." She describes the extent of her "sharing it" with others:

> I might go to a training on something, and then come back and mention it in staff meeting, but that is not the same as getting trained yourself. It just isn't enough. (Harriet, family service worker)

Staff also received only limited training regarding working with parents or promoting parent involvement. When I asked staff about such training, their responses ranged from reports that they had received none; they had received some, but it had been a long time ago and it had been perfunctory; or they could not remember.

> Honestly, nothing. I came from a public school setting, so I assume that they figured I knew how to work with parents. (Sally, nurse, Harbor Street Center)

> Yes, a long time ago. I can't remember much, to tell you what it was about. I think about making them [parents] feel good about the things they are doing with their child, stressing their role as primary caregiver, their role with their child. (Miss Jinny, teacher, Downtown Center)

Despite the need for all staff members in the program to know how to work with parents and promote their involvement with their children and with the program, not all staff saw their role as being important to parental involvement. Instead, many of the teaching staff preferred to ignore the parents.

> I recognize that many people in Head Start aren't trained properly to work with parents. At my former program, even though it was a great program, when I came in as education coordinator I realized right away that no one was doing anything meaningful with parents. So I

> made it my business to make sure that programming was set up so that parents knew what it was we were doing with kids. (Elizabeth, special needs coordinator)

> Teachers do not like interacting with parents, they do not feel equipped, and are uncomfortable with it. I think they have a hard time switching gears from working with children to dealing with parents. They are just not trained in doing this with parents. (Candice, education specialist)

Both the family service workers and the administrative coordinators concurred that there was a huge need for staff training regarding involvement with parents. While in agreement that more training was needed in this area, once again their views differed along the lines of the need for "professional" preparation and skills, and "grassroots" experience and perspectives.

> It has everything to do with training, and they aren't skilled enough or educated enough to know how to work with them. . . . Many are not sure of what role they should convey to parents, one of authority as teacher or not, since they are not professionals and are often unsure of what they are doing. (Candice, education specialist)
> They need more training about working with parents. How to understand them and what they are going through. (Harriet, family service worker)

Family service workers received the most training about program planning and implementation regarding parent involvement, parent education, and leadership development, yet their skill and competence level was questionable. For example, Doris, upon taking the position of family service coordinator, expressed to me that her main concern was trying to provide leadership to staff members whom she perceived as lacking preparedness and skills in a range of areas related to parent programming. Furthermore, in her opinion (and in the opinion of others), the component was in disarray, and had been for some time.

LITTLE SUPERVISION

In this context, and in lieu of adequate levels of training and expertise among the staff, the importance of supervision and guidance was especially evident. Yet, little meaningful supervision was provided to the staff, and they often simply relied on what they thought was best. Their judgment, though, was not always prudent, and unethical or deleterious practices were the occasional result.

One example of the lack of accountability and supervision in the program was a situation involving Josephine's granddaughter and one of the bus drivers. One morning, shortly after boarding the bus, the four-year-old got off the bus while it waited at a red light. According to the driver, the little girl had started coughing, and since children were not to come to school sick she had told her to get out and wait for her mother's car, which was three or four cars behind the bus. While this situation was horrendous enough, it was made worse by what was perceived to be the administration's seemingly unconcerned response.[11] Josephine was near tears as she shared this story with me:

> They're telling me that this bus driver could know that it was my daughter [the girl's mother] in the car. . . . Now I'm a crossing guard, and I know for a fact that you cannot recognize people through a windshield, from any distance away, until they come right up along side of you. These people are either evading the situation, or they think I'm stupid. All Head Start did was give her a written reprimand. This woman lost nothing, absolutely nothing. A written reprimand that goes in her file and will get forgotten. Until the next time. And I hope the next time is nothing serious. (Josephine, grandparent and guardian, Downtown Center)

Thus, another key complaint among the staff was that employees were often not supervised well, nor held accountable to do a good job. In the words of Edward Zigler (1994, p. 38), in his analysis of Head Start, "the best standards in the world are meaningless if they are not enforced." But assessing what skills were needed and then working towards providing the staff with upgraded skills were also often problems. According to Candice, the teachers and teacher aides in the program resented the fact that their work had to be monitored.

> Observation of them in the classroom is very threatening. . . . I also have problems with staff who don't want to stick to a job description, and find some of the work demeaning, like cleaning up. Some aides think that the early morning clean and prep work is beneath them, and want to share that with the teacher, rather than do it themselves. But the

> teacher has her own things to do at that time, if they are doing their job right.

Many at this program concurred, and could not understand why certain staff were allowed to keep their jobs despite the fact they were not doing them right. In fact, it seemed as if the administration had simply given in, and had quit resisting problematic behavior. Instead, inadequacy was accommodated, and personnel problems ignored. As one staff member commented: "Some of them just don't have it. They yell at the kids, or don't do their job. But there's no accountability" (Elizabeth, special needs coordinator).

Doris, the temporary family service coordinator, quickly realized that the administration was accommodating, and in fact, encouraging poor performance. She had been having problems supervising Joyce, Debbie's replacement at Harbor Street. Joyce was a close friend of Desmond, the executive director of Head Start's sponsoring agency, and as such, she had gotten the job through that route, and not, as Doris explained, "because she was qualified." Because of her lack of qualifications, and her seeming sense of impunity as a result of being connected to Desmond, Doris had been having numerous problems trying to get her to do certain aspects of her job.

> I can't get any work out of her. She won't turn in her reports on time, or do anything that I tell her to. You know what her response to me is? "When I get to it!" If I complain to her, she then takes everything to Desmond [who then tells her to ignore Doris], so I have no power to supervise her. (Doris, interim family service coordinator)

PERCEPTIONS, POSSIBILITIES, AND THE LIMITATIONS OF THE FAMILY SERVICE/ PARENT INVOLVEMENT COMPONENT

Competent leadership over this program's family service component did appear to have been lacking over the years. For instance, while action plans regarding social service and parent involvement were to be developed on a yearly basis, both were outdated by two years. The staff's referral and resource book was also outdated by two years, and a required community-resource book that was supposed to be available for distribution to parents no longer existed. Similarly, a newsletter that was scheduled to be issued during the previous spring had never been completed.

Furthermore, as mentioned previously, the required Social Service Advisory Committee had not met in previous years, nor was it formed during the year that I was with the program. In fact, in all aspects of this program component, it appeared as if things were either done in a haphazard fashion or not at all. Given the inadequate levels of staffing, and the material resource constraints, this is not a surprising situation.

Valerie had warned me at the beginning of the study that she felt the entire family service staff was difficult to work with, resistant, and overall, not competent.

> It's important that parents have positive experiences with their children, and with the school. Like doing a parent activity that's productive, learning how to make toys or creative play. Being with other parents who have children the same age also helps. It's the positive experiences that can affect their own negative experiences in their lives. But that takes social workers who can get resources for these parents, find out what they need for the family, and learning how to work with the social service system. (Valerie, Head Start director)

Despite this however, Valerie also recognized that the family service staff in the program were "resistant" to changes she had attempted. So, over the years, despite the importance of parent involvement to the goals and mission of the program, she began to ignore the situation, viewing it as unresolvable. The result was a parent component that was largely unsupervised, stagnant, and inept.

One example of the lack of skills found within this unit related to the part of Harriet and Fran's job that entailed organizing and facilitating the parent orientation that was to take place every year. Held in early September, it was to welcome families and inform parents about the overall Head Start program, their particular center, and what they could look forward to in terms of activities for themselves and their children throughout the course of the Head Start year. Yet, as the following scenario illustrates, even this most basic function went amiss.

Parent Orientation Night. The noise level in the room was deafening. Of the two hundred parents at the Downtown Center, fifty had assembled in the cafeteria and were talking amongst themselves; the children who had come with them were running around screaming. It seemed as if everyone had brought their children with them to the meeting. The memo that had been sent home on the bus had promised child care, yet no one was organizing it. Instead, Harriet was standing in the middle of the chaos, waving some yellow papers in the air, and shouting, "This is for us to keep track of how many people come to meetings and volunteer. It is very important that it is filled out!"

The meeting had begun fifteen minutes late, and it was the third time she had tried to shout these orders over the din. Yet few parents were paying attention, and fewer still had a pen with which to write. Harriet did not have any for them to use, and I found myself fishing them out of my purse and lending them to those seated around me.

As the parents had come into the room that night, they had taken seats on the tiny chairs that were placed around each of the lunch tables. As I had selected a seat, I had noticed that most of the chairs and tables and the surrounding floor were still dirty from that day's lunch and snack time, as bits of food and dried puddles of milk were crusted on them. Crumbled napkins also lay on the tables, chairs, and the surrounding floor.

The tables at which the parents sat were scattered around the room. Some were pushed too close together, while others were in far corners of the cafeteria, apart from the others. Since no one had bothered to rearrange them, as parents took their seats some ended up facing the front of the room, others, the back.

Complicating this seating arrangement was where Harriet had placed herself to lead the meeting: instead of standing at the front of the room, she stood in the middle. Therefore, her back was towards at least half of the parents, and it appeared from their frustrated looks that they were having a hard time hearing her. I was also having a hard time hearing, despite being seated on the side of the room that Harriet was facing. Little of what she was saying could be heard over the din, so when she waved more papers around, I was only able to catch part of what she was saying: "These are fund-raising items to look at! Later, everyone will vote on what to sell!"

Judy, a parent, was one of those seated far off in the corner. Finally, she let it be known that she had had enough, and she shouted at the top of her voice: "No one on this side of the room can hear! It is too noisy, I can barely hear!"

Earlier that day, the family service workers had told me that they had organized everything for a successful meeting: the refreshments were ready, the parent speakers lined up, the meeting notices sent. Lorna had explained how the meeting was planned and organized:

> The orientation involves parents from former years. They and the staff plan it, getting together in meetings at the beginning of the year. Invita-

> tions are sent out, and refreshments are offered to get parents to come. Transportation is provided to parents if they need it, as is child care. At this meeting, the program is explained, as well as how they can get involved. (Lorna, family service coordinator)

Harriet had also told me what types of topics would be discussed.

> Committees and projects that happen throughout the year are discussed. Basically, the session explains what can be done in the year, and how committees work. Fund-raising, so that parent activities can take place, are stressed. Different types of topics are brought up, like aerobics, parenting, different guest speakers, arts and crafts, sewing. It's up to the parents to decide, though. (Harriet, family service worker, Downtown Center)

I had also probed Fran about what was being planned.

> The main idea is that parents get to know each other a little bit, so they know each other before they vote on representatives and officers [at the next month's business meeting]. First there will be a meeting with everyone, and then they will break down into groups and do an interactive exercise; things that the children do in their classrooms. Then they'll go into their children's classroom to do this. (Fran, family service worker, Downtown Center)

I asked whether the design for this meeting was something that was a mandatory part of the program, or whether it was a plan that the staff here had created. "I'm not sure," Fran said tentatively, "but I think it was something that Head Start had suggested."

She also showed me the handouts that they would distribute, that were supposed to "orient" the parents. There were four of them: one discussed the center's parent committee, another was advice on how to participate in a meeting, and yet another suggested ways to run a meeting. The last one briefly described the roles of parent-committee officers.

Nothing else besides this perfunctory type of information was to be given to them in writing that night. Nothing — however briefly — about the mission and scope of the program, the goals of the parent participation component at Head Start, the rich variety of ways that parents could get involved, or the ways in which it would benefit themselves and their children. Since the lack of written information was striking, I anticipated that what the staff would verbally share with the parents would be quite extensive. Yet the comments about Head Start and parent participation that Harriet gave them that night were just as brief and uninformative:

> Head Start is a parent program, not just a children's program. It is very important that you get involved to help make decisions, and volunteer in classrooms. We also need you to help with events. It is your program.

After that short description, Harriet then introduced Judy, the woman who had stood up to complain about the noise level. Judy was a good speaker: plain, but to the point. In a five-minute presentation, Judy told the others in a matter-of-fact manner that all three of her children had gone through the program, and that, as a parent, she had seen how she and others working as volunteers had helped her own children and the entire program. She encouraged those present to become active:

> Parents are also needed in the classroom, kitchen, on field trips, and at lunch. You cannot depend only on the teachers. This is a parent-run program. It is not like a public school, we need everyone to get involved. . . .

Her main emphasis, however, was on the need to do fund-raising so that the children could do "fun things in the program," as she explained that "fund-raisers go to extra activities that Head Start would not be able to pay for, like field trips." Interestingly, while Judy had been asked to speak to promote parent involvement, her final comment also offered a mixed assessment of her experience over the years, as she concluded: "I've learned a lot. I have had a lot of good experiences. Some bad ones, too, I'm sorry to say."

Harriet introduced Juanita next. She was a grandmother/guardian who had been last year's parent chairperson. The sole focus of her brief comment was on the importance of raising money, and the threat of what could happen if they did not.

> You are here for your children. The teacher can only do so much; your children need you. I came from a sick bed tonight to tell you this because I love my children, and I love this program. [But] you must sell something, or children can't go on trips or get Christmas presents. . . .

After hearing the comments by Judy and Juanita, Harriet then stood up and mentioned the ways the parents could volunteer. Her entire message in this regard was the following:

> If you can't come in, there are things that you can do at home to help. You can make calls, cut and assemble things for teachers, be on the phone committee. (Harriet, family service worker, Downtown Center)

Judy then interrupted Harriet to say a bit more about the phone committee.

> The phone committee must have updated phone numbers for all parents. These numbers are important for emergencies and for noting changes in school issues. (Judy, parent, Downtown Center)

Yet neither woman actually explained what the "phone committee" was. So two of the teachers present (who at this point had not yet been introduced) called out from their seats that the staff needed current addresses and phone numbers, in case they needed to reach parents. Another teacher then yelled from across the room about the need for parents to supply clean sheets for nap time, and extra clean clothes for the children.

Up to this point, the other staff that were present had been sitting silently, dispersed around the room. Now that a couple of them had spoken up, Harriet took a minute to introduce Marlene, the branch manager, who in turn introduced the staff who were present. While all Head Start staff were required to attend the session, only five of the thirty Downtown Center employees were in the room. As Marlene introduced the other three teachers present, each one stood up and the parents politely clapped. One of the bus drivers was also present. When Marlene asked her if she "had anything to say about the bus system," the driver shyly shook her head no, and sat down. With that, Marlene stood silently a moment, then sat down.

Juanita quickly stood up to fill the void, saying:

> I forgot to tell you that in two weeks we'll have our business meeting, and you all need to come back for it. We will need a president, a vice president, a secretary, and a treasurer. But you need to come back and elect them.

Harriet jumped up to expand on this point, by noting, "Yes, meetings will be held monthly, and at them you can do whatever you want, have speakers, movies, videos, whatever." She then told the group that it was time to vote on the fund-raiser project for the fall. No one listened to her instructions however, and since none of the handouts that Harriet had been circulating about the fund-raising options had made their way to my part of the room, when she called for a show of hands, none of the parents around me knew what to vote for, and so they didn't participate. Rather, after a glance at Harriet, they shrugged it off, and instead of bringing up this point, just kept talking to each other.

Despite this, after scanning the room for a show of hands, Harriet announced that the group had decided to sell holiday gift items for the fund-raiser. Upon announcing this, people began to get up and leave, so Harriet started yelling, "No! Go to the classrooms, go to the classrooms!"

But the idea of going to the classrooms to meet with the teachers and "have an interactive exercise" had not even been brought up, so it was not surprising that most parents left. Some parents yelled back, "Where do we go? We don't know where our child's classroom is!" A few parents wandered up to the refreshment table, although the refreshments had not been mentioned either. The Head Start handouts lay scattered on the tables and the floor; these papers had not made it to my table either, and many of the parents who had received them had chosen not to take them home.

I noticed that one of the parents that I had met earlier was now leaving with another parent. They had disgusted looks on their faces, and were shaking their heads. I could not hear what they were saying, but I imagined that their comments reflected my own thoughts: the situation was ridiculous. I looked at my watch. It was now 7:45; the entire meeting had taken fifteen minutes.

Perspectives of Possibility and Change. By mid-year, Barrie, Elizabeth, and Candice were secretly planning steps to work around the deficiencies they saw in the family service workers. They were tired of "putting up with" the way parent involvement efforts were organized, and in separate conversations Elizabeth, Barrie, and Candice each shared with me some of the plans they had been talking about together.

> We've been talking about this lots, that we should take the responsibility for the orientation session away from the family service workers, and have the coordinators do it, so it gets done right. Candice, Barrie, and I have been talking about this, and we have decided to try to institutionalize [a parenting workshop], and simply have it at the beginning of the year. (Elizabeth, special needs coordinator)

> We've talked about this again and again, and we agree that they need an orientation for parents that addresses how to get involved, and the

> worth of it. We want to take it over from them [the family service workers], and make sure that it gets done professionally. (Barrie, health coordinator)

> The family service workers here let the parents do whatever they want instead of guiding them. They have no facilitation skills, and no rhyme or reason for their actions. Elizabeth, Barrie, and I have talked about this problem a lot. We really see a need to direct parents more. (Candice, education specialist)

Candice, the education specialist, was also convinced that the family service workers just "could not see the larger picture." She felt they had a narrow view of what educational activities could entail, and what the possibilities were for parent involvement, not only in the program, but in the lives of their children. The differing perspectives of these two camps became apparent one morning as Candice, Harriet, Fran, and I began to chat about ways to help parents understand how they could use everyday settings for learning.

Candice had commented that it made her angry when she saw parents in the grocery store who did not let their children make choices regarding food items, or even talk about the different foods in the store. She noted that if parents discussed foods with children and encouraged them to participate, shopping could be a wonderful learning experience.

To her great surprise, Harriet and Fran disagreed. They took the position that children should be kept quiet in the store. After all, they reasoned, a parent might not have the money to buy the things that the child wanted. The argument between the three of them became heated. Candice left in a huff, but not before making this point: "Even if you don't have a lot to spend, you can still involve your children!"

This scenario illustrates the power that perspectives, class, and context have in shaping one's view of the possible, and the potential, for learning outcomes. From Candice's middle-class perspective, the supermarket offered parents and children a way to explore and learn about their world as they compared and contrasted the various items and their attributes, as they counted, sorted, and weighed them, talked about nutrition, and where the different foods came from. In her mind, it was foolish to ignore the abundance around them, and hence, the unlimited learning opportunities.

As former parents in the program, however, Harriet and Fran knew the bite of hunger, and the experience of living in poverty shaped their view. Hence, the point they were arguing was based purely on economic realities. Instead of viewing the market as a positive place of possibilities, to them it was a place that taunted and tempted their children with tantalizing and expensive goodies. A place of promises, yes, but ones that were mostly out of their reach. Thus, their comment, "why even talk about it, if you can't buy it," was indicative of the way in which economic constraints shaped their broader view of life's possibilities. To Harriet and Fran, life offered only limitations; to Candice, life offered an abundance of learning opportunities.

STAFF VERSUS ADMINISTRATION

The center-level, nonprofessional staff blamed the county-wide Head Start administration for most of the program's limitations and problems, which included the lack of staff and resources, a lack of training, and inadequate levels of supervision and accountability. Yet the staff at all levels felt frustrated in this regard, as they were rarely allowed to give their input, regardless of their role in the program, professional or not.

> He [Desmond, the executive director] had a consultant come in, on a big salary, to do a needs assessment, and supposedly we were to find out what she found. Nothing came of it though. Staff were upset about personnel kinds of issues when she was here, and everybody talked to her about them. We thought it might do some good, but nothing has come of it. (Barrie, health coordinator)

> The staff don't really have any say around here. Administration just does what they want, and we have to live with it. (Harriet, family service worker, Downtown Center)

> Sometimes we staff do get our way, but not very often. (Miss Jinny, teacher, Downtown Center)

One gripe that the staff had regarding the administration was related to the way in which the management issued orders that made no sense to the staff, or were not workable. And getting the administration to see their point of view was, according to them, fruitless, and sometimes, as in the case of Miss Charlotte,[12] resulted in threats of dismissal. One example of the lack of regard for the staff's opinions about their working conditions and roles related to staff assignments at centers. Staff would periodically be bumped from center to center within the county, with no explanation and with no appeal. Harriet had been transferred from a small suburban center to the Downtown Center several years earlier. She told me how she had felt about being uprooted and moved to this site.

> I was so mad I didn't even unpack for the whole first year. It was bad, 'cause a lot of the plans that I had going on over there didn't get done after I left, and when [the new family service worker] came in, she had a different way of doing things. It made for a lot of tension. The second year, after I got back here, I felt more at home, and unpacked, but it took awhile. I don't look forward to moving again. (Harriet, family service worker, Downtown Center)

The administration also appeared to make capricious decisions in other areas. For example, as Columbus Day arrived that year, the staff, who had been granted time off for the holiday in previous years, were informed one week in advance that the holiday policy had now changed, and they would be required to work. Although the school would not be open for classes, they were to report at their regular times. The staff responded angrily, and threatened to form a union to protect them from such fickle treatment. Slowly, however, as time passed that year, the effort of trying to organize the staff ebbed as most, fearful of losing their jobs, chose not to press the issue.

Lack of Coordination and Teamwork. In theory, everyone at Head Start was supposed to work together to implement a safe, supportive, effective program for children and families. And yet, coordinating their efforts into a cohesive, integrated whole was rarely tried, let alone accomplished, despite the national Head Start focus on "component integration" and its stipulation in the policies of the program. Furthermore, while these policies indicated that all staff were supposed to be apprised of these policies through orientation and training processes, and once on the job were to work together in an integrated way in order to meet the needs of parents, families, and children, as Valerie had indicated in Chapter 2, no common mission or purpose of the program was ever discussed or developed among the staff.

The importance of coordination is underscored by the research on effective educational environments, which indicates that organizations that are effective are those that "maintain a pleasant and orderly atmosphere that promotes school coherence and positive, rather than competitive relationships among the school's members" (Stockard & Mayberry, 1992, p. 34). As has been illustrated in this program, however, numerous factors constrained the staff and administrator's capacity to coordinate efforts. The program's poor material conditions, human resource problems, and the distrust and division that marked the culture of the organization all impeded cooperative behavior.

Barrie spoke to me of the national Head Start office's promotion of coordination among components of the program. She also noted some of the drawbacks of the setting that were preventing this from happening in Morrison County:

> One emphasis of the feds right now is component integration at both the micro and macro level. Programming must be approached from a teamwork approach. For example, on immunizations. All staff, not just nurses, but bus drivers, teachers, family service workers, everybody must know the importance of them, so that all staff are on the same wavelength about why they are important. That way, all parents will get the same message. This of course leads to training. Everybody has to agree to carry certain things out, approach problems from the same perspective. We really do all need to work together. A lot of the staff don't see the bigger picture, but if we don't empower them, we can't empower parents. (Barrie, health coordinator)

Saranson (1982) has commented that the reason change is not made in schools is due to the fact that people cannot or do not feel they can express their ideas, believing that no one else feels the same. His research indicates that communication in schools is based on an avoidance of controversy, and feelings of individual impotence. This research resonates with the reality of poor communication in Morrison County, where ideas about programming were not shared between program components within centers, or between the centers. Information and ideas regarding the parent involvement program were not shared either, despite Lorna's initial point to me that "parent involvement includes all aspects of the program." Many other employees besides Lorna also espoused the view that everyone had to work together to get parents involved. For instance:

> Well, it's got to be more than just one staff person working at it [parent involvement]. It's got to be the branch manager, the teachers, everybody, working together, to make sure that parents feel welcome. We got to tell them, we need you as much as you need us. It's up to the

> teacher though, to get involved in this. Not only us, though, bus drivers, everybody. (Miss Jinny, teacher, Downtown Center)

Yet despite these views, the opinions of staff other than family service workers was consistently resisted or ignored as it related to suggestions about programming for parents. As Billie, a teacher aide at the Downtown Center, observed, "We give suggestions only if they want us to. More staff involvement, everybody working together on this would help."

When a staff member did make a suggestion to a family service worker, if it was responded to at all, the comment was typically negative. As a result, several staff had told me that they felt "their hands were tied" even though they might have good ideas for each other about parent programming. Candice, for example, had shared with me her belief that "the education and family service component needs to work more closely together for parents," but also noted that "it is important to not step on toes."

An example of the problematic social dynamics that were evident around such "turf issues" occurred one day regarding an idea that Candice had for parents. I had noticed Candice walking down the hall, chatting with another woman. When the woman left, Candice came into the family service office and told Harriet that the woman was a nutritionist who was willing to do parent workshops. She explained that the nutritionist could prepare and serve food while teaching about it. Candice then suggested, in a tentative way, that Harriet should invite this woman to a parent meeting. In response, Harriet just nodded her head and said "thanks" in a cold, disinterested manner. She then turned her attention back to the paperwork on her desk. Apparently angry at this dismissive attitude and lack of interest, Candice turned on her heel and left the office.

In talking with each of them later about this situation, both felt in the right for responding the way they did. Candice expressed anger and frustration over the lack of response when trying to provide some "professional expertise and direction to parents." Harriet also took the position that her resistance to "outside" suggestions was justified, for "if the parents didn't pick it," if it didn't arise from their own volition, then in her view, it wasn't something that should be offered.[13]

Like Candice, others not on the family service staff resented this lack of common vision and focus of purpose. In fact, this lack of coordination was a major source of tension that pervaded the program. And, as the comments below indicate, staff were frustrated because they couldn't get beyond their own roles, statuses, and duties to focus on their common purpose. As several staff related to me:

> Trying to get people to work together in this place is the pits. There is no communication with the staff, it's really poor. (Kathy, teacher, Downtown Center)

> We should be working together, but we don't see eye-to-eye on what should and needs to be done with parents. (Elizabeth, special needs coordinator)

> We need to get staff on the same wavelength about parents . . . (Doris, interim family service coordinator)
> The bottom line is that we have to work together or sink. (Sally, nurse, Harbor Street Center)

Furthermore, as a result, they didn't even know that in some ways, they were saying much the same thing. For example, in Harriet's comment (below), it is evident that she did not realize that some teachers did have a "two-generation" perspective about Head Start programming.

> The teachers forget that this program is not just for kids. It's for the whole family, and we are supposed to be working together. The teachers just don't see the whole picture. We have to work together, and we don't. We aren't together.

The lack of coordinated efforts was not just evident regarding parent involvement and programming at the center level. The administrative staff also had problems among themselves regarding other issues as well. For instance, Valerie felt Desmond (the executive director) continually overstepped his role in the program. Recently he had demanded that the volunteer Board of Trustees for Head Start[14] approve everything, such as staffing and expenditures, although, as she saw it, this was not their role.

> With Desmond's controlling manner, everything is bogged down. And while he tells parents that they can make decisions about things, he has changed the rules on them and now needs the Board of Trustees to approve everything. That is so unnecessary, and totally not within the rules. He is very difficult about it though, and that's the reason why we haven't been able to get much done this year. (Valerie, Head Start director)

Other staff members had also had experiences with Desmond stepping in and reversing decisions they had made. One staffer (a white woman) anonymously related this incident:

> The man [Desmond] is totally inappropriate. I worked eight months to try to get a child evaluated because I was convinced that she had neurological problems. I worked with her parents little by little, educating them about the importance of testing, explaining what I thought might be some of her problems, and what does he do: he accuses me of being a racist 'cause the child was African American. Then he calls the parents and tells them to go to [a major university out of state]; that he knows someone there who will treat them right [in a nonracist way]. So then I get a call from the doctor at the Medicaid office who says that they won't pay for an evaluation out of state. Of course not! Well, I didn't even know he was doing this. I had to call the parents and try to mend this whole thing, convincing them all over again that what I had suggested was the appropriate thing to do. (Head Start staff member)

The resentment and anger that these types of situations caused the staff influenced not only how they viewed their organization, but such negativity also shaped how the culture of the organization developed. Thus, one explanation for why staff did not talk about their beliefs, values, and understanding of the mission of the organization is related to the divisions extant within the staff, the level of distrust, and the resulting isolation expressed among them.

ON DIFFERENCE, TRUST, AND EXPECTATIONS

The skills and resources that the staff had available to them shaped their expectations about each other, the programmatic possibilities, and their own unique role with parents in the program. When low levels of skills were combined with a lack of adequate material resources, it was not surprising that conflicts among the staff were numerous. Blase (1987) has also noted the way in which such resource issues divide staff in educational settings. In this setting, struggles over the allocation and use of resources (such as volunteers and consultants), control over the means of production (i.e., planning programs for parents), differing values (about the importance of experience or formal education), and divergent perspectives (about what competent programming entailed) were but a few of the conflicts that arose in relation to resources.

In this setting, the issues of needed skills and appropriate levels of supervision were expressed as among the most vital, yet missing, resources. Because of the realization that many of the staff in the program were not highly skilled, and were not being held accountable to do a good job, trust of each other had been eroded, and this lack of trust was a source of tension. Professionally trained staff typically distrusted the grassroots experiences and perspectives of those staff who began as former parents, and likewise, those personnel did not value the formal education and experience that their administrative, supervisory colleagues brought to the setting. Neither group felt that they were understood or that they were allowed to do their work to their maximum capacity. In fact, relations were so tense that many staffers did not know what others did in their jobs. Because of a lack of trust of each other's qualifications or abilities, each one's judgment was also suspect, and as a result, open communication, the airing of opinions, and the exploration of possible programming and activities was avoided or resisted.

The result of these resource constraints and subsequent expectations was that staff who truly wanted to pursue programming for parents felt a deep sense of disappointment in not being able to do more. Others simply expressed feelings of malaise and disinterest regarding parents. In fact, most staff had expectations that within the present conditions, little could be accomplished regarding parent programming.

Thus, in this situation, the lack of material resources was a reality, the enormity of the job and the level of service they were expected to provide was extensive, and the levels of prior formal education and in-service training and development were not adequate. Therefore, it is not surprising that almost everyone struggled to fill their roles. In combination with the lack of trust and subsequent isolation, most not only struggled, but were unhappy doing it.

The result was that an air of negativity hung over the program. Rather than being a joyous place of possibility, it was the limitations of what couldn't be done that were consistently expressed. Such attitudes, and the corresponding staff relations had been formed in material conditions of poverty — programmatic poverty in an organization that had consistently been underfunded. In such a setting, and because of their very real personal, material, and interpersonal struggles and limitations, the staff expressed feelings of negativity about each other, and about themselves, their own abilities and perspectives. And, as will be illustrated in subsequent chapters, some of this negativity was also projected onto the parents in the program — interactions that the staff often avoided and resisted.

Therefore, in the same way that material, informational, and skill-building resources were low, so were the expectations of staff members. Ultimately, it was this low level of expectations about the possibility of working together and of doing something meaningful with parents and families that affected the overall culture of the staff and organization at this Head Start. Because of their disparate views on ways to implement — or whether to implement — the parent involvement program, each group saw the other as the problem, and a siege mentality of "us" and "them" was the result.

Hence, another result was an organizational culture marked by overt silence and covert turmoil. Compounded by the differences among the staff, the distrust among them fostered the lack of interaction among them, and staff members used what little power they had to deflect each others' input, relevant experience, and point of view. Combined with the lack of accountability, little supervision, and little coordination, the staff politics of mistrust and blame at this Head Start program appeared to prevent the implementation of any solutions. While individuals had personal conceptions of how the program might serve parents, the wealth of ideas among them was not welcomed as being relevant or possible. The staff resented this, and they resented the dictatorial leadership that promoted the silence; as we shall see in subsequent chapters, they "coped with the institution" (Pollard, 1982, p. 26) by replicating it in their interactions with parents.

Watkins and Marsick (1993), in their work on human resource development and learning in organizational settings, note that "organizations can foster passivity as a natural outgrowth of a rigid hierarchy and overbureaucratization" (p. 244). According to them and others researching this area (Martinko & Gardner, 1982, in Watkins and Marsick, 1993), individuals in organizations become "desensitized" to problems, and, hence, do not act to change their situations. Furthermore, Watkins and Marsick (1993, p. 244) point out that "decisions about how to act are made with an expectation of either success or failure. These assumptions about how things are likely to turn out influence behavior." Sheared (1993) has also addressed this dynamic, but even more specifically in regards to the relationship between an organization's evident resource constraints, and "the irrational bureaucracy" that subsequently results. Each of these factors, the inadequate physical and human resources, the infighting, and the poor communication that was endemic to the organizational setting, had a significant and discernible negative effect on individual staff member's understanding of their own role as one who was to promote parental participation and involvement in the program.

Therefore, thus far it can be seen that program staffing levels, inadequate skill levels, limited on-the-job training, and the lack of supervision and accountability were major problems that characterized the organizational culture of the program. While a lack of training, supervision, and accountability were recognized as being critical to the performance of the program, the interpersonal politics found among the staff were perhaps most influential in creating the negative tone that pervaded the organizational culture. Furthermore, when considered in combination, these issues synergistically affected the entire climate of the program, with the ultimate result being highly pessimistic expectations about the overall program's potential to optimally serve parents, children, and families.

Apple (1982, p. 82) has emphasized that "ethnographic analyses are dependent upon the accuracy of their view of the labor process," noting that only when the work culture is understood can the act of teaching and the content of teaching be comprehended. Each of the Head Start workers characterized here, through their day-to-day labor in this educational setting marked by scarcity and silence, had developed a perspective of what was possible in relation to parent programming. In the following chapter, the stories of parents reveal the way in which this program's organizational culture and the staffs' resulting negative, limited perceptions influenced the social relations between staff and parents.

NOTES

[1] As noted previously, children, staff, and parents typically referred to teachers and teacher aides by the title "Miss."

[2] After much begging by Barrie, Lillian did come back that year, but not until several months had passed since Gina had left.

[3] The Education Advisory Committee, the Social Services Advisory Committee, and the Health Advisory Committee were all stipulated within the original *Head Start Performance Standards* as key components of the parent and citizen participation emphasis of the program. Each of these three committees was to meet at least once yearly. In this particular year, only the Health Advisory Committee met — however, without any parent representation. The Social Services Advisory Committee had not been active for several years.

[4] As noted in the Introduction, prior to and during this field work I was a consultant at a local agency, and was affiliated with numerous social service initiatives, community projects, and committees. Hence, I had regular contact with a range of many different types of community and corporate representatives.

[5] Ironically, while Head Start promotes the hiring of parents, once hired they may not vote or have formal input into management or administrative decisions.

[6] Bolman and Deal (1991, p. 186) define the sources of political behavior as consisting of five factors: 1) coalitions or interest groups of individuals; 2) enduring differences among groups regarding values, preferences, beliefs, information, and perceptions of reality; 3) decisions about allocation of resources; 4) the

reality of conflict in organizations and the notion that power is the most important resource for dealing with conflict; and 5) bargaining, negotiating, and jockeying for position (i.e., power) is how organizational goals and decisions emerge.

[7] The professional-level positions — director or coordinators — typically held a B.A. degree, although this was not universal, as in the case of Lorna.

[8] Furthermore, within each of these two groups (professional and non-professional), additional "class" and functional divisions could be discerned in relation to a staffer's educational level and programmatic responsibilities. One example of how mid-level managers aligned themselves by education and expertise can be seen in the way that the education specialist, the special needs coordinator, and the health coordinator looked down upon the family service coordinator, who had only a high school education. Divisions were also present between employees of similar levels, but with differing duties. For instance, tensions existed between the family service workers and the teachers.

[9] Interestingly, while Harriet was typically an advocate regarding parent hiring, she also noted that sometimes hiring parents as staff wasn't always for the best, since they could be critical of others as well. For example, she once noted: "Take Kathy, she's a good teacher, but she really gets down on parents . . . She always says, I did it, they can too! . . . Sometimes it isn't always good to have former parents as staff, 'cause they don't put themselves in their shoes."

[10] For example, family service workers went to sessions about human service issues, but if a teacher wanted to attend, for example, a session on AIDS or drugs, the response was typically that it didn't fit with the duties of that job, and therefore was not needed.

[11] As in this situation, the case of the bus driver who revealed the AIDS case also had little administrative action taken against her.

[12] See Chapter 1.

[13] Chapter 6 examines issues regarding the development of parent activities in the program and the way in which the rhetoric of choice was a form of control over parents.

[14] The *Head Start Performance Standards, Appendix A,* provides guidelines about the responsibilities of each administrative entity in the program. These are: the "governing body" (at this site called the Board of Trustees), the Policy Council, and the Head Start director's functions. For some management functions, the governing body is responsible for guiding and overseeing the carrying out of the functions described for the group (Policy Council) or individual (Head Start director) charged with the actual decision-making function. In other words, the governing body is not required to vote on or make all decisions for the program, as Valerie states Desmond is requiring.

CHAPTER 4

Some Parents Are Better Than Others

The Politics of Class, Race, and Gender in Head Start

As families walked into this Head Start program, they encountered inadequate facilities and resources, poorly trained staff, and the undertow of staff politics. And, as this chapter will illustrate, they also came face to face with the negative perceptions and prejudices of staff members who often saw them as deficit-ridden, suspect, and having little to offer the program. In reality, the Head Start parents in Morrison County constituted a group of richly varied individuals of differing races and ethnic groups, social classes, genders, education levels, experiences, and resources. While each individual typically had challenges to overcome, they also had attributes and assets — strengths that not only were often ignored, but were sometimes openly denigrated.

I found this to be surprising in a program that was both literally and figuratively supposed to give children and families a "head start." Yet, while I was told that the program made an effort to enroll the most needy, "at-risk" families, it was ironic that those very families were then disparaged for being needy or having special concerns or problems. Some were young and had struggled with teen parenthood; others were grandparents now raising a second generation of children. Some parents were employed, while others received welfare, unemployment, or disability benefits.

This chapter addresses the reality of parents' lives from their perspective, and describes the material and symbolic resources that they brought with them to the Head Start program in Morrison County. Equally important, this chapter also explores the way in which the staff perceived the parents in the program, and the expectations, attitudes, and views they expressed about them. Embedded within this discussion are issues of race, class, and gender, and the ways in which biases about these constructs affected the programmatic and personal approaches that Head Start staff took with parents.

Although rarely acknowledged in Head Start's literature or programming initiatives,[1] biased expectations about the poor, people of color, women, the disabled, and others outside the normative white, male, middle-income reality are important to address because of the way they influence our actions as educators. As Rist (1970, 1972) first began to point out in the 1970s, and others (Good & Brophy, 1971; Rubovits & Maehr, 1973; U.S. Commission on Civil Rights, 1973; Persell, 1976; Tisdell, 1993; Sadker & Sadker, 1994) have expounded on into the late 1990s, the expectations of educators[2] are political. The views they hold about students affect how and what they teach, to whom, and whether or not they privilege students' life experiences, perspectives, and participation — or work to diminish those insights and efforts.

Swadener and Lubeck's (1995) recent book entitled *Children and Families at Promise: Deconstructing the Discourse of Risk* cautions us that the language we use to describe low-income children and families mirrors not only how those individuals are viewed in the present, but also reflects educators' perspectives of how they view what is possible for them in the future. In a culture that lauds the accumulation of capital above all, low-income families are considered "failures." Low-income status may be compounded by race, ethnicity, gender, and other markers (such as disability) considered to be "risk factors," and Swadener and Lubeck argue that it is this constellation of factors that explains why low-income people, people of color, and others "at risk" are then perceived as lazy, stupid, unreliable, unstable, and dangerous. Their careful analysis further asserts that racism, classism, and sexism is inherent in popular discourse about children and families, and that beliefs about low-income peoples' "defective tendencies" have historically pervaded social policy and public debate (Reed, 1992, in Swadener and Lubeck, 1995; Polakow, 1993; McCarthy & Apple, 1988).

Indeed, racist, sexist, and classist perspectives about the worth, potential, and reality of economically disadvantaged children and parents continue to influence public policy in areas as divergent as welfare reform (Miller, 1990; Sheared, 1993; Edin & Lein, 1997; Hayes et al., 1998) and school funding and facilities (Kozol, 1991; Wilgoren, 1997; Edwards, 1998), and subsequently affect educational programming (Lubeck, 1988; Hayes & Colin, 1994; Cuban & Hayes, 1996). Such policies and programmatic outcomes then shape the expectations of individual educators and others who are in helping roles. Slavin (1989, 1990) and others have documented that educators who have high expectations of students and families, regardless of their "risk factors," create environments that allow everyone to perform at optimum levels.

Indeed, at the Morrison County Head Start, instead of being viewed as having potential and "promise" (Swadener & Lubeck, 1995; Polakow, 1993), parents, children, and families were labeled as "at-risk," in need of fixing, or ignored as being more trouble than they were worth. Furthermore, entire centers were sometimes written off as being problematic, or not worth the staff's time. Because of these perspectives, the "privileged place" (Washington & Oyemade, 1987) that parents were to have in their child's life at Head Start functioned only for those who were privileged enough to be invited to participate.

This chapter begins with a demographic overview of the families at the Downtown and Harbor Street Head Start centers. During the study, I interviewed over fifty parents, thirteen of which are highlighted here. Their stories have been selected as representative of all parents with whom I met and worked during the study. In these stories of struggle, parents continually speak of their hopefulness — even in the face of some very difficult problems — and their desire for wellness, betterment, and change for themselves as individuals and for their families. Unfortunately, as will be seen, Head Start's role of building on this hopefulness, on the strengths and dreams of parents and families, was often not apparent.

DEMOGRAPHICS OF FAMILIES AT THE MORRISON COUNTY HEAD START

Head Start families in Morrison County were like many of the families who have participated in Head Start across the country. Because Head Start has an explicit mission to serve children and families with income and assets below the poverty level, the families involved in Head Start are typically members of the working poor or families who rely on welfare benefits. In Morrison County the majority of families at the Downtown and Harbor Street centers fit this description. While many were receiving Aid to Families with Dependent Children (AFDC) or some other type of government subsidy, such as disability benefits (60 percent at the Downtown Center, and 30 percent at Harbor Street received such benefits), substantial numbers of the heads of these households were employed. Whether receiving welfare benefits or employed, however, the

Table 4.1. Percentage of Children Served in Head Start by Racial and Ethnic Designation

	Nationally				Morrison County
Race/Ethnicity	**1983**	**1986**	**1993**	**1996**	**Year of Study**
Black	42%	40%	36%	36%	35.3%
White	31%	32%	33%	32.3%	37.1%
Hispanic	20%	21%	24%	25.2%	27.6%
Native American	4%	4%	4%	3.5%	0%
Asian	1%	3%	3%	3.0%	

Source: U.S. Department of Health and Human Service

majority at both the Downtown and Harbor Street centers reported yearly earnings of less than $12,000 (87.2 percent and 80 percent, respectively).

Over the years, while African Americans have been representative of approximately 12 percent of the U.S. population, because they are over-represented among the poor, they have been a much larger proportion of the children served. Table 4.1 compares the racial and ethnic designation of children served nationally to those served by Morrison County during the year of this study.

These county-wide figures were distributed across centers in varying patterns. As noted in Chapter 1 of this book, the Downtown Center was majority African American (87.2 percent) and at Harbor Street the majority of children (and by extension, families) were white (65 percent). There were also significant demographic differences between these two centers in the area of educational attainment (48 percent of Harbor Street parents had a high school diploma as compared to 73 percent of those Downtown), and percentage of two-parent families (the Downtown Center was mostly single-parent [84.5 percent], while 65 percent of families at Harbor Street had two parents in the home). In addition, differences existed in the numbers of children in the home (6.25 percent of families at Harbor Street had four or more children, while Downtown, 22 percent of families had this number of children). Similarities between the parents at the two centers were found in the age ranges of the mother (90.8 percent and 95 percent of mothers were between twenty and thirty-nine years of age at Downtown and Harbor Street, respectively), and in the gender of the primary contact parent listed at registration: the parent of contact was almost exclusively female.

Thus, while some variation existed in the demographic profiles between the two centers and among the individuals themselves, there were more similarities than differences. A typical parent of record at Head Start could be described as a woman with little income, little or no education beyond high school, and having two or more dependents. She was also the person who had primary responsibility for overseeing their child's schooling experience, regardless of whether they were in a two-parent household or not. Moreover, whether they were African American, white, or Latino, young or old, everybody seemed to have had their troubles to one degree or another. Yet, despite their problems and resource concerns, inherent throughout this chapter is the message that parents (most often women) consistently imparted to me: the desire — and the assumed capacity — to be some type of partner with the staff at Head Start, as a means of helping their children.

PRIORITY FAMILIES AND FAMILY PRIORITIES

At least 90 percent of all enrolled families in Head Start must meet income guidelines that hover at or around the federally established poverty levels. Within this group, families with the greatest needs are to be considered high priorities for enrollment into the program. In Morrison County such priority families were defined in numerous ways: single-parent households, grandparents acting as guardians, children and families referred by Child Protective Services, and families with intractable problems such as ongoing struggles with illness, addictions, and AIDS, and those experiencing immediate crises such as domestic violence. While some families were accepted into the program as "over-income" families (up to 10 percent of Head Start enrollees can be above the stipulated poverty threshold), the majority of families fell within the distinction of being a priority due to a constellation of factors.

These problems, and the constancy of poverty had worn them down, physically and mentally. As a result, isolation, financial constraints, problems with "the system," and fears for the present and future welfare of their daughters and sons were themes woven into their stories of struggle. Nina, Bobbie, Bess, and Carmen were examples of women who were able to articulate their priorities. Some women, like LaVerne, were so worn down by their struggle that they had difficulty in expressing an expression of the need for change, for betterment, for a future. Yet, each of them in their own way addressed the victimization and powerlessness, as well as the required resiliency that had framed their experience as low-income women. With major problems at home and few immediate solutions at hand, they had each sought assistance and support in Head Start.

NINA

Nina was a short, heavy Puerto Rican woman in her early twenties. Her bloated face was covered with acne, her teeth were pitted and brown and needed dental work. Occasionally she wiped her nose with the back of her hand, for either a sinus condition or drug habit left her constantly sniffling. Her hair was dank and lifeless, her clothes were too tight and were ill-fitting, and the overall effect was disheveled and dirty.

Having been in and out of relatives' homes and mental institutions as a youngster, Nina had not been successful in school, and she did not know how to read in English or in Spanish. While she did not share this information with everyone, she proudly told me when I interviewed her that she was enrolled in a literacy program. Until she became more skilled, she did not want others to know that she lacked this ability, and so put people off from learning too much about her by acting aggressive and talking tough.

Despite her air of bluster, Nina often looked depressed. In fact, Nina currently received Social Security Disability payments because of her poor mental health status. Despite this reality, she described herself to me as a "pretty proud person" who wanted to make people think that she was okay. She shared her life story with me one chilly fall day as we sat outside on the steps of Downtown Center:

> My mom died when I was five, and first I lived with my father, but he didn't want to keep me and sent me to Puerto Rico to live with my aunt and uncle. My uncle started raping me when I was nine; that went on till I was thirteen. I tried to tell my aunt but she didn't believe me. Then they sent me back to my father, and he was beatin' me, locking me up, hitting me with belts. He wouldn't let me have no black friends either.
>
> I tried to kill myself when I was fourteen. They sent me to mental health and I tried two more times. Therapy helped, but I still feel dirty, like I ain't worth nothin'. That's how I felt then and that's how I feel now. I feel like I never really had a shot. If I could live my life over again, I wouldn't have it that way, no way. Nobody ever really showed me love.

After I got out of the hospital, I moved in with my aunt, but she kicked me out too. So, I lived in a foster home till I was 17, and then I got pregnant. I guess I did that 'cause I was wanting love, to get it and to have something to give it to. I was so happy when I got pregnant with Jetta 'cause I knew it would be something to love. Her father didn't want her. He asked me to have an abortion. After she was born though, he liked her.

While I was pregnant my boyfriend and I didn't have no place, so my aunt let us sleep in her garage. Then he got a job, and would give me money. He helped for awhile, but when Jetta was about a year old, he lost his job. I have a son, too, now, so I get welfare for both my kids.

When I start working and making my own money, I'm leaving my boyfriend. He puts me down, tells me I'm stupid, that I can't read, that I'm fat. He hits me, hurts me bad sometimes. I hit him back. I s'pose I shouldn't, 'cause it just makes him slap me back. I hate him. I thought he would stick by me 'cause I have his babies, so I stayed. I work and struggle for my kids and here he is, healthy and doesn't support them at all. He just hangs out and does nothin'. He doesn't even help with the kids.

He accuses me that I don't love my son. But I spend more time with Jetta 'cause she's a girl. I was raped and if you were, you want to spend more time, you want to keep them from having to go through something like that. I'm worried about her 'cause of what happened to me, I don't want it to happen to her.

I want to work for my own money, I'm tired of being on assistance. . . . I'm workin' on my reading now so I can get my skills up so I can work on my GED. I really need that piece of paper, you know. . . . I want to get a job, and give my kids everything they want. (Nina, parent, Downtown Center)

BOBBIE

Bobbie was a white woman in her mid-thirties. She was tall and lanky, and had eccentric blond hair that formed a fuzzy mass of yellow around her head. She chain-smoked cigarettes, and the nearly continuous movement of her hand to her face called attention to the long, deep scar that ran from her upper lip to her cheek bone. Her freckles stood out against her fair skin, as did her sad blue eyes.

She had been married once a long time ago, and two of her three children were from that marriage. None of her children had contact with their fathers, whom she described as losers. Neither man sent her any child support.

Bobbie was not in good health, and her condition seemed to deteriorate as the year progressed. A chronic neurological condition impeded her from working, and as a result she received SSI disability payments. Between her symptoms, and the side effects of her medication, she rarely felt well. However, despite the fact that she didn't "exactly feel great all the time," she noted that "I don't take it out on the people around me."

Despite this caveat, Bobbie had many complaints about life, her church, the medical community, the schools, and Head Start. Having learned much from a difficult life, she appeared to be a woman of principle who tried to do what was right. Because of this she had volunteered to be Parent Chairperson at the Harbor Street Center. Her experiences as chairperson were difficult and stressful however, and she handled them with this philosophy: "just because somebody is in charge does not mean that they are doing the right thing, or are doing things in your best interest." In her stories to me, she always stressed this point: "you must take charge of your life, or be stepped on."

She and her children lived on a noisy street, in a ramshackle house, just a few blocks from the Harbor Street Center. While we usually met at the center, I visited her there one day, and we sat and drank lemonade on her patio, which was a cracked cement slab overlooking an alley filled with garbage. She described her life and her views about it:

> I graduated high school. I took classes in psychology, and I was gonna go into psychology, but it was bad timing. At the time I would have been going half time, part time, and at the time I couldn't drive, so that would have been a problem. But I try to tell people what I've learned, help them, and whatever. Maybe someday. . . .
>
> How would I describe myself? Well, I would describe myself differently now than I would years ago. I speak up for my kids, defend somebody when they're right. A person who likes to get involved, you know. Not always shut their eyes to situations and pretend that everything's okay when it's not. Years ago I was very quiet. It's the people in my life that changed me. I've had a lot happen to me in my life. Getting royally screwed, in plain English. I mean, you're talking about an alcoholic father, my husband. . . . Just things that happened in the family, outside friends, landlords. . . . The system. . . .

> You go into a school . . . and a lot of times they'll say, single parent, that's the problem. But I know a lot of single-parent kids, including mine, that are doing a lot better off than people's who are married. It's got nothing to do with being a single parent. It's what you want to accept and how you deal with things.
>
> It makes you realize that you have to defend yourself, you have to stick up for yourself. The way people look at you is the way you look at yourself. Take your kid to school, and one person can say something stupid to your child. . . . All they need to say is one line, and it'll stick with them for the rest of their life. . . . The most crucial age is between the ages of one and five, you know? Society needs to open up its eyes. [But] politics rules everything. . . . (Bobbie, parent, Harbor Street Center)

BESS

Bess was a wonderfully engaging African-American woman with a friendly smile. She talked easily with everyone at the Downtown Center and was eager to chat with me. She admitted that she was eager to socialize because she rarely got a chance to get out of the house and be with other adults.

Bess had dropped out of high school to have her first baby. She now had seven children,[3] and spent the majority of time with them at home. Now and then she was able to get factory work, and at one point had been a lunch aide at a local school. That didn't last long however; she had quit since she felt the principal always "picked" on her. Along with these job hassles, finding reliable child care was hard, so she ended up staying home.

Bess was rarely able to come into the Head Start center because she had no babysitter. On this particular day, her fifteen-year-old son Tyquinn was home with three-year-old Brenda and nine-month-old Dante. Tyquinn had been suspended from school for fighting, so she took the opportunity to have a little time to visit her four-year-old son, Ronald, here at Head Start. Next year, when both Brenda and Ronald would be in Head Start, she was hoping to be at the center much more frequently, but for now, because her youngest child suffered with asthma, she rarely took the children out.

> It will be good, 'cause at home it will only be me and Dante, and I don't hang around with other parents. I want to get to know other parents next year, when both Ronald and Brenda be goin' to school.

> They [Head Start staff] say that you can come to the school and what not. But see, me with seven kids, and needing a job, it drains me. I mean, it's enough taking care of Brenda and Dante at the same time. And I don't really bring them out, 'cause they suffer from asthma. If they feel bad, I don't get 'em out, 'cause they get worse, and then I have to bring 'em to the hospital, and stay at the hospital.
>
> If they [Head Start] had somebody that would, like, watch little kids, so that the parents could stay with the other kids in school, I'd like that. I would have liked to have gone on some [field] trips [with Head Start]. Like if each parent could take turns watchin' each other's kids. Or, if they had a room that the kids could stay in. If they said, like, this time you watch 'em this week, and then next time you do it. That would be good. A lot of these parents, they by themselves.
>
> I raised all my kids by myself. My kids' fathers, I don't ask for nothing. Not a dime. I don't want nothing from them. I'd like to go back to work, either work with kids, or in a factory. That's what I know. I used to do factory work, but, I couldn't get good people to watch my babies. I would come home and the baby would be wet, or didn't get fed, and I couldn't take it. Now, welfare gives me $734.00 a month, plus I get food stamps, which is about a total of a thousand dollars a month. I just make ends meet.
>
> I think I'm a pretty good mother. I'm a loner though, I keep to myself. I don't want no trouble. When it's about four or five o'clock, it's just me and my kids on the porch. (Bess, parent, Downtown Center)

LAVERNE

The first time I met LaVerne was at one of the Downtown Center's commodity food-distribution days. She and a girlfriend, along with three small children, were standing next to a pile of food stuffs, wondering how they would get it home. Realizing that there was no way that they would be able to carry this mountain of food, I offered them a ride home in my car. Her girlfriend chatted the whole way home, but LaVerne was mostly silent and spoke only to correct the children.

LaVerne did not look well. She was so thin, I could barely tell that she was five months pregnant with her ninth child. She had a ghostly look about her, as if she were exhausted and malnourished. Her eyes were sunken, and her dark brown face had an ashiness to it. A spattering of hairs ran along her jaw line and just above her lip. The pregnancy had been a problem, and she had been experiencing what she called "sugar."

This gestational diabetes had hospitalized her several times in the past few months, and she said that right after the baby was born, she was finally going to get her tubes tied.

At thirty-four years old, she had never worked outside the home. Having had a baby about every two years since she was sixteen, she had not thought much about what she might do if she was employed. Now she thought she might want to become a teacher someday, although she had difficulty articulating what that might mean. A high school graduate, she was soft-spoken, and while she had very little to say to me about what she might want out of life, and Head Start, she was very polite. She had recently applied for a teacher's aide position at Head Start but then became pregnant again, and her current condition prevented her from acting on the job opportunity, or doing much of anything really. She just did not feel up to it. Yet she was determined someday to get a job, since, as she put it, she was "tired of sitting around" for all these years.

Interestingly, it appeared to me as if she did little "sitting around." As a single mother there was no way of avoiding the day-to-day tasks of cleaning and caring for her children and her home. The home, which stood next to a railroad track, was only an alley's width from the foundations of the train trestle. The noise of the train was deafening as we chatted that day. Still, she made it home, and it was quite tidy. She told me that with no vacuum cleaner, she was left with the hard work of trying to brush the carpet with an old broom that had been worn down almost to the binding. With no working refrigerator, she was forced to find a way to buy perishables on a daily basis, and because of this she offered items such as fresh milk to her children only once a day. She needed other basic household items too, things that she had no ready cash for, as the monthly rent alone took almost her entire welfare check.

This daily experience of struggle had worn down LaVerne, and like other women with whom I spoke, she wanted more from her life, and for her family:

> I have to do somethin' besides sittin' around. But there aren't too many jobs that they're [her physician] gonna let me take now. But I just can't sit around. It's boring. I have to do something. I applied for a job at Head Start, 'cause that would be the easiest. I don't have to do no heavy lifting or anything. And the children, you know, they'd be right there, in the program.
>
> As a teacher [aide], maybe I could learn, like how, well, to be with the kids. Like, it's their first time, right? Their first time going to Head

> Start. Maybe I could learn to handle, you know, the kids. Maybe they got a different way than I do. Maybe they could learn from me and I could learn from them.
>
> I'm hoping that Tarique [her boy in Head Start] and Shahaira [age three, and signed up for Head Start next year], that I can get them into day care, 'cause you know, I don't want to be sittin' around. 'Cause that's what I would be doin', anyway, sittin' around. (LaVerne, parent, Downtown Center)

CARMEN

The first thing I noticed when I met Carmen was her pierced nose. She wore a small gold nugget in it, and she fiddled with it — twirling it around from time to time, as if to reassure herself that it was still there. Carmen was a young Puerto Rican woman in her early twenties. She had dancing black eyes that looked straight at you, as if in defiance. A chronic chain-smoker, she would jab her cigarette into the air to accentuate what she was saying. She spoke with a similar one-two punch as she told me about this habit:

> I hate these cigarettes. I been smokin' since I was ten, 'cause my mom used to ask me to light hers for her. Here she was dyin' of lung cancer and emphysema, and she asks me to light her up. It's 'cause of her I started, I got hooked right away. I'm twenty-three now, and been smoking since I was ten. That's thirteen years. I've tried to quit, 'cause I know it's bad for me, and for my girls.

She was as beautiful as she was articulate. Her skin was creamy and her dark hair fell to her waist. Carmen was overweight, but her roundness suited her. One could imagine that, if all dressed up, she would be a lovely sight. Instead of nice clothes, however, I always saw her in the same pair of tight jeans, one of a handful of sweatshirts or teeshirts, and an L.A. Raiders jacket.

Although I occasionally saw Carmen at the center, catching up with her was always a problem. As she put it, "all of her phones were out." Furthermore, the back-up, emergency numbers she had given the center to use were no good either, so reaching her by phone was impossible.

Carmen was Latina, but the father of her two children was African American. This had caused her and her dad to have a falling out. Her dad could not understand why she would stay with a Black man, and he had kicked her out of the house because she refused to break it off with him. Since her family did not approve of her relationship, they rarely helped her. If they did give her money, "it always came with strings" about how she should spend it, and why she should leave her boyfriend.

Carmen was a second-year parent at Head Start. Last year she had two daughters in the program, but one was now in kindergarten. While the public school system in the community was not considered to be very good, the school her daughter attended was regarded as the best in the city. Carmen was glad that she lived in the area so that she could send her daughter there. She felt that school was very important, and doing well in school was a goal for herself and her children, a point that she frequently referred to as she talked about her life experiences and her outlook:

> My mom died when I was thirteen. I had brothers and sisters that I had to take care of. I got in trouble when I was young, and I don't want that for my girls, pregnant at sixteen and such, with no money for an abortion. I dropped out in tenth grade due to my baby. I didn't have no money for a sitter. Besides, I don't trust my girls with a sitter. I don't trust anyone with my girls. I'm afraid for girls, they have it rough in life, you know? I was sexually abused when I was a girl, that was that trouble I was telling you about. If anybody ever touched mine though, I would kill 'em in a minute.
>
> Anyway, I was hopin' that if I got them in here at Head Start, that then I could maybe get back [to school]. I still haven't finished though. I was doin' my GED, but they told me with my level, it would take about three years to get it. I gotta get it though, that's my ticket.
>
> I am so sick of welfare I could puke. I had a job at an apartment complex, but the guy put too much on me. At the end of ninety days, he said I was out because I couldn't do all the work. I had another job before that, but my oldest got sick and I had to take off. My boss wouldn't help me, and let me go. I feel like people say that I don't want to get on my feet, but that's not true. There's no job that works around school hours. And if you do find something, and your kid gets sick, you're fired.
>
> Now, I can't find a job, and it's gonna be a year and a half before both my girls are out of kindergarten. I want to get off welfare, but how could I and still pay a sitter, make the rent, buy food and the other stuff? I babysit, and make twenty dollars a week walkin' a kid in my neighborhood to school. I get help from my dad, and my family sometimes too, but then they make you feel like you owe 'em. I'm fixin' to

> lose my WIC now too, 'cause it's only till the baby is five. I don't know what I'm gonna do then.
>
> I'm sick of welfare. I been on it five years now, and I'm sick of struggling to get by on $433.00 a month when my rent alone is $500. Five hundred for the place I live in, I still can't believe I pay it, but I can't get no better. Now, if I had section 8 (the federal subsidized housing program), I'd be home free, but I've been on the list for five years. I was number 956, and now after all these years, I'm only in the 300s. If I had a job, was on drugs, or on the street, then I could get on, but 'cause I play it straight, I don't get nothin'.
>
> I know how you get up the list, everybody does. My girlfriends tell me, "Carmen, it's only 20 minutes outta your life, give it to the man." But that makes me sick. There ain't no way that I'm gonna fuck him to get a place to live. I ain't no hooker! So, I'm stuck.
>
> I am sick of everything. Sick of welfare, sick of men, sick of everything. I'm not married, and I never want to be. Once that ring's on your finger, men think they own you, even more than they already think they do. But I love my kids. The girls see their dad every day, but he only comes over to play with them. He gives me money sometimes, when he's got it, which ain't very often. (Carmen, parent, Downtown Center)

Throughout their comments, the isolation and the need for support and child care were dominant themes among these women, each of whom aspired to something better than their circumstances presently allowed. Each wanted to work, yet work was no guarantee of having an adequate income. As the parents in the following section illustrate, simply having a job was not enough to keep families out of distress.

THE WORKING POOR

Approximately 40 percent of families at both centers were employed full-time. Some of these families were members of the "working poor" who had always barely made ends meet. Yet, even families from financially stable working-class homes now reported struggles with layoffs, downsizing, underemployment, and minimum wages. For those with no other options, sporadic periods of welfare assistance felt frustrating and demeaning.

For example, Francine and Pamela had come from families that, while sometimes struggling to make ends meet, had managed to provide adequate resources and support. Theresa, Maggie, and Garnet had been raised in families with stable resources of high skills and good wages. While all parents interviewed expressed the perception that education and employment were important, unlike the other parents already highlighted, each of these women had a good support network, and a good educational foundation, which helped them to seek jobs, get work, or further their training. None of these women considered themselves to be "poor", even though at times they had to rely on welfare. Instead they thought of themselves as "struggling."

FRANCINE

Francine was a sturdy, round African-American woman in her mid-twenties. Francine was friendly, had clear opinions about how things should be done, and she offered a good argument when challenged. Her mother had worked as a teacher's aide for Head Start, and Francine had attended that program in another state when she was four. She was bright, had received good grades in school, and had been a leader in school activities. After high school, she had attended business school where she received her Associate's Degree, and had worked for several years in clerical positions.

She had been raised in the rural south, but often came north to visit relatives. During one visit, she met and married a college student from Africa. The marriage lasted only five years. She now had custody of Andrew and Brianna. The children had regular contact with their father, but he could not contribute much toward their support. The family received AFDC and lived with her mother in a house just around the corner from the center. In fact, she had specifically chosen that flat because it was so close to Head Start.

Francine wanted to do something meaningful in her life. She was interested in nursing school, and had wanted to return to school through a welfare program, but could find no one to watch her children. Family members were committed elsewhere, and the day-care programs had long waiting lists. However, as soon as her youngest child was ready for Head Start, she intended to pursue this further.

Francine perceived her role as parent as being especially important, noting that this was a lesson that she had learned from her mother. To Francine, being involved with your children meant more than coming to an occasional parent meeting. She explained:

> I myself had attended Head Start, so did all my sisters. We all attended Head Start. And I knew what Head Start was all about, 'cause my mom

> was a Head Start teacher. My mom went to every parent meeting for all of us, all through school, and she had been urging me to get involved.
>
> When Andrew started coming [to Head Start], I said, I have to get involved, because my mom was involved with us up until the time we graduated. But last year I didn't get involved, but my mother was, with Andrew. I had to be with Brianna at home 'cause she was sick.
>
> Now, the kids like to see me in class. It makes my son feel good to have me there helping. And now that I have been, I really see the importance of it.
>
> I want to go back to school. Actually, I was supposed to start nursing school this year, and I had signed up through the REACH[4] program, but I couldn't afford a babysitter. I wasn't a priority, 'cause Brianna wasn't two yet; once she becomes two, I will be. They'll pay for my day care, provide me with transportation.
>
> I'm not one to sit there quietly. I do a lot of listening, but I also speak up. I've always been that way. I'm just that way. If you tell me that I can't do something, and I know it can be done, then that just makes me even more determined to do what I gotta do. (Francine, parent, Downtown Center)

PAMELA

I met Pamela early in the year, at a parent meeting at the Downtown Center. She had a beautiful oval face. It was smiling and open, and her eyes were just a shade lighter than her rich brown skin. She also stood nearly six feet tall, and the night I met her, she was wearing a bright pink sweatsuit. Such a bright expanse of pink most certainly caught my eye, but the most striking feature of the outfit was the tightly laced, black army boots she also wore. While the color of the sweatsuit varied, the boots never did.

Pamela was interested in everything, motivated, friendly, and eager to learn. She had grown up in a loving, working-class family. She was the youngest of ten biological children, but the family also had an assortment of foster children living with them. Both of Pamela's parents were deceased, but the family was still very strong and supportive. They kept in touch with one another, and helped out when needed.

She and her daughter, Zena, lived near the Downtown Center with two of her girlfriends. They shared a tiny house in the middle of a low-income neighborhood, on a street that was dirty and dim. Pamela complained that the abandoned buildings surrounding her house were fire hazards and drug dens.

Inside, her living room was paneled with dark wood, and little light came through the heavy curtains on the window. Photos of her family hung on the walls, along with several pictures of Dr. Martin Luther King, Jr. When I asked Pamela if this was the home she had grown up in, she responded proudly that she had been raised in "a nice place, not like this." This was only temporary, she explained, while she got back on her feet.

Pamela had recently been laid off as a phlebotomist,[5] and was unable to find work. She wanted to get work in another medically related position, and so was now attending community college, studying radiology full-time. She received welfare, and hated it. But Pamela was very motivated and determined to get the most out of everything, for both herself and her daughter. In fact, the reason she had switched her daughter from a day-care program to Head Start was because she wanted more of an education for her, not just "babysitting."

> It's more educational, they teach the children, and I think it's a good head start for a child, to have that before they go into kindergarten. Well, she's been in day care since she was 6 weeks, so she's used to children. But I wanted that educational background before she got into public school.
>
> Zena is really smart, and really outgoing, so I did it. I want her to have a good future, because, if you ask her right now, she wants to be a lawyer or a doctor, so I mean, she has a great goal that she wants to accomplish, and I'm gonna help her accomplish it.
>
> I got good grades in school, a B average. In school I was a very active person. I was on every committee there was. I'm a very outgoing person. I'm a senior advisor for [a local girl's drill team]. I've been with them for nine years. Zena's a part of it too.
>
> I enjoy helping other people. My heart goes out to other people, and I really enjoy helping them. I wish that more parents at Head Start would come and get involved. 'Cause like, when we vote on something, parents get upset, because they say, "well, we didn't want that," but they don't show up. I do understand that a lot of them have children at home, so they can't come. But, I would hate to say it, but I think that a lot of them just aren't interested in their child. (Pamela, parent, Downtown Center)

GARNET

Garnet was a petite Black woman who spoke with a lilting Caribbean accent. She was an intelligent woman in her late thirties who had taught high school home economics in her native country, but then came to the

United States to work on a bachelor's degree in food service. After graduation, the only work she could find was a low-paying position in a nursing home, where she now worked full-time. Garnet hoped to complete a certification program that would help her get a better job. But her real dream was to move back to her home island in the Caribbean, where she could earn more and have a better standard of living.

Garnet was married to an African-American man. Since their marriage, he had become disabled, and when he lost his job, the family lost their health insurance. The surgery he required in order for his full recovery was beyond their means, so he remained unable to work.

They had one son, Andre. He was personable, bright, and fun to be around. Andre was the gem of their life, and Garnet spoke of him with pride. Garnet tried to be upbeat about their troubles, and her religious faith helped her cope. She was active in her church, her neighborhood, her job, and with her family. She discussed her situation with me:

> I think I'm outgoing. I have a lot of friends that could tell you about me. I'm deeply religious, I go to church, and I think that's it. It takes a lot to get me down. There are times I get down, but I pop back up, so I guess it's optimism.
>
> I was a teacher before I came here. That was my career before I started in food service. My area of work is food service, and I belong to a food service organization. I go to a lot of seminars connected to work and whatever. Sometimes it's continuing education, and sometimes it's like, food shows, and things like that. I'm kind of used to being in activities, and in positions of responsibility, and whatever. I'm really involved in my church. I'm on the vestry at my church, I'm involved. . . . Ha, ha, ha, too busy. I try to help everybody, and I enjoy being of service to others.
>
> Friends told me about Head Start. At the time that Andre was ready to go to school, our finances were really bad. My husband needs to have a total hip replacement, and his disability has run out. It's just my salary that we are living on, and we wanted Andre to mix with a lot of other kids, without spending a lot of money.
>
> I want to be involved in anything that my child is involved in, because I want to know firsthand what's going on. So that if I know what's going on, I can do as much for him as I can. So, like if there are parent meetings, and I go just as a bystander, to listen, I don't feel that I'm adequately . . . that I am doing an adequate job. I want to go and be involved in decisions that will affect him. If there's anything that I can

> change I would, because of him I would like to change it. And just sitting back as a bystander you won't be able to really do nothing much. (Garnet, parent, Downtown Head Start)

MAGGIE

Maggie had also emigrated to the States from the Caribbean, and as a result had seen her standard of living decline. Like Garnet, she had also been a teacher, but she could not work in that capacity in the U.S. until she finished her degree. She began to pursue this, but soon became discouraged by the lack of discipline she had found in classrooms here. So, instead of teaching, Maggie worked as an entry-level clerk in a hospital. Her husband was a laborer. They had four children, three of whom had attended Head Start. Their youngest was currently in the program, and she was sorry that her Head Start experience would soon be over, for she enjoyed meeting with other parents.

Maggie felt education was important, and she hoped to go back to school to become a nurse. Her mom and her aunt were both nurses, and most of her immediate family were employed in the medical field. All of them had college training, which is what she wanted for her children:

> Well, just like me, I want them to go to school, right up through high school. I will help them. We want them to go to college. We already told them, that if they go to college until twenty-two years old, we will help you, if you want to continue college, we will help you. But if you gonna drop out of college, that's it. We're not gonna help you do nothing.
>
> Yeah, 'cause like we tell them, you know, you can't get a job without going to college. I tell them you used to be able to take your high-school diploma and get a job, and now you can't do it. You can't do it, you have to have college.
>
> Education is important for me, yes, it is. I want it for me. I wish I could quit my job right now. I want to go back to school. I'm trying to see if I can go into the LPN[6] program right now. 'Cause I can't get into the RN program, it's a three-year waiting list for it. So I was thinking about going into the LPN, work my way up, take classes, and then get into the program, which I'm on the waiting list. I felt that I should have continued on with school, at the time. It would have been something for me to fall back on.
>
> I'm motivated to better myself, not only financially, but educational wise, I definitely want that. I'm trying to and working hard towards

> it. . . . I'm a good mother, I would say. A hard worker, a very hard worker. One of these days you'll see me as a nurse, probably. (Maggie, parent, Downtown Center)

THERESA

Theresa was a white woman in her early thirties. She had a beauty reminicent of a renaissance madonna, with creamy skin and long, wavy, dark hair, and her easy smile and her friendly, personable manner were inviting to both adults and children. Theresa had grown up in a large, close-knit, working-class Italian family in a community near Harbor Street. Despite these strong roots, her own children had no contact with their father. He had abandoned them after the second child was born; she had not heard from him since and received no child support.

She and the two children lived in a run-down apartment on the far edge of town, a good distance from Harbor Street. She had moved to that particular location because it was cheap. The only income she had was her welfare check and some occasional money from making and selling decorative crafts to friends and family.

Theresa had graduated from high school and had worked as a bookkeeper prior to her marriage. Her dream, however, was to work with children. In fact, she had wanted to be a kindergarten teacher for as long as she could remember, but with a lack of money, and then her marriage, she did not go to college. Despite this, she found ways to work with children. Prior to the birth of her children, she had been a volunteer for a Head Start center in a different part of the county. Then, when she enrolled her children in Head Start at Harbor Street, she offered to volunteer there, because, as she explained:

> I love children. I always have. As a kid, I used to watch the neighborhood children, and my sisters and brothers. I'm the oldest of seven, so I've always been involved with children.
>
> I volunteered a lot of time last year, and I enjoyed it. I helped out a lot, but I enjoyed it, and I loved it. Sometimes, like if Miss Winnie was gonna be out for the week or part of the week, I'd try to get in every day. Last year, at the end of the year, I was given an award for volunteering, at the picnic. And I was shocked, 'cause I wasn't one of the mothers who handled the meetings. I never dreamed. It never entered my mind.
>
> I can never have them [her children] around me enough, I guess. You know, if I didn't care to have children around me, and it was just to

> look in on my son, I probably wouldn't have volunteered. But I'd send him off to school, and then drive over to be with him. . . . I should have been a teacher, because just sitting with the children, I would watch, just watch the things that they would do, and how they interact with each other. . . .
>
> I felt happy helping out. And, I guess I pretended to be a teacher. The dream that I didn't fulfill. . . . Miss Theresa this, Miss Theresa that . . . a couple of them still call me that. You know, it got me right here (pointed to her heart) where I live. My father tells me all the time, "it's not too late. You'll be forty-something when you get your degree. It's not too late." But that, that has always been my dream. To be a kindergarten teacher. (Theresa, parent, Harbor Street Center)

Clearly, each of these women viewed education as a way to move up and out, the ticket out of their current, low-income status; the key to a more prosperous future. While this dream involved continuing education for themselves, it also consisted of one day seeing their children with a college education, and good-paying job. In essence, being a part of the middle class.

THE MIDDLE CLASS

As some Head Start parents could tell you, however, being a part of the middle class was no guarantee of immunity from financial disaster and personal crisis. Job loss, disability or illness, and fractured marriages wreaked havoc on what had once been a stable lifestyle. While not necessarily in dire poverty, these families were also struggling, and were enrolled under Head Start guidelines that allowed up to 10 percent of families to be above the poverty level. "Over-income" families[7] at this program fell far below the 10 percent cap however, for only 3.9 percent of all families were within this category. Most over-income families were let into the program because their children had a special need, or the family was experiencing problems. Three of these parents were Heather, Christine, and Raymond, who was one of the few men overtly involved as a parent in the program.

HEATHER

Heather was a white woman in her late thirties. She was petite and slim, and had enormous green eyes that were hidden under a continually furrowed brow. Although she and her son had applied to Head Start several weeks after the program had begun in the fall, due to her personal crisis her son was admitted as soon as a slot opened up at the Harbor Street Center.

Heather had been raised in a white-collar family, and before getting married she had worked for years in clerical positions. Then she married am upper-middle-class, professional man and the family moved frequently due to his job. He began battering her, and away from home and family, she had few places to turn. The longer she stayed, the worse the situation got. The first time she tried to leave, her husband had chased her down and almost killed her. Still determined to get out, however, and with the help of a relative, she had recently escaped. Packing in two hours' time, she fled the house with her three-year-old son, Jordan, and moved back to the town of her youth.

Despite leaving the marriage, life for Heather and Jordan was not easy. While the physical abuse had been frightening, the scars from the emotional abuse were what remained. Now describing herself as anxious and passive, she told me that the confident Heather no longer existed; instead, she felt isolated and fearful. She was particularly concerned about the welfare of her son, and had been thrilled to hear about the possibility of Head Start, hoping that it would be a safe, supportive environment in which both of them could begin to heal. She described her situation:

> We live with my dad who's retired. I moved back home 'cause I had no place else to go. . . . I needed desperately to put Jordan with the children, in a good, healthy surrounding. 'Cause between my father and me, I don't know what was happening to him. For example, Jordan started stuttering real bad, and my dad thought it was a joke. That's just the way he is, and I can't wait to get a job, so I can get my own apartment.
>
> I was always very independent, responsible. I would laugh myself out of any situation. . . . Now, I'm deathly afraid of confrontation, and I didn't realize it till after I was in counseling. It's like a part of me wants to take a stance, and the other part is scared to death; because of what I went through, you know. And things happened with Jordan, too, so I want to be on guard.
>
> One time, when he was five months old, he was in his walker in our room. My husband came flying out, pushing him all the way down the hall, saying to get the fuck out of here, then punched a wall next to him. I pulled Jordan into the kitchen, and he was bone white, shaking, and he was not breathing. He held his breath, he was scared to death. . . . Jordan got to the point where he [his dad] would just say boo, and he was afraid of him.

An old friend of mine told me about Head Start, and told me to check it out, 'cause it might be what I needed. It was right up my alley, 'cause I couldn't afford anything, I wasn't getting child support at the time, and I was more concerned for Jordan than for me. Still, it was rough starting [at Head Start], because we're from an abuse situation. I was very scared to put him into anybody's hands. (Heather, parent, Harbor Street Center)

CHRISTINE

Christine was the vice chairperson at Harbor Street. A white woman in her early thirties, she had carefully styled, shoulder-length blond hair, dark tanned skin, twinkly blue eyes, and a smattering of freckles. She dressed in stylish, expensive sports clothes, and looked as if she should be on her way to a golf date at the country club. On close inspection, however, you could tell that the clothes had been worn more than just a few seasons.

Christine was married to an alcoholic who, as a result of his drinking, had lost his high-level job with the government some time ago. He had just recently been in treatment, and Christine hoped that his newly sober condition would continue. The family had gone through his benefits and their savings account long ago, and they now had little money. She went to Alanon daily to try to stay sane.

Christine tried to stay upbeat. She was friendly and outgoing, and admitted that she did not like confrontation. She was learning to deal with it at Alanon, however. Christine had worked as a bookkeeper, but with the birth of her two sons, had decided to stay home "since they were only little once." Even with their financial problems, she still did not feel that she could return to work full time, for she felt that her husband was not reliable enough to take care of the boys. So, even though Head Start only offered half-day sessions at the Harbor Street Center, when she found out about it, she jumped at the chance to enroll her oldest son.

I couldn't afford preschool, and he needed something. He was climbing the wall at home. He needed some friends, he needed some kind of school atmosphere. I can't afford to go back to work, not with two of them. It's just too much money for sitters. It just would have been too hard. Plus, I wanted to be home, you know, be a mother for a few years, you know. They're only little once.

I happened to be in McDonalds one day [across the street], and they were having an open house. My son had been on a waiting list, a long waiting list. And when I found out about this open house they were having, I rushed right over.

I grabbed all of his papers, you know, his immunization records, his doctors, everything I needed. They put me right at the top of the list, 'cause I had everything ready. . . . And that fall, there was an opening. I had to wait a couple weeks, to see if anybody would drop out, or if somebody wouldn't show up, and then when there was this opening, they took him.

I'm grateful that they have programs like this for people who can't really afford to put them. And I feel happy to help out when I can, 'cause I don't believe in getting something for nothing, you know? I do what I can. I've brought things in, I've tried to contribute as much as I could. I do it for my kids, and I do it for the other kids too. I've been involved from the very beginning, but that's the way I am. I want to know what's going on, and I wanted to, you know, be a part of it. So, I'm not working full time, but I am busy constantly, and at nights it is hard, I do have to squeeze things in sideways. (Christine, parent, Harbor Street Center)

RAYMOND

Raymond was a soft-spoken, African-American man in his late thirties who was now disabled, out of work, and trying to put his life back together. Slim and quite frail, one could imagine him as having been constantly on the move in his better years. A college graduate, he had been a manager with a major company, but he became ill with cancer and he lost his position, which had required extensive travel. Now he spent his days at home with his young daughter. He had taken his illness with good stead, and shrugged off his pronounced limp as matter-of-fact. He was determined to make the best of life.

Raymond loved being a dad, and being of service at Head Start. He served as representative to the Policy Council, and was the chairman of that committee. Because of the lack of overall male presence in the program, he felt that his volunteer work was especially important.

Raymond's wife worked at a job that also required much travel, and so for extended periods was on the road. This, in effect, put him in the role of single father, keeping house and caring for his daughter much of the week. While his wife focused on supporting the family, he focused on getting better, and spending time with his daughter. His cancer was now in remission, and he hoped to get back into the work world. He spoke to me about his life, his illness, and the support that the program had given him and his family:

> The tumor was so large it was pressing against my spine, so there was nerve damage. My doctors were honest. They told me it could take anywhere from a year to eight years to regenerate. Who knows, 'cause of the nature of the cancer, and the seriousness of the operation.
>
> It was a blessing, though, 'cause I was able to spend quality time with my daughter. She was about two years old, something like that. She's my only child. And that's when that bonding started. My wife was working, but daddy became the housewife. That's when I took on a different role. Prior to that, I was involved, but it was not the involvement that I have now.
>
> A good neighbor of mine, she told me about Head Start. As a matter of fact, she recommended my daughter for it. We never realized that it was available in our area. It was a good idea too, 'cause at that time, I was just out of the hospital, and a few hours, the four hours that she had here in the afternoons, did me some good, it let me rest.
>
> The first meeting came at the center, and I attended. So, that's when it really started. I can't work right now due to my disability, and I did not want to sit home and get bored. I'm not just home trying to recuperate. I started meeting the staff, I liked what I saw, I liked the surroundings, I enjoyed the staff.
>
> I'm always hearing about parents not being involved with their children. And that's where it starts, at a young age. You have to get involved at a young age. So, I'm spending time out there, trying to do something for the community, and for the county. I'm proud of that.
>
> Sometimes I go into the classroom and just watch the children. It kind of makes you see the world differently, when you see it through their eyes. Everything is so new, you know. Their wonder at the world is amazing. It really teaches you to stop and look at things again. We, I mean, adults, don't do that enough. (Raymond, parent, Morrow Street Center)

STAFF EXPECTATIONS ABOUT PARENTS

As is evident in these stories, Head Start parents in Morrison County represented a range of backgrounds, experiences, circumstances, and resources. Some came to the program abused and battered, with no clear sense of where to turn. Others had a clear sense of purpose and direction, and carried with them a wealth of social and educational successes, while others needed a variety of skills and experiences that would help them to develop such successes. Some parents were in transitional periods of past successes and present difficulties. Francine, Theresa, Bess, Carmen, Pamela, Nina, LaVerne, and Bobbie exemplified the efforts that women everywhere must undertake when trying to maintain the health and well-being of a family alone, and spoke to the entrenched nature of some parents' problems, while Garnet, Raymond, Christine, and Heather addressed the sudden unpredictability of life and their resulting hardships. Regardless of their past and present struggles, however, each wanted a future that would offer a better life for themselves and their children.

Thus, both crisis and opportunity presented itself in the lives of these families. And yet, as Swadener and Lubeck (1995), Polokow (1993), and others have pointed out, when individuals or families are only identified by their weaknesses, problems, or constraints, their potential is overlooked. Furthermore, as will be addressed below, when families and parents are viewed in negative terms, when they are seen as too much trouble, not worth the effort, or hopeless, they are sometimes ignored, not welcomed, or otherwise dissuaded from participating. This is particularly ironic in a program that was specifically designed to address the needs of families, to build on their strengths, and encourage participation and involvement.

PARENT INVOLVEMENT: WORTH IT OR A WASTE OF TIME?

The Head Start program in Morrison County had the potential to offer tremendous opportunities that could have lead to growth and development of parents and a more prosperous future for their families. As stated in previous chapters, the mission of the program details a variety of experiences that were to be offered to parents to help them develop leadership skills, job skills, and parenting skills; provide informational and material resources; and help them assess their needs, goals, and options. Key to providing such a program agenda for parents was the view that creating and implementing programming for parents was worth the time and effort of the staff. In this regard, what was expressed by the staff was contradictory. For example, staff generally expressed a view that parent involvement was important, yet clearly wondered whether it was "worth it" to try to work with certain groups of parents or with specific individuals, because of characteristics or concerns that they viewed as problematic. Some broadly stereotyped parents as either stupid, or resistant to involvement with their children and the program. And, when these negative expectations about parents intersected with the lack of programmatic resources (facilities, time, expertise) available to work with parents and develop meaningful programs, then the expectation that parent involvement is an effort well spent is even further diminished.

In probing this area, I asked staff if working with parents was "worth it." Some staff members stressed that the level of need that these families had was what convinced them of the importance of their time with parents.

> If I can make one parent more aware of the world outside, it's worth it. (Miss Billie, teacher aide, Downtown Center)

> Oh, yes. If I can make a difference with even one parent, help them understand something better, or change their lives, then it's worth it. (Miss Charlotte, teacher, Downtown Center)

Only a few staff members — typically family service workers — expressed their belief in the strengths of parents as a rationale for involving them, and making them "key to the whole program."

> The key to the whole program is the parents. Without them it would just be another day-care center. It is trite to say this, but parents are the first teachers of their children. (Debbie, family service worker, Harbor Street Center)

Others typically noted that parent involvement had the potential to be valuable, although it was often frustrating.

> Feel? It's satisfying, but frustrating too. I guess I have all sorts of different emotions about it. Some things you try don't work out, but in the end, it's great. (Fran, family service worker, Downtown Center)

> Some of them are more responsive than others, and you really get to know them. Like, with Natalie, this is a big part of her life now. With parents like her, it's like working side by side, together. (Miss Carla, teacher, Downtown Center)

> Well, it's sure frustrating, but it's rewarding too. When it works out, it feels great. (Miss Jinny, teacher, Downtown Center)

> Okay, if I can help them. Some are really nice, and you really want to go the extra mile for them. Others, well, they use us. They take advantage of the program, or they just don't care. That's frustrating. (Miss Marlene, teacher, Downtown Center)

> It depends. It's not [worth it] if it just involves fund-raisers and graduation ceremonies.[8] (Valerie, Head Start director)

Others on staff felt that it was not worth their time and energy to involve parents, and were adamant in this regard, telling me that it was definitely a waste of their time.

> No. No way. For the kids, yes. But parents, they should just skip it and give us the money to teach the kids. No matter what you do, if a parent doesn't want to get involved, they won't. (Miss Kathy, teacher, Downtown Center)

> They try to tell you how to run things, but don't have the proper information to make decisions. (Rhonda, teacher, Harbor Street Center)

SOME PARENTS ARE BETTER THAN OTHERS

While some staff made these kinds of generalizations about parents, others recognized that parents were all different and had varying needs and circumstances. They expressed this differentiation by saying that "some parents were better than others." Some were helpful, and nice to have around; others were no good, and should be avoided or ignored. In fact, the way in which the staff viewed parents, interacted with them, and planned programming with and for them had foundations in classist, racist, and sexist beliefs and prejudices. The way in which these biases were played out in staff expectations and behaviors toward parents is the focus of the next section.

Contempt or Pity: Class Counts in Head Start

In the comments of the Head Start staff quoted above it can be seen that most implemented parent involvement efforts "with a grain of salt." In fact, they expected little from parents, a view that, for some, seemed to stem from pity for families; others, however, seemed to have outright contempt for their life situations. As Swadener and Lubeck (1995) and others have pointed out, the poor have always been suspect, not only because of their inability to achieve material wealth in a culture centered on that goal, but also because of the way the lack of money manifests itself in the limitation of options in terms of safe housing, adequate food, equitable education, and other fundamental material needs. Lacking such benefits, the poor have been theorized, not as victims of an unequal system, but as victimizers of their own lives. Such "culture of poverty" theories (Miller, 1965; Lewis, 1968; Schiller, 1980; Auletta, 1982) focus on the individual as having a flawed character, and depict them as disorganized, aggressive, and fatalistic. Furthermore, because of these negative attributes, they are seen as actively choosing a lifestyle marred by violence, illness, and want, and when they make attempts at meeting their needs, their actions are seen as being largely misguided or criminal. Such theories, therefore, place blame on both the individual and the immediate members of his or her family or social group, not on broader social forces that limit their opportunities.

Washington and Oyemade (1987) have pointed out that although there have been a variety of scholarly responses refuting the culture-of-poverty theories over the past twenty-five years, in the 1960s when Head Start and other social programs aimed at eliminating poverty were developed, it was this deficit theory that provided the foundation for the creation of the program. They note that it was "assumed that the life-style of the poor was complex and defined by characteristics of dependency, illegitimacy, instability, psychological deficits, and behavioral deviance" (p. 49).

With such a foundation, it is not surprising that the politics of parent involvement at the Morrison County Head Start were grounded in much the same classist, deficit perceptions. For example, at this Head Start, most parents did not actively participate in the program, and while many parents would initially indicate that they were willing to help, many did not follow through. The staff blamed parents (and their flawed characters) for this reality, rather than looking to themselves, to the program, and to the material conditions of parents' lives as being a part of the problem that limited parent access and impeded their opportunities to become involved.[9] Their lack of participation prompted anger and contempt among some of the staff, which in turn was translated into a negative depiction of the way in which parents were interacting with the program. For example, many staff felt that parents did as little as they could, and tried to get the most out of the situation. Many used the phrase "taking advantage of the program" when they described parents.

> People try to work the system, and get as much out of it as they can. (Joyce, family service worker, Harbor Street Center)

> Sometimes it is hard to find a way that they will take help, others will get all they can. (Sally, nurse, Harbor Street Center)

> Sometimes it seems as if they are using the program. They just take and take, and if you can't give everything they want, they get angry. For example, at Christmas, if we do something here, have a tree and give out gifts, it is as if that absolves them of doing anything at home with their children. It makes you wonder what else they don't do with their kids. (Miss Marlene, teacher, Downtown Center)

> Right now, parent involvement is for the parent only, and it should be for the kids too. Parents either don't know, or they don't care about what we do here. They need to come into classrooms, to see us do assessments of kids so they can find out about them. Many just see us as a babysitting service. Parents should understand what kids do here, and how to work with their kids. (Miss Kathy, teacher, Downtown Center)

Valerie, the Head Start director, depicted some parents as pushy, greedy, and arrogant. She felt that some parents undertook activities for their own gain, and they had no regard for the children's needs, or for the program. Those who complained, tried to act as an advocate for the needs of disadvantaged children, or otherwise tried to make changes in the program were not her favorites either. For example, Valerie had described Bobbie as a "lulu" who continually made trouble, and Francine and Marilyn as "pushy."

> Yes, Bobbie. She's something, isn't she. Always complaining. People get turned off by that. . . . And people don't want to come and hear Francine and Marilyn raise stupid issues like this cap and gown mess.[10] I'm convinced that these two want this, and are pushing it, and nobody else cares. They just want to push though their agenda, and other parents say, well, forget it, they don't want to listen to me. (Valerie, Head Start director)

The irony in all of these comments cannot be underestimated. First and foremost, the fact that parents were perceived as taking advantage of the program indicated the resentment that the staff felt about their jobs and those they were to serve. After all, Head Start was supposed to be giving parents an opportunity to access help, support, and services, as well as develop leadership skills, make changes in their own and in their children's lives, and help them develop in their children skills that promote academic success. In other words, creating a program that parents *could* take advantage of. Yet, instead of embracing a parent's desire to enroll their child in and optimally make use of the program as provided, parents were covertly blamed for needing the service in the first place.

Second, while the behavior of individual parents elicited these comments, the result was that all parents were then suspect. Swadener and Lubeck (1995) point out that deficit-model thinking separates us from each other, and results in an approach that negates the strengths, knowledge, and attributes of parents, who are continually asked about their failures and problems instead of what they do know and can offer. Such thinking makes it easier to place all parents — or significant groups of them — outside of our own experience of struggle and oppression. This application of a deficiency-based appraisal to a collective is the way in which any bias or prejudice is legitimated (Derman-Sparks & Phillips, 1997).

Third, the critical nature of the comments of these staff were firmly grounded in the poor material conditions in parents' lives. In effect, such comments denigrate them for being low-income. For example, instead of seeing parents as being resourceful for utilizing the program (for example, to help provide Christmas presents to their children), Marlene blamed parents for not having access to resources akin to a middle-class existence. In fact, a variety of situations and their related material conditions were discovered as being significant factors that parents indicated as affecting their participation in the program. Little money for transportation or child care, tenuous employment situations, poor health, problems with living conditions, and long lines at welfare offices meant that for some parents it was all they could do to come in and visit the center now and then.

Because of this clearly negative view about parents in general, teachers were always quick to point out to me their "good" parents and their "bad" parents. This dualistic way of thinking about parents, which separated them into categories of "normal" and "abnormal" (Foucault, 1980), was both ironic and dangerous: ironic because although staff reported that they wanted "all parents to participate," in effect they wanted only those who acted in ways that could be depicted as typically middle-class behaviors; and dangerous because of the moralistic judgments about parents' behaviors, which can only lead to divisiveness (Hodge, 1990). For instance, Fran, a family service worker, indicated to me that the program only wanted "the mild ones" to be involved; therefore, vocal advocates like Bobbie were then considered to be troublemakers, and avoided or ignored. Others, like Miss Carla, who had expressed to me that she was grateful that she only had one "project mom" this year, talked pejoratively about the mothers who lived in the public housing near the Downtown Center. As a group, these women, because of their living conditions and geography, were seen as particularly dysfunctional.

Even Miss Billie, a teacher aide who was generally supportive of parents, told me that she could think of only one "good parent" this year (meaning that all the others were "bad"). Her comment was particularly ironic given the fact that while the program purported to want many parents involved, she saw too many different volunteers in a class as potentially disruptive:

> I don't think these parents realize how important it is to get involved with their kids and their schooling. If they don't, who will? This year, Pamela is the only one who has been helping. Some years are better than others, but it seems like it is getting worse. Now Pamela is a good worker. I'm happy that she had been able to be here so regular. New faces can really disrupt the class and upset certain children. (Miss Billie, teacher aide, Downtown Center)

Rhonda's comment regarding the differing values of parents spoke even more clearly to this view, for her analysis of a good or bad parent was clearly grounded in economics and culture. She had told me that since she had worked with both upper-income and low-income families, she had decided that the "best ones" were middle-income parents. This was because they shared her own views about children. Gwen fit this description, and the result was that she was one of the few parents whom Rhonda allowed to volunteer in her class.

> People with middle incomes seem to have the most even-keeled approach to their kids. Now Gwen, the parent who is helping in the class today, comes from a middle-income background. She shares my view of what can and should be done for kids. I feel really comfortable working with her, 'cause, well, how would I put it — I guess I feel like she is equal to me. (Rhonda, teacher, Harbor Street Center)

Miss Kathy was not shy about giving her opinion of the parents either. She had described some parents as being "so unintelligent that the children were smarter than they were." I knew that she felt a lot of negativity about parents, but it was not until the following situation arose that I realized just how strongly she felt. I had been looking for Nina at the Downtown Center, and since her daughter was in Kathy's class, I asked if she had seen her. Kathy asked why I was looking for her, and I told her that I was interviewing her for my research. In response, Kathy interjected:

> Oh, you picked the wrong parent to interview! She complains all the time, about everything. About little things, like that I won't call her daughter by her first and middle name. I keep telling her that we don't do that here, we only use one name, it's easier for the kids. *And*, she's in literacy classes, you know. . . . (Miss Kathy, teacher, Downtown Center)

She said this last remark with a sneer, as if learning to read was a bad thing. At this point in the year I had not been aware that Nina was working on her literacy skills, but I thought that was great news, so I said: "Well that's good, isn't it?" She responded by exclaiming: "WHAT?" I repeated myself. "I said that's a good thing, that she's working on her literacy skills." In response to this, Kathy's face took on a quizzical look, as if now she did not quite know what to think about Nina. "Oh, yeah, I guess so," she mumbled.

Later that day, without revealing identities, I shared the gist of the conversation with Fran. She was appalled.

> I can't believe that. I'm so proud of my parents that are learning to read, I don't know why anybody would look down on somebody trying to improve themselves. Hey, you know what, besides my four parents in literacy classes, one of my parents just became an American citizen! Isn't that great? I'm so proud of her. Anyway, some of these teachers, though, I think they look down on them. (Fran, family service worker, Downtown Center)

Thus, classist prejudices against parents were found among the staff at the Morrison County Head Start. This is ironic, not the least because such staff and client relations were found in a program that was developed for the poor, but also because a large percentage of the employees were, and are, former parents in the program — parents who had also struggled with poverty, and thus were qualified for enrollment in Head Start. Such class bias subsequently reinforced existing power relations between the staff as "helper" and the parent as "client" (Fraser, 1989), even though for many these boundaries were vague and frequently shifting, particularly as it related to those staff members who had been parents in the program. These staff tried to impress upon me that they had not enrolled their children (and thus been a Head Start parent) because they had been low-income like the others, but because their child had been experiencing some type of problem, such as a speech difficulty, or they themselves had been a teen mother, living at home, and trying to finish high school or college. But regardless of why they had enrolled their child, these staff typically did not align themselves with the struggles of other parents in the program. Instead, they positioned themselves as being separate from them when they angrily expressed "I participated [then], why can't they [now]?"

It is the connection between staff and parents that purportedly helps to develop support and solidarity among the adults in Head Start. As has been illustrated in the previous chapter, however, little solidarity existed among the staff at the Morrison County Head Start. Instead, divisiveness grounded in differing levels of education and life experience was evident among their ranks. Still, within this group of employees, it is probable that the parents who got hired were the ones who "fit in," and who were probably pinpointed because they had had the time, energy, resources, and capacity to be active volunteers in the first place. Therefore, it could be argued that a program with a goal of providing jobs for the poor separated out individuals as either "good" or "bad" based on their material resources and "cultural capital" (Bourdieu & Passeron, 1977). From this perspective then, silent LaVerne, who had health problems, no experience outside the home, and who had no pressing goals to articulate, would have never been hired — even though she was one of the "mild ones."

ADDING A DYNAMIC TO THE DEFICIT: RACE AS A TABOO TOPIC IN HEAD START

As Cornell West (1993) so aptly stated: race matters. Yet race as a factor that mediated the experiences of the lives of children and families in Head Start was not explicitly recognized, was programmatically ignored, and was, in fact, a taboo subject that was alluded to, but not talked about at the Morrison County Head Start. Indeed, at the Morrison County Head Start, overtly racist actions and behaviors were not in evidence, and on the surface it appeared that race as an issue in Head Start did not matter — that interactions among and between staff and parents were not laden with racial bias, and that equity and fairness existed as it regarded opportunities for involvement, empowerment, and participation of families and parents in the program. That race was largely ignored in Head Start was not surprising, given the fact that race as an issue was also "invisible," in the liberal policies and programs that birthed Head Start — one of the programs formed under the umbrella of the War on Poverty (Scott, 1997). Yet, as has been pointed out by scholars such as Rist (1974), Schofield (1986, 1989), Dovidio and Gertner (1986), Gates (1987, 1990), Goldberg, (1990), Hayes and Colin (1994), and, most recently, Derman-Sparks and Phillips (1997) and Scott (1997), the lack of acknowledgment of race as mediating unequal social relations, and an uncritical acceptance of racial dynamics, promotes racist thinking and racist practices. In other words, by not actively working against racism, one is complicit in reinforcing it.

At the Morrison County Head Start, the oblique way that racism was expressed and reinforced in the program could be found in the attitudes and expectations about parents in the program. As already noted, the staff frequently talked about parents in ways that both showed their disapproval of them, and in ways that accentuated the differences between themselves and the parents. An example of this is the fact that staff sometimes referred to entire groups of parents as being unreliable or undesirable. Comments in this regard, while not explicitly racist, appeared to be thinly veiled prejudicial opinions that had distinctively racial overtones. In sweeping generalizations, parents at particular centers were talked about in relation to being either "good" or "bad." For example, the old North Branch Center[11] that had recently been shut down and about which the Head Start employees had wistfully spoken as having been the "best center," had been virtually all white.[12] The Porterstown Center, a large center that primarily served Latino families, was viewed as "good, " and proceeding down the continuum, the Downtown Center parents (the center with the largest percentage of Black families) was typically talked about in pejorative terms, including that parents there were "bad," not as interested or not as reliable as parents at other centers. For example, Marlene said the following about the parents at the Downtown Center: "At this center, parents have so many problems. The poverty is so different, so ingrained, and it makes for a lot of apathy and lack of motivation. I always had volunteers at the other center I was at."

Behaviors that promoted racial divisions were seen in other ways also, for some centers with mostly white parents were also criticized when they didn't hold up to the standards of the other majority-white centers. Joyce, who was the Black family service worker at Harbor Street, was highly critical of the Harbor Street parents (who were majority white or Latino), complaining that they were not as good or intelligent as parents at other centers. Joyce often compared the parents at Morrow Street to the ones at Harbor Street. Thus, white parents were supposed to be "good," and when they were not, they were harshly criticized in terms such as Joyce's: "The Morrow Street parents are a joy, a real breeze to work with, but these, ugh! Morrow Street doesn't need it [my help] and neither should they."

The parents at Harbor Street knew that Joyce did not like them, and with little to go on regarding her reasoning, some parents whispered among themselves that it might be race related. In fact, as the new family service worker assigned to the Harbor Street and Morrow Street centers, Joyce was determined not to share anything about her personal life, which included having been brought up in a family of intellectuals and policy-makers, who engaged in frequent international travel. She perceived her lack of candor about her class status as being important to their acceptance; she did not want to alienate parents by acknowledging the differences between them. Interestingly, however, just the opposite occurred: they resented her secretiveness, and viewed her as racist — which in turn fueled their own racist thinking about her. In fact, one could view Joyce's lack of acknowledgment of her background as being duplicitous and promoting of the status quo, since Joyce's actions perpetuated another type of stereotype about Blacks: that they are not capable of being members of the upper-middle class.

Rist (1974) has noted that not being cognizant of an individual's racial, ethnic, or cultural membership results in a lack of acknowledgment of the positive attributes, values, traditions, and behaviors of that group. Furthermore, what happens is that this invisibility leads to publicly unchallengeable deficit-based assumptions and assessments of children and families.

Ladner's (1987) analysis of deficit-based assumptions by race noted that "placing Black people in the context of the deviant perspective has been possible because Blacks have not had the necessary power to resist the labels" (p. 75). Also connecting class-based deficit theories to those of race, Scott (1997) argues that in the same way that "the poor" have been described as deficient in the culture-of-poverty theories, historically, much of social science has posed Blacks' psyches and behaviors as also being nonnormative, damaged, and even pathological. Moreover, he traces the roots of this deficit-based assessment to racist perspectives held by both conservatives and liberals, and examines how such "damage imagery," when used as a basis of social policy, results in racist, reactionary programming. Swadener and Lubeck's (1995) deconstruction of the word "at-risk" reveals the way in which this label is automatically used to describe low-income families and their children.

Scott (1997) elegantly traces the social construction of the rationale for why Blacks as a group are labeled as "at-risk," revealing the structural invisibility of Blacks in social policy and programs:

> On the surface, the debate over the cultural and personality damage of the poor had nothing to do with the image of black Americans. It was a debate about the lower class, regardless of racial or ethnic identity. The operative terms used were *lower class, the culturally deprived, the disadvantaged* — not *Negro*. The studies they produced were rarely organized under the rubric of black identity — not even as poor blacks. Nonetheless, at the very moment that the debate raged over the permanence of the poor's pathology, the lower class was becoming increasingly synonymous with black. (p. 144)

To illustrate this point, Scott quotes the sociologist Nathan Glazer, who in 1963 stated that the phrases "culturally deprived" and "disadvantaged" "are only euphemisms for the Negro child." And yet, despite the reality that the face of poverty in the U.S was, in the 1960s, becoming more frequently black or brown, the issue of race in antipoverty programming and a focus on racial uplift were missing. The reason for this invisibility was structural, argues Scott, and was based in issues of power and politics. In the 1960s, as today, the issue of race was highly charged and Blacks were perceived as being dangerous. Thus, Scott argues, policy-makers posed social problems and legislative "solutions" as being grounded in class (and cast issues revolving around the poorest of the poor — not the working poor) rather than race, in order to make the passage of such legislation more palatable and less volatile to neoconservatives. Citing Daniel Patrick Moynihan's call for a "benign neglect" of the race issue (*San Francisco Sunday Examiner*, March 8, 1970, in Scott, 1997), such shifts in the debate also functioned to discourage critiques of the underfunding of these social programs as being racially motivated. This distinction was vital, as he sees it, for at the time policy-makers did not want Blacks, who were developing a power base and becoming organized around civil rights, to become further politically empowered through public discussion of racism and racist programs.

Thirty years later the lack of political power among the poor and minorities was still in evidence. The political power of the parents at the Morrison County Head Start program was very limited, and the language and actions that the staff used about them were symbolic of their judgments about parents and the power that they held over them. For example, Desmond's emasculation of Raymond[13] was symbolic of the lack of support of Black consciousness, the lack of support for the development of strong Black leaders, and the denigration of the idea that parents — of any race — should have a central role in the administration of the program. Instead of supporting Black leadership, Desmond's act connoted the idea that they should be kept in their place: disempowered and disenfranchised. As an African-American man engaging in the overt acts of emasculating Raymond and sabotaging Francine's desire to undertake an authentic program review,[14] Desmond represents some of the struggles that the oppressed face as they sometimes dehumanize others[15] in their search to "regain their humanity" (Freire, 1970), and the contemporary problems with Black leadership that Cornell West (1993) depicts as a crisis (p. 33). In his view, this is a crisis that can only be remedied by "a race-transcending prophet who critiques the powers that be (including the black component of the Establishment) and who puts forward a vision of moral regeneration and political insurgency for the purpose of fundamental social change for all who suffer from socially-induced misery" (p. 46).

In fact, a strong ethnic or cultural presence that positively promotes community building within and between races, cultures, and ethnicities may be important to the success of the parent involvement program. Although this has not been adequately addressed by research, some research on tribal Head Start programs (Williams, 1975; Coleman, 1978) suggests that an emphasis on strong ethnic and racial affiliations may be important in efforts to involve and empower parents. While Head Start does encourages programming that addresses local needs, there is little emphasis in promoting racial identification and pride.

Rist (1974) and Schofield (1986, 1989) have addressed the way in which racial invisibility perpetuates hegemony, noting that when programs and schools focus only on class and ignore race as a dynamic in the lives of individuals, families, and programs, they promote a public perspective that such programs are "color-blind." Ironically, in both liberal and conservative frameworks, personal and programmatic "colorblindness" is equated with the concept of justice and fairness — key principles which are overtly used to promote good community relations. And yet, in Rist's research (1974) it was revealed that the less that Blacks were visible in the setting, the more likely a school system's integration efforts were viewed as successful, thus establishing the invisibility of race as a key structural component of modern systems that purportedly value egalitarianism.[16]

There is a danger in the honoring of racial invisibility, however, for not only is a color-blind perspective disingenuous, but as Schofield (1986, 1989) also reveals, ignoring race as a dynamic which affects social relations in schools and programs leads to issues of race becoming taboo as a topic of discussion. Such a taboo then increases the likelihood that issues and conflicts related to race become submerged and not negotiable. As a result, any opportunity to capitalize on diversity or to work toward real equity is also thwarted. In the words of Stanlaw and Peshkin (1988, p. 209): "what we choose not to see, we need not deal with; if blacks are invisible, we can ignore their plight."

Washington and Oyemade (1987) raised the issue of race in relation to Head Start in two conferences held in 1983 and 1985, with the rationale that minority children comprise over two-thirds of enrollees, and thus are represented at proportionally higher rates than their representation in the general population. Recommending both an increased emphasis on parent involvement and a specific focus on minority issues and concerns in Head Start, the minority scholars convened at these conferences appear to have clearly understood the connection between visibility, empowerment, and positive outcomes for children and families. It is a connection that others (Nunez, 1993; Arnold, 1995; Darder, 1995) have stated since then, and must be revisited in Head Start.[17]

Thus, class and race can be seen as interlocking social signifiers that influence life in anti-poverty programs such as Head Start. In the same way that the Head Start program reproduced classist and racist relations, the sexism inherent in the program was also apparent.

GENDER AND ENGENDERING CHANGE: SEXISM AND THE STATUS QUO

In the same way that Ladner (1987), Scott (1997), and others have linked deficit theories to racist mentalities and institutional structures, so too have feminist scholars exposed the way in which women's social and sexual identity and experience have been shaped externally and constructed by sexist stereotypes, institutions, frameworks, and theories

(Rosaldo & Lamphere, 1974; Reiter, 1975; MacKinnon, 1981; Harding, 1987). Feminist analyses have revealed women as being viewed as deficit-ridden and nonnormative in relation to men (Gilligan, 1982, 1987), as having been spoken of and studied as object (Tetreault, 1985; Harding, 1987), and laid bare the fact that women are treated as marginal and invisible (Reiter, 1975; de Lauretis, 1990). These analyses have revealed the depth of the oppression of women across cultures, thereby arguing that females are consistently considered secondary to men — and therefore can be constituted as a gendered class. Furthermore, the second-class status of women in relation to men is in evidence regardless of their economic class or race (Wittig, in de Lauretis, 1990).

Compounding the oppressed status that all women share, however, is the reality that the overlapping signifiers of class and race intersect with gender to give measures of power and privilege to some women — white, middle class — and further negate the experiences of others — the poor, and people of color (Andersen & Collins, 1995). This understanding of gender as but one aspect of the multiple, interlocking forms of domination and exploitation, power and privilege, serves to better reveal the multiplicity of ways that both women and men exist in the world and negotiate their realities on a day-to-day basis (hooks, 1984; Collins, 1991).

The ways in which parents experienced the Morrison County Head Start, and the day-to-day expectations and stereotypes about their participation that were found in this setting, are best explained through this lens of interlocking notions of race, class, and gender, and the issues of power and privilege that were the result. Chodorow's (1974) classic work and others' later discussions (Swadener & Lubeck, 1995; Polakow, 1993) have noted that children's social, emotional, and academic welfare always implicates the mother. Symbolic of the home and private life, women have been seen as the parent primarily responsible for the care of the child. Therefore, women are blamed for the inputs they do or do not provide as parents, and for their child's experience and outcomes as students and as social actors. Furthermore, society situates women as being the primary conduit to children's literacy, and positions them almost exclusively as the liaison to schools (Luttrell, 1990, in Cuban and Hayes, 1996). Because of this, social institutions that are designed to intervene in the lives of children have focused their attention solely on women as the source of wellness or pathology in their child (Fraser, 1989).

Women, who had already been stereotyped as nonnormative, deviant, and pathological (e.g., Freud, 1943; Maslow, 1970; Kohlberg,

1984) are thus not only the assigned interlopers in children's lives, they are also suspect simply because they are women. And the parenting behaviors of women who happen to be nonwhite and/or low-income are then especially questionable. Polakow (1993) addresses the intersection of gender and the way in which racist, sexist, and classist beliefs have "confined single mothers and their children to a zone of deviance and moral suspicion" (p. 5). Thus, the logic can be seen as follows: women are deficit-ridden, yet responsible for the behavior and outcomes of their children. Poor women and women of color are particularly problematic, especially when they are single mothers.

Head Start, as one of the social institutions that Fraser (1989) comments on as being designed to intervene in the lives of needy children, reflected this line of thinking, so much so that the expressions of the staff were typically congruent with such stereotypes. Yet the question remained: where were all the men? Where are the men situated within societal conceptions of parenting and, consequently, where were all the men in Head Start?

As may be apparent, Head Start as a program is full of ironies: for example, over the years it has been women who have typically been the ones who came to parent meetings, special events, and helped at the Head Start centers around the country. Men, on the other hand, were rarely seen, and for the most part have been overlooked and ignored in Head Start, nationally and locally.

From this framework, the invisibility of men in Head Start is not surprising. In fact, one rarely finds information on any aspect of male involvement in the program, whether it be programmatic data or research reports. Levine (1993) speaks to the lack of focus and available information on men in the program, and notes that data on fathers in Head Start families is typically not collected at either the local or federal level. Moreover, with the exception of one study that is now ten years old (Gary, Beatty, & Weaver, 1987), little has been published regarding their participation in the program or their involvement with their Head Start children. Despite the fact that Head Start policy-makers and advocates have periodically called for research on fathers since the late 1980's (Washington & Oyemade, 1987; U. S. Department of Health and Human Services, 1987; National Head Start Association, 1989; U. S. Department of Health and Human Services, 1993; Levine, 1993; Phillips & Cabrera, 1996), the absence of such a focus in the literature remains striking.

Some data about fathers is available. For instance, it is known that 41 percent of all Head Start families are intact, with both parents living in the home (U.S. Department of Health and Human Services, 1993). A study of selected sites around the country that used an expanded definition of "father" that included boyfriends or other significant male relatives found the number of men present in the home and acting as father-figures to be upwards of 60 percent (Levine, Murphy & Wilson, 1992, in Levine, 1993).

In Morrison County, at Harbor Street, for example, 65 percent of families had fathers living in the home, and Downtown, while this figure was only 18 percent, large numbers of women reported that their children's fathers were actively supportive and saw their children frequently. Nevertheless, few were ever at the Head Start centers.

Women such as Garnet, Gwen, Lily, Christine, Ivy, Charlene, Maggie, and Josephine were all married. Each of these men had the potential for getting involved at the center. Except for an occasional holiday, they were not active. The same was true for the fathers of Francine and Judy's children: these men regularly interacted with their children, as did those of Kimberly, Karen, and Carmen. Both Lily and Charlene had told me that their husbands simply did not feel comfortable at the center. Lottie, too, referred to her man's discomfort, noting that "their dad helps out a lot with them at home, but he doesn't come in here."

Men sometimes came when prodded, however. For instance, Garnet explained that she sometimes assigned her husband to go to the center. The purpose of "sending him" was "to fill in for her," since at times her work schedule prevented her from certain activities. She explained this by implying that the responsibility for doing things at the school and communicating with the teacher was her duty as the woman in the family:

> I cannot be involved in actual classroom stuff, I really would like to be, but I can't. But if there is something, like the Thanksgiving dinner, I asked my husband to go, and he did. If there's anything where a parent would really be needed, or if they invited a parent, I would ask my husband to go. He has visited a few times, in the classroom too. (Garnet, parent, Downtown Center)

Other women also worked to involve their men. Judy convinced her ex-husband to play Santa at Christmas and Kimberly tried to get her son's father to be active.

> He came when they had the Easter party and when they went on the Easter egg hunt. He was here. He was gonna play the Easter bunny but

> he backed out at the last minute, because of the costume. It didn't hide his face, and they would know who it was, so he said he wasn't gonna do it. So, he helps out. Once I had to cut out things and he cut out things for the next day. He's involved. (Kimberly, parent, Downtown Center)

The typical attitude among these families was that the children's education was the woman's duty, not the man's. For instance, one night I noticed a man at a parent meeting. This was the first male that I had seen at a parent group, so I approached him. Rather than answering any questions about the meeting, he told me to "go talk to my wife, she is over there." It was Francine's ex-husband. She told me that he had not really come to attend the meeting, he was simply there to pick up her and the children for dinner.

Another example of this expectation was the fact that Maggie's husband refused to help the children with their education, saying that it was her role, not his. She attributed his reluctance to having dropped out of high school. He did not read well either. Although she tried to emphasize the importance of him being a role model for the boys, he refused to discuss it. Now their youngest son was failing the second grade, and complained that learning was a girlish thing. Their older boy was also resisting school, and had not been doing his school work.

This gender-based notion that educational issues and school relations were inherently part of the feminine role was also reinforced by the program. While men were not formally excluded, the setting did not encourage them either. For example, many teachers at the centers wanted a "class mother" for their classroom. Furthermore, even if there were two parents in the family, the woman's name was invariably listed as the volunteer and emergency contact. The staff reinforced the idea that women should be active, not men. I asked about the fathers' participation at the Downtown Center, and was told by Harriet: "We call them if we need something, like carpentry, done."

The irony in this statement was profound. While the policies of the program explicitly stated that the children's materials in the classroom were to be gender-neutral and not promote gender stereotypes, the programming and practices that Head Start engaged in with parents were both sexist and stereotypical. In essence, parent programming was essentially only targeted at women: programming that focused on deficits, and not their strengths. Men, in contrast, were ignored, dismissed, and excused for their lack of participation. Furthermore, since all of the onus for parental involvement was on the woman, it was she — individually and collectively — that bore the brunt of the criticism for what she did or did not do. The real danger of this dualism was found, as has been mentioned previously, when staff talked to me about "good" and "bad " parents. They only focused on the woman, blaming or praising her for what took place with the child. They never spoke of the fathers, and whether they were missing or present, nor of the positive or negative impact that their presence or absence played in children's lives.

The general lack of attention to fathers in Head Start is beginning to change, as Head Start has recently initiated a series of efforts to focus on male adults' involvement in the program (Levine, 1993; Levine, Murphy & Wilson, 1993; Fagan, 1996; Bradley & Sissel, 1997). However, the distance that remains to be covered in creating fully family-focused programming is great.

CONCLUSION

Parents are supposed to be developed as first teachers of their children and as leaders in Head Start. Yet, in both policy and practice they are people who are conceived of as being seriously flawed, in need of fixing, and marginally valuable because of factors of race, class, and gender. Therefore, they were deemed not worthy of the time and energy of many of the staff, who, having been in their place in many different ways, were now accommodating and reproducing the prejudices of the dominant culture, and subsequently reproducing the unequal power relations that typically exist between those in "authority" and those who are not.

Furthermore, it appeared that in their roles of authority, the staff in the program — who were largely parents of Head Start graduates themselves — supported the deficit perspectives that the program promoted about parents. For example, from a gendered perspective, women, the mothers of Head Start children, were not thought of as leaders, but (as will be more fully revealed in the following chapters) were instead seen as troublemakers. In typical sexist fashion, while men who take charge are seen as leaders, women who take charge are seen as shrill and inappropriate. Yet, paradoxically, low-income men, who have not lived up to the societal stereotype of being adequate bread winners, or as in the case of Raymond, men who are disabled, are not leadership material either. Because of these perspectives of their deficits, their voices and opinions did not merit any weight, and they remained marginalized in the very system that was designed to empower them.

Thus, it is not surprising that the program gave parents mixed messages about other aspects of the program as well. Chapter 5 reveals some of these mixed messages, and parents' reactions to the way in which Head Start in Morrison County used information to reinforce their marginal status in the program.

NOTES

[1] Washington and Oyemade (1987) are early exceptions as they critiqued the deficit perspective pervasive in the program and addressed issues of racism and gender. Ellsworth and Ames (1995, 1998), Ames and Ellsworth (1997), Mickleson and Klenz (1998), Spatig et al. (1998), and Kuntz (1998) offer recent work related to race, class, and gender issues in Head Start.

[2] This has been documented in educators in areas ranging from K–12, higher education, and adult education settings.

[3] Despite societal myths that perpetuate the idea that the poor have large numbers of children in order to collect larger welfare benefits, large families were not the norm among this population. While Bess and LaVerne had large families, only 6.4 percent of the families at the Downtown and Harbor Street Centers had four or more children. In fact, many women told me that they were actively limiting their number of children since they found it so difficult to make ends meet with the one or two that they had now.

[4] REACH is a welfare-to-work project for recipients of Aid to Families of Dependent Children.

[5] Pamela had been trained as a medical technician whose primary duty is to draw blood from patients.

[6] LPN stands for Licensed Practical Nurse, which is a two-year degree program. The RN, or Registered Nurse typically requires a four-year bachelor's degree program, and demands a much higher wage.

[7] Over-income families are those who are above the poverty-level/income guidelines that Head Start uses to define the target population to be served by the program.

[8] Valerie is referring to the parents' desire for a graduation ceremony, which was first addressed in Chapter 2.

[9] See Chapters 5 and 6 for in-depth discussions of the variety of programmatic barriers that actively impeded parent opportunities for involvement. In the same way that parents on Policy Council here were limited in terms of power and decision-making capacity, Mickelson and Klenz's (1998) study of parents in Head Start revealed the same lack of authentic power, viewing this as a reproduction of class relations among staff and parents.

[10] See Chapter 2.

[11] See Chapter 1.

[12] Lubeck (1995, p. 70) has noted that "Head Start frequently segregates students according to class, and frequently by race." This was true at this Head Start. When the old North Branch Center closed, the children assigned there were bused from the suburbs to the Downtown Center. When this happened, it meant that their class was mostly white, in a center that was almost all Black. This pattern continued after this year, with all the kids coming from that service area being put in the same class. Thus, though majority Black, the classrooms at the Downtown Center were in fact, segregated.

[13] See Chapter 2.

[14] See Chapter 2.

[15] Recall that Desmond was an African-American man, and while his motivations and rationales for working with the Policy Council can only be guessed at in this context, what was observable were behaviors that were seemingly disempowering.

[16] In a critical, postmodern analysis of the history of Head Start, Kuntz (1998) and Ellsworth (1998) explore some aspects of racial dynamics that were present early in the public messages of the program. They cite the program's frequently segregated settings and centers, and the overtones of white racial superiority in the program's early public relations literature.

[17] Faith Lamb Parker and her colleagues (1997) at Columbia University are making strides in this area. They have recently produced a training program for the National Head Start Association that has a component in it that encourages Head Start employees to address their prejudices and work to overcome them. See Parker, F., B. Clark, L. Peay, S. Young, A. Fernandez, R. Robinson, and A. Baker. (1997). *Parent involvement: A training manual for Head Start staff.* New York: National Head Start Association.

CHAPTER 5

Mixed Messages

Information as Political Resource in Parent Programming

As is apparent in the previous chapters, the parents in the Morrison County program were not viewed by the staff as having a variety of strengths, talents, and capabilities that could benefit their children, themselves, the program, and their community. Instead, they were seen as having various deficits, and were talked about and treated differently depending on their gender, race, and class. And, while the staff in its entirety did not view parents in a negative way, all realized that the resources needed to support their programmatic efforts to involve parents were largely missing. As a result, they were negative about parent involvement as an activity. Based on these realities, parents collectively could be collectively viewed as a separate "class" within the Head Start structure — one that had little status, and was further marginalized by little power, few resources, and few powerful advocates.

And yet, Head Start has been credited with starting the trend toward parental involvement in the nation's schools (Slaughter & Kuehne, 1988) as well as developing school-based support systems for parents and families (Kagan et al., 1987). What can explain the disjuncture between the lived reality of the parents and staff at the Morrison County Head Start, and the situation they may exist in other locales, where parental involvement has been established as credible, powerful, and transformative of institutions and communities?

In one of the early (and few) in-depth qualitative studies of parent involvement in Head Start, Adams (1976) pointed out that parents could either "passively participate" on the most minimal level, such as during a home visit, or they could be "actively involved" in helping to plan the program's activities and agenda. It was the reality of this qualitatively distinct difference in experiences among parents in Head Start that compelled Washington and Oyemade (1987) to note that while some parents benefited greatly from Head Start, others got little from it. In particular it was those who had functioned in real leadership roles — those who were actively involved, not merely acted on — who received the most benefit.

This conceptual difference between "participation" and "involvement" is important to address for several reasons. As Bagnall (1989) has pointed out in the field of adult education, the act of an adult "participating" in a learning environment can, and is, constructed and construed in differing ways. He clarifies the term "participation" as connoting the simple act of attendance at a training and the willingness, therefore, of the adult to be instructed or otherwise acted on. The word "involvement" implies engagement in the planning, development, and assessment of that activity or class. This difference is critical, since it is known that individuals feel more satisfied when involved in decision making (Rosenblum, 1985; Jurmo, 1989), and that in programs for low-SES adults such involvement can sustain attendance, recruit and motivate additional participants, and increase self-confidence (Balmuth, 1987, and Lerche, 1985, both cited in Jurmo, 1989). In addition, shared norms, meanings, and goals emerge within groups who are involved in planning functions (Galbraith, 1990), thereby fostering community building and support.

If we make this distinction between mere participation and active involvement, it then causes us to recognize the variability that exists in the social relations between the adults who enroll in, seek help from, or otherwise engage in human service and/or education programs and those who are responsible for this assistance and education-related programming. Secondly, recognizing this, it also urges us to reflect on the way in which we as educators may be reproducing unequal and disempowering social relations, and the way power and privilege (or lack thereof) affects the assumptions, biases, and expectations that we hold about the other, and how these views are played out in day-to-day practices (Rist, 1970; Giroux, 1981; Tisdell, 1993; Ginsburg, et al., 1995). In other words, the views that human-service workers, helping professionals, and educators hold about their "clients" or "learners" play a strong role in what these people perceive as being appropriate roles and activities for their clientele. Because of this, we must make efforts, as McIntosh (1988) has said, to work to "unpack" (p.10) the meaning and measure of this privilege. To do so means we must reflect on the level of involvement and the measure of power or control that we believe these adults should have in developing their own agendas, plans, or goals.

If the emphasis is on creating empowering environments and building partnerships with adults, then this implies several things: first, that educators and others should have expectations that the adults with whom they interact have the capacity to be active agents who can authentically articulate a sense of their needs (Freire, 1973). Second, that educators view these adults as having the capacity to critically reflect on and make responsible choices about how, when, and what to learn for their personal lives, their work lives, and their communities (Knowles, 1970; Niemi, 1985; Jurmo, 1989). Third, educators themselves need to engage in critically reflective practice and continually assess their role regarding the facilitation of this reflection and learning among their clientele (Brookfield, 1995).

The notion of including adults as collaborators and creators of their experience is key in the field of adult education — this is central to Knowles's (1970) individualistic, instrumental, humanistic perspective; Freire's (1973) social change, critical theory approach, which promotes reflective communal dialogue about social problems; Mezirow's (1991) psycho-social theory of perspective transformation; Hayes's (1989), Hart's (1990, 1992), Tisdell's (1993, 1995, 1998), and others' (Cuban & Hayes, 1996; Flannery & Hayes, in press) emphasis on emanicipatory action in feminist pedagogy; Colin's (1988) focus on collective, empowering education through Africentrism; and Sheared's (1994) polyrhythmic, womanist framework that accentuates "giving voice" to the multiple realities of race, class, and gender as essential contexts in learning. Furthermore, the centrality of adults being thought of as capable of being developers and evaluators of their experience is fundamental. Equally foundational is the realization that when adults jointly collaborate in the development of their goals and activities, power becomes more equalized (Cervero &Wilson, 1994, 1996). Yet only those who truly buy into the perspective that their clients have the capacity to be involved in such a role will foster this collaboration (Sissel, 1997; Bounous, in press). As Galbraith (1990) has pointed out, this view is critical to creating in learners "a sense of hope and dignity, a sense of responsibility for their own communities and lives, and a voice in the social and political arenas (pp. 7–8)."

One key to involving adults in empowering ways is providing them with access to information — or helping them discover how to find the information themselves — that they can use to weigh options, plan actions, and evaluate outcomes. At the Morrison County Head Start, however, very little information was given to parents about the mission of the parental involvement component, and what the benefits of their participation might be. Furthermore, the invitation to involvement that parents did receive was filled with contradictory, mixed messages that were rarely offered in a comprehensive, cohesive manner. This was paradoxical, however, for having information about parent opportunities was essential if parents were to become at all inclined to try to overcome their constraints of lack of child care, transportation, or time, in order to participate. And certainly, if a parent saw no reason to participate, had never heard about this possibility, or was not encouraged to do so by the staff, then they would not attempt to participate on any level. Without information about the program and how it might benefit them and their children, it was also less likely that they would actively try to find solutions to the resource problems that were potential barriers.

The connection between parents having adequate information about participation and their role as parents was inherent in Winnie and Debbie's comments to me. They noted that there were many reasons why parents lacked an understanding of what participation in their child's education might mean:

> They think that the teacher has to do it, that the teacher has all the know how. I guess not all of them feel that way, but some of them think that the teacher has to do it all. (Miss Winnie, teacher, Harbor Street Center)

> Some of them are probably resistant due to bad experiences with schooling themselves. Yes, shyness, isolation, not knowing how or being too scared to speak up. (Debbie, family service worker, Harbor Street Center)

Marshall and Mitchell (1991) have said that "power is enacted through language." Thus, this chapter focuses on the ways in which the staff communicated with parents, what it was that parents knew about participation in the program, and the types of expectations they held about it. It will also address parents' views of the information that they were provided.

This chapter also illustrates that parents' access to information differed in the program. Not surprisingly, those who were the most accepted and welcomed by staff (hence, those with the most power and privilege) were those who typically had more information. The frequent result was division and distrust between parents and staff. Anita, a long-time employee and former parent in the Morrison County Head Start, speaks here about the paradox in the program, and the reality of the mixed messages that parents were given:

> A lot of times it's just really discouraging. . . . It's hard to do what you want to do for parents when staff don't work together to make it successful. So, they [the parents] get mixed messages about what they should be doing with us. . . . What happens is that some staff actually shoo parents away. . . . She [pointing to a staff person] does her best to make sure that parents aren't around. I just think that it's important that everybody work together with parents. (Anita, branch manager, Cedar Heights Center)

INFORMATION OR OPPORTUNITIES

A parent's first introduction to the idea of parent participation and involvement was often at registration. At registration parents completed a host of forms, some of which included questions regarding whether they were available to volunteer. But available to do what? This was not always clear. While registration would have been a good opportunity to let parents know about the full scope of the parent involvement program, according to both staff and parents such disclosure did not occur. Some parents, like Garnet and Natalie, were certain that they had been told nothing about it at all.

> No. I remember. They didn't say nothing about it. (Natalie, parent, Downtown Center)

> No, everything was more, just business. It was nothing saying, when your child gets in here, we usually have meetings, and things like that. That probably would help, like on the day of the registration. They could say, oh, we have PTA meetings and would you be able to come, or whatever, and you'll really learn a lot about what your kid is doing. (Garnet, parent, Downtown Center)

Other parents said that a staff member had "mentioned it," but did not make it clear or emphasize it.

> The only thing they said was that sometimes you can come in and help out the teachers, and you know, 'cause sometimes during lunch time, they, you know, need to have a break, or something like that. (Maggie, parent, Downtown Center)

> When I came to register [my son], she just said, "are you available?" I wrote the times down available, and that was it. Other than that, she

didn't mention certain things, or anything. (Cynthia, parent, Downtown Center)

Oh, if I'm not mistaken, when we were interviewed, I think Debbie had mentioned the parent group, and they wanted parents to become active, to come to meetings, to voice your opinions. (Gwen, parent, Harbor Street Center)

I had asked Debbie why parents were not given more information or more encouragement to get involved as they went through the registration process.

Registration can be stressful for both staff and parents. The staff are often rushed if there is a large line of parents waiting. . . . Parents are stressed because the questions are personal, and the whole process is bureaucratic and intimidating. We do mention it, but not forcefully, since it is an overwhelming process. (Debbie, family service worker, Harbor Street Center)

Written program materials did not provide much clarity either. While various booklets, handouts, and forms noted activities in which parents could participate, there was no single piece of literature that addressed what parent participation was all about: its goals, purposes, activities, and outcomes. A booklet about Head Start that was produced for the parents held the greatest amount of information about parent participation, yet in its entire sixteen pages, only five paragraphs addressed this issue. The two most explicit were the following:

Parents are the most important influence on a child's development. Head Start helps parents learn more about the needs of their children, and about educational activities that can be carried out at home. Parents are encouraged to volunteer in classrooms and with many other vital Head Start activities. Many parents and community members serve as members of Policy Council and committees, and have a voice in decisions about program planning and operations. . . .

The aim is to work with the whole family, as well as the enrolled child. . . . Family service workers help families to obtain the social services they need, and help parents to become actively involved in Head Start . . . activities. (*Head Start Parent Handbook,* Morrison County)

Because little specific information was available (in addition to other constraining factors that will be addressed in following sections), parents sometimes reported that they found each other to be the most important sources of information.

> I didn't even know about parent meetings, and other things, but my cousin told me they were going on. (Lily, parent, Downtown Center)

> Another girl, she told me about it, 'cause she's a parent also, and so I came to a parent meeting. They had said that parents could be involved as much as they want. They could come to classes, and stuff like that. That's how I learned about it. (Richelle, parent, Morrow Street Center)

> I saw other parents playing roles. Like, when I came to the meeting, I saw how involved other parents were. So that made me want to get involved . . . it gave me a little push on it. You know, sometimes, you be like, oh, when you see other parents there, you feel good about it, you feel good that you decided to go, even though you at first didn't want to go. So it kinda like changes your mind into a more positive attitude. (April, parent, Downtown Center)

Thus, few concrete explanations were provided to parents regarding the ways in which they could become active as volunteers (or paid employees) in the program. To make matters worse, when a parent did take the initiative and came into the center to help, the staff had very little idea about how they might meaningfully volunteer. I discovered this lack of systematic thinking as it related to volunteer roles and specific tasks when, as a new volunteer at the Downtown Center, I had needed some information and guidance about my helping role — both as an aide to the family service workers, and in thc classroom. Yet, the family service workers had problems giving me directions. Despite mountains of paperwork, and constant complaints of being overloaded, they had difficulty articulating what they might need help with. When they did think of specifics, they had few clear thoughts on ways to do them.

There was also little planning or direction as to what other volunteers might do if they came in, or who would supervise them. For example, one day Fran and Harriet had asked me to telephone parents to ask them to volunteer at the center. Yet, when I asked the two of them what parents might do, I was simply told that they could "help in the classroom."

Having been a volunteer coordinator myself, I knew that one volunteer job did not fit all volunteers. So I asked them, "What if someone was not interested in that? What else might be done?" After much prodding on my part, they remembered that the nurse needed help sometimes, but doing exactly what, well, they were not quite sure. They also said, "Someone to answer the phone would be nice." However, they did not know where a parent would sit to do this. In fact, neither family service worker could spell out what the possibilities were regarding the tasks and duties that volunteers at the center might do. They admitted that, despite years on the job, they had never really thought about it.

I also found a lack of information and supervision in the classroom. While Miss Carla had always given me specific activities to do with the children, she did not discuss the purpose of the activities, nor had she given me any basic information about my role. For example, I was not told the rules of the program, nor what was considered proper and safe behavior when working with the children. It was just assumed that I would know what to do and how to interact with the children.

INFORMATION AND EQUITY ISSUES IN PARENT PROGRAMMING

While the invitation to involvement that the program gave was muddled, parents' expectations about many other aspects of the program were quite clear. They expected that they would be able to communicate with the staff, be made to feel welcome as a parent at the center, and be provided information, advocacy, and support when it was requested. This included support for themselves, their child, their family, or their Head Start parent committee. They also expected to be treated fairly, and with dignity and respect. Unfortunately, my notes were filled with parents' unfulfilled expectations regarding the way the program was organized, and the way in which they were treated by the staff.

Information and Assistance

One key expectation that parents had about the program, and their interactions with the staff, was related to the forms that they had completed during the registration process. On these forms, they were repeatedly asked to respond to questions such as the following:

> Do you need information or assistance with: ( ) Food Assistance, ( ) Legal Services, ( ) College Education, ( ) Clothing, ( ) Baby Cloth-

> ing/Furniture, ( ) Education: Reading and Writing, ( ) Education: High School Diploma or GED, ( ) Budgeting, ( ) Alcohol Problems, ( ) Drug Problems, ( ) Family Therapy/Counseling, ( ) Tenant's Rights, ( ) Other. (*Head Start Family Assessment*, Morrison County)

Parents expressed the view that, if they checked it on the form, they should have received the requested information or assistance. Yet, time and time again they reported that they had not.

> I would have liked the schooling, or even housing to get out on my own, but they didn't help me. They never offered any information about the schooling, and I would have felt that was a plus. But they never even looked at it. I can't really say that I'm disappointed anymore, because the way that it has worked out, I'm going back to school anyway. (Cynthia, parent, Downtown Center)

> Yeah, I checked the financial, and the schooling, and some other stuff, I don't remember. But the things that I did check off, I never saw any of it. As far as the housing, they said they had aid, and whenever I called about it, the lady was like, no. As far as getting any schooling, they never sent any information or give me a telephone number. And I would have liked the CPR lesson. I wanted to learn that, but I didn't get a chance to. (Maura, parent, Downtown Center)

As Maura noted, parents were also asked about the types of workshops that they wanted. However, this too was not followed up on when parents had checked the following types of interests:

> ( ) Making children's games ( ) Activities with children ( ) Selecting safe, educational toys ( ) What happens in Head Start classrooms, and why ( ) Effects of television on children ( ) Discipline ( ) Child development and behavior ( ) Balancing children's needs and parents' needs ( ) Arguing between brothers and sisters ( ) Other. (*Head Start Education Component Questionnaire*, Morrison County)

As a result, parents were disappointed when they were not given the requested information. Francine noted that since she had not been active during her first year, she had assumed that they put on a lot of workshops.

> But I found out that they don't do them. They don't do everything that I thought they did. At the end of the year, they send out a form, asking

> what you have attended, and last year I didn't put anything, 'cause I didn't go. But it turns out that they didn't offer anything either. The program could be lots better than it is. (Francine, parent, Downtown Center)

Heather went even further with her complaint.

> I think it is unprofessional that I put the things down that I wanted to learn, and no one got back to me about it. I filled out the form saying what it was I wanted to learn, and nobody ever did anything with it. (Heather, parent, Harbor Street Center)

Knowing the parents felt this way, I had asked Harriet and Fran (the family service workers), and Candice (the education specialist), about these forms, and what they did with the information that parents gave them about their needs and interests. Harriet and Candice both responded that they didn't do anything with it — they just didn't have time to compile the responses and then work with each individual. And when I asked Fran about this particular form that parents filled out, she did not know what I was talking about. She had never paid any attention to the questionnaire.

Even when parents tried, in a very pointed way, to get desired information and help from the staff, they were often rebuffed. Heather tells here of her efforts:

> When I sat with the nurse originally, and we went over the guidelines, she told me that you'll get the menu once a month so you can see what they eat. Well, they never did it. When I told them [the cook and the teacher] that I didn't get my menu in the package, I was told, oh, we don't have that here. [I said,] but the nurse told me that I'm supposed to get one. And they just said, we don't have that, we don't have that. That's the kind of answers that I constantly got. (Heather, parent, Harbor Street Center)

The lack of information provided to parents was a problem at all levels. According to Bobbie, parents had a variety of questions about the program that should have been answered at the very beginning of the year. This included information such as what goes on in the classroom, and what types of resources the program had for children and families. The result was that in March, parents assembled for a meeting at Harbor Street to air complaints that they did not know what was going on in the program. Despite the fact that the program year[1] was almost over, at this meeting it was revealed that parents did not know several things about the program, including: what Policy Council was, that their children were being given health screenings, or that the program had a family therapist available to them at no cost.

Information and Access

Clearly, the capacity of the program to communicate with the parents was poor. Some of this was related to problems with the centers' telephones; in other instances it had to do with the system of sending notes home with children on the bus, or with the staff's lack of organization and willingness to pass along the information. In some cases, a lack of communication between parents and staff was simply the result of staff who chose not to provide information to particular parents. When parents were not informed, frustration and confusion resulted.

The telephone would have been an ideal way for parents to communicate with the staff, but there were many problems in this regard. Because of their problematic finances, parents often reported that they had their phones cut off for lack of payment; therefore, it was difficult for the staff to reach them. Therefore, since they couldn't always be reached, it was essential that the phones at the centers be in working order when a parent tried to call there. Yet, the phones at the centers were often in need of repair. Furthermore, the staff would not always answer the phone. Because of this, parents told me they could not return calls or get messages through to the staff.

This was a chronic concern at the Downtown Center. Many times I, too, could not get anyone to answer the phone when I called. Sometimes, if someone did answer, I was told to call back, since the person answering did not want to try to locate or leave a message for the person with whom I needed to speak. Others spoke of similar experiences:

> And then there's this place. I try to call and get my questions answered and I can't get through. And the bus, it hasn't been working for four weeks. I just find this whole place unprofessional. I tried to talk to Harriet about it, and all I get is nasty looks. (Gaylynn, parent, Downtown Center)

In lieu of the telephone, parents were sent letters about center activities, notes from the teachers about the child's progress, and permission slips for field trips and medical visits. Yet written notes did not always make their way to the parents, and when they did, the message was not always clear:

> Sometimes they throw it away, or they leave it on the bus, or the bus drivers sometimes don't give it to them. My daughter missed her dentist appointment because of that. (Nina, parent, Downtown Center)

> If you don't go to the meetings, half the time, I don't think you'd probably know what was going on, I mean, you just wouldn't know. 'Cause, they'll send home permission slips and stuff like that, but they don't really tell you what's going on. (Karen, parent, Harbor Street Center)

A notice sent home on the bus was the primary way that parents were informed of parent meetings at the center. Some notices never made it home and at other times meeting notices were sent to the parents only three days ahead of time. In fact it was not uncommon if parents only had one day's notice, or none at all. Parents bitterly complained that the short time spans between announcements and meetings meant that they could not plan it in their schedules.

> And as for parent involvement . . . how can you get to a meeting when you get the notice two weeks late? Or on the same day? They should be more flexible about meeting times, too, and not always have them in the evening. (Gaylynn, parent, Downtown Center)

> And then this last meeting. We get the letter the day of the meeting. It's dated the 26th of May, and we get it June 2nd, the day of the meeting. Most of the time, I come in, and I don't even read the notes till later on, and I would have missed the meeting. (Theresa, parent, Downtown Center)

> I sometimes get my announcements about Jamal two or three days after the thing happened. Can you fix that? [she called over to a staff member] Make sure that they all get sent out. (Sherrill, parent, Downtown Center)

And, while parents whose children rode the bus might get the notices, those who picked up their children at the center often did not know about meetings at all, for the teachers themselves did not hand out meeting notices. So while there were always problems with notes and telephones, there were also problems with the staff communicating in person with parents.

Heather and her son were examples of how simple procedures could become a problem when staff did not take the time to explain the school's routines. When Heather's son began at Head Start, the staff did not explain the daily routine to her. When she did something incorrectly, such as putting his coat in the wrong place, the staff took it out on her son. And, if she dropped him off too early, the staff would ignore him. He became so uncomfortable there, that he did not want to go to school. Heather was angry when she discovered that the staff was treating her son this way, for it was not his fault; she felt it was hers. No one had explained about the drop-off time, or where to put the coat, and she did not think it was right.

> I'm like, I wish you people would tell me what goes on. I wasn't told where the coats go. I put it on the wrong table. I only did that 'cause I saw what other people were doing. So my son was sitting at the wrong table. I still don't understand where they are allowed to sit. I still don't understand that.
>
> Lunch took me the longest time to figure out. Jordan first started coming home saying, if there was school the next day, I don't wanna have lunch there, I don't wanna have lunch there. For some reason he had a big hang-up about lunch.
>
> I was dropping him off at a quarter to one, and they didn't sit down to eat till a quarter after one. That poor thing had to sit there, with his hands on his lap, waiting to eat lunch. So, I decided, I'm not bringing him in till the bus comes. And that corrected the problem. But you see how they don't tell you? (Heather, parent, Harbor Street Center)

Edna had also experienced problems with getting needed information. She explained the situation as it related to her granddaughter, Tonette:

> They need more feedback to the parents about the kids. The teachers need to be in contact more. My Tonette was having a problem wetting herself, and nobody was talking to me about it. We worked it out, getting her to the bathroom more, and limiting her drinks. But it took me to talk to the teacher about it. (Edna, parent, Downtown Center)

April had similar complaints about the lack of communication with her daughter's teacher:

> One time they had parent conferences. It was like, one day, out of the blue, they just decided to have them. This was a day that the children weren't going to be in school. But they didn't inform the parents. I shouldn't say all parents. Well, they didn't inform me. But they did not send home letters saying we are going to have parent conferences on such and such a day, so there will be no school, and I was not informed by my daughter's teacher.
>
> So she didn't schedule me for a parent's conference. I guess she was expecting me to come to her and ask, when do I have it, but how do I know when to have it, when you the one [the teacher] supposed to schedule it? You know what I mean?
>
> Ever since that day, I felt kind of funny about it. I thought it was her business. I thought she should have made it her business to let me know as a parent that we are having a parent conference on this day, and I want you to come in at this time.
>
> But I had to find out from another teacher. So I went and asked her about it, and she was like, oh yeah, you can come in, I had a little letter posted up there. And when I went and looked at that letter, it was behind some books, and it was, you know, very small print that you really couldn't even see. (April, parent, Downtown Center)

Information and Advocacy

In addition to expectations regarding the various types of communication with staff, parents also had expectations about other types of staff behaviors. They assumed that staff would be competent and act professionally, so when they were informed of meetings and subsequently attended them, parents expected that the meeting itself and the staff who ran them would be organized and orderly.

But, like the parent in Chapter 3 who had left the orientation shaking her head in disgust, others had similar reactions about the way in which meetings were typically facilitated. They always began late — often forty-five minutes behind schedule. The noise level was usually uncomfortable, facilitation was often inept, and order and discussion were largely absent. Therefore, when parents did try to fit the meetings into their busy schedules, they were not satisfied with such experiences.

> I am thoroughly disgusted and upset by this whole thing. I never get the meeting notices on time. It was difficult getting here tonight, and when I do rush here, look what happens. It was a mess. (Esther, parent, Harbor Street Center)

> I would like to see the PTA meeting more structured. And have it start on time, and get on with the business of the meeting. I would just like to see a little more structure than it is now. And sometimes, like the secretary is late, and we are all sitting there. I would like it to be more business-like than it is. (Garnet, parent, Downtown Center)

Part of the problem had to do with the lack of child care. Although promised, it was usually not present. Instead, children ran around screaming, and parents had to yell to be heard. One night at the Downtown Center, parents were trying to listen to a guest speaker on child abuse. The children were so loud, the guest speaker was the one who kept asking them to "be quiet, please!" It was frustrating for all involved.

> They say that babysitting is available, but then the kids come and they run all over, and you have to really strain your ears to hear. I would like it to be a little more organized, like the kids go into a room, and somebody watches them play, and whatever. (Garnet, parent, Downtown Center)

> Have child care sometimes, 'cause, some parents say, "I'm not gonna go there to a meeting. Ain't nothing there. Because, they ain't got no day care, and I can't bring no kids with me." (Jasmine, parent, Downtown Center)

According to Josephine, the lack of child care at meetings was common. In years past, she made a point of asking for it.

> One of the teachers is supposed to step in and babysit. They should have insisted. Because that's what I have done a few times when I've come here, and they've taken a teacher and put a teacher in there to babysit. Or a bus driver. You offered this, this is what it is supposed to be. I'm here with my child. And I don't want to go home. (Josephine, parent, Downtown Center)

While Josephine reported that staff attending the meeting were sometimes pressed into service, staff who were supposed to attend the meetings usually did not attend. Their lack of attendance was related to another parent expectation: having the staff's support for their activities and interests.

Parents at both centers expected staff to be supportive. After all, parents had been told (albeit not well) that this was their program. Therefore, they expected assistance with their activities, guidance and instruction, access to community resources, and support and advocacy when problems arose. Unfortunately, even when parents had requested that staff come to their parent meeting, they did not come. This was evident the night that Valerie had opted not to attend the Downtown Center meeting to discuss a graduation,[2] but it happened in other circumstances as well.

During the spring, the Harbor Street parents had asked the administrators (Valerie, Barbara, and Candice) to come to the meeting to discuss their concerns about the way that their children were being treated by Rhonda. While Rhonda and the center's other teacher, Winnie, attended the meeting, Valerie did not come, nor did Candice, Rhonda's supervisor. Thus, there was no supervisory personnel there to handle the complaints of the parents. Joyce, the center's new family service worker, was also absent. As a result, not feeling safe or supported, the parents raised no problems or concerns, and the session turned into a brief presentation by Rhonda about things parents could do at home with their children. It was frustrating for the parents, and Bobbie told me that the parents felt ignored:

> We don't have anybody in administration backing us up. Everybody was supposed to be there, Valerie, Joyce, Elizabeth, and Candice, 'cause it was supposed to be a time to check out Rhonda and some of our complaints, but no one, no one showed up. Nice, huh? They made up a bunch of crap stories about why they couldn't come, but we didn't buy it. They think they are fooling us . . . (Bobbie, parent, Harbor Street Center)

Support to parents was also to include fiscal assistance for their parent group activities. As described in the program guidelines, each center was allotted a special account for parent activities; some brought in speakers, others organized something fun with their money. The amount that each group received varied; the rate was three dollars per child. Therefore, larger centers received more money. The Downtown Center's total was approximately $600; Harbor Street was to have $240. But Harbor Street Center, it seemed, always had problems getting their money:

> We didn't get it at all last year. First we were told that we couldn't request it until the spring, and in the spring we were told it was too late to request it. It just seems like the administration hampers our efforts at

> every turn. In October, we requested our parent activity money so that we could pay a sitter for our kids during the meeting. [But] they said that we never sent in the minutes about it, and they're full of shit, because I talked to Desmond [the Executive Director] about it. I talked to Candice too, before a meeting in December about it. They requested to see our checks [for the child-care worker]. We sent it [the request] to them, and then they told us it would be in with the next pay checks. And now they tell us we didn't give them anything. (Bobbie, parent, Harbor Street Center)

I asked Valerie why it might be that a parent group wouldn't get their money, and she explained that there were procedures that they had to follow, and paperwork to fill out. She also suggested that it was Joyce's role to help them with these procedures and paperwork. But, by the end of the school year they still did not have access to their parent money. So, as with the previous year, they were not able to offer any special parent activity. Bobbie felt the situation was due to two reasons: Valerie herself was not supportive of the parents' efforts, nor was Joyce.

In fact, when such problems arose, it was the family service worker's job to be a liaison between the parents and the staff at both the center and the program level. Unfortunately for the parents at Harbor Street, Debbie left in November and Joyce was not hired until February. This meant that for about three months there was no family service worker to handle concerns; thus, many of the parent complaints fell on Bobbie, the chair of the parent committee at Harbor Street. Bobbie felt that she had no allies, and she sensed that the staff thought she was a pain.

> That's one of the problems this year, with me being blamed for things not being done, or done the wrong way, which is staff's job. I'm not staff. Somewhere along the line they forgot I'm not staff. I'm the chairperson, I'm a mother just like everybody else. (Bobbie, parent, Harbor Street Center)

Bobbie was relieved when Joyce came in as Debbie's replacement. However, she soon realized that the parents still did not have an advocate on whom they could rely, for Joyce was not the least bit helpful; instead, she berated the parents.

> I was hoping that Joyce would be a help, but she is just on our case, snooping in our business and accusing me of taking drugs. She just

> cuts me off and is rude. I had to hang up on her once. It probably wasn't right, but I didn't have the patience to listen to her anymore. I wasn't feeling well, and she was accusing me, and not listening. She has a real attitude. (Bobbie, parent, Harbor Street Center)

It did appear that Joyce was overwhelmed, and didn't understand her job. She had admitted to me that she hadn't been well trained or oriented, and her lack of preparedness was evident in her defensiveness, and in her reticence to be available. For example, the first night the parents met Joyce, they had asked her to schedule another meeting with her soon, since they had not had a staff person for so long and had several items to address and activities to pursue. But despite their request, Joyce adamantly refused, citing more important business: "I just cannot meet again this month, it is just not possible. I'm just too busy getting situated on the job."

Her reluctance to help parents became even more evident when parents tried to organize the commodity program for the Harbor Street families. Unlike Harriet and Fran, who worked side by side with the parents at the Downtown Center, Joyce told the parents that this was "their baby," and she would have nothing to do with it.

> These commodities, they need their hand held to get it going. But I've told them that it is their baby. I'm not gonna do a thing to help them. Morrow Street doesn't need the help and neither should they. I figure that they can sink or swim on their own. I'm gonna make a point of not even being at the center on that day, 'cause I don't want to be stuck cleaning up after them. (Joyce, family service worker, Harbor Street Center)

She had made this point to me in private, earlier in the evening. Later on that night, however, she directed her remarks to the parents. When I had told Joyce, "I'll see you at commodities on Friday," her response was clearly meant for the parent to hear: "Oh, no you won't! I'm not gonna be there. That's their project, I don't have anything to do with it. I'll be at Morrow Street that day, like every Friday."

The day of the food program arrived, and I found Bobbie standing alone in the office, nearly in tears, surrounded by boxes of food, trying to figure out what to do. No one else was there to help her; the teachers were downstairs with the children, but they did not know what to do either. So, she asked me to help her figure out how to process the paperwork, and how much food to give out. Luckily, I had assisted the

Downtown parents with their food the week before, but I was no expert either. It was quite confusing, but together we read the allotment form and handled the paperwork.

Other parents began arriving to volunteer, and people started picking up their food. But Bobbie soon realized that Joyce had given her too many names: there was not enough food to go around. She panicked, and decided to call Joyce on the phone. Joyce was angry about the imposition, and when she arrived at the center, made a point of saying so in a loud voice. She was also so rude to the parents that she almost started a fistfight with one of them. Bobbie had this to say about the situation: "That was totally unprofessional if you ask me. There ain't no way that I'm doing another one of these things. It got all messed up, thanks to her, and then she almost starts a fight."

Joyce's disdain for parents was apparent to all. For instance, one night after a meeting, Joyce literally screamed at Theresa. It was an embarrassing situation for all in the room; no one could escape overhearing what Joyce was saying to her. Theresa had expressed concern that her child was not being treated right in the classroom, and she was now considering taking her child out of Head Start. She had written a letter to Valerie, but nothing had been done. Joyce insisted that she not withdraw her son, saying: "You can't quit. You've got to stay. Do you hear me, you have to do this. I'm here now, you're just gonna stay."

Several weeks later, Theresa had this to say about Joyce's lack of support for her and the letter that Joyce herself had made her write.

> Joyce wanted it [the complaints] in letter form. I had to write Valerie a letter, which I believe backfired in my face. Joyce led me to believe that other mothers were going to put it in letter form too. I was the only mother that did this, from what I hear. And I didn't get nowhere with it. I'd bet money that my letter was shown to Rhonda. If anything, Rhonda likes me less now.
>
> I had decided to handle it myself that night and that woman blew up at me. She jumped all over me, and then she said, "oh, I can't talk to you." She twisted everything I said. I don't believe that Joyce is so professional. I trusted her with it and all. . . . (Theresa, parent, Harbor Street Center)

Theresa cried angry tears as she told me about this situation. Yet, she was not the only parent that shed tears over the program. For instance, Bobbie confided to me:

> I started crying the other day, talking to the bosses [Valerie and Candice] over at administration. Do you know that Joyce gave me a hard time over it, telling me to "be professional." Well, I'm not a professional. I'm just a parent who cares about their kid, all these kids. I couldn't help it, it makes me so mad what goes on around here. (Bobbie, parent, Harbor Street Center)

The reality was that the parents required staff assistance in order to carry out events and programs. Some staff were more willing in this regard, others less. At the Downtown Center, Harriet was known for her willingness to act as an advocate for the parents, and her readiness to try to help. While committed, however, Harriet was not perfect. Sometimes, whether it was due to incompetence, overwork, or disorganization, she did not follow through and it created bad feelings. Judy told me of one such situation. Judy had been a leader at the center during the previous year, and that summer she and some other parents had held a car wash for the program, and made seventy-five dollars. After turning it in to Harriet, however, the money disappeared.

> I had a problem at the beginning of the year. I ran a fund-raiser before the school even opened. Through my church. We had a car wash to raise money for Head Start, just to give them a jump on things. We raised seventy-five dollars. And son of a bitch, Harriet supposedly left it in a locked desk over the weekend, and she came into work Tuesday and it was gone. Why didn't she go to the bank, that's all I wanted to know. So the way I see it is she is responsible, and I'm sure she found out through word of mouth that that's how I feel. (Judy, parent, Downtown Center)

In addition to staff assistance with parent activities, parents also expected to receive their assistance with personal needs such as food, clothing, shelter, and services. But, according to Nina, not all parents got the assistance they needed or requested. Her story in this regard illustrates what can happen when a parent is a nonreader who cannot adequately read the program literature, and the staff does not take the time to help him or her understand procedures and programs.

> I came here, and I filled out the papers, but Harriet never told me when to get the food or anything. She just told me "fill out this thing," and the day the food would come. She never told me what time. She just told

> me to pick the food up. So I figure, I'll pick the food up when I pick up my daughter, you know? So, I come pick up my daughter, and she tell me that it's too late. Well, how did I know that it was supposed to be at a certain time for me to pick it up?
>
> Well, last year I didn't get none of that food, this year it's the same way, I didn't get no food. This is what I think. They treat other ones better than they treat some parents. You know what I mean? I feel that we all, we should all get treated equal the same. While some of us act like we got everything, it doesn't means we have everything, you know what I mean? (Nina, parent, Downtown Center)

While parents expected help from the family service workers, teachers were also seen as resources, although some provided better guidance and assistance than others. Nina reported that she had experienced differing treatment in this regard as well.

> My daughter, she comes home and says she gettin' beat up by the kids. She don't speak up about it, like she afraid to. And now she say she want to leave school, so I'm thinkin' of takin' her out. Miss Kathy, she ain't been real helpful about it, she means well, but I don't think she is that good a teacher, not like Miss Charlotte. In a way it make me feel frustrated. See, to me, the teacher that I had last year for my daughter [Miss Charlotte], to me she's a beautiful lady. I got so close to her, and if it's not nobody else, I think the teachers should try to get to know their parents better, you know what I mean? (Nina, parent, Downtown Center)

A personalized approach with parents was appreciated by them. Cynthia found it disappointing that, despite having arranged her schedule so that she could meet with Ms. Carla alone, she did not have some individual time with the teacher at the parent conferences:

> Well, I worked my schedule out so that I could be there for that [parent conferences]. And, you know, pretty much, they just discussed the class, and the things that they were gonna do at that particular time, and that was it. I didn't find it helpful, not really, no. It was geared more like a PTA, and I thought it was going to me more of a one-on-one basis. And they had that afterwards, but they didn't have no scheduled meeting time. All the parents were coming, so it wasn't like a one-on-one thing. I would have preferred a one-on-one. (Cynthia, parent, Downtown Center)

Like Cynthia, Heather had also expected more of a personalized approach in all areas, and from all the staff. Since she had revealed so much important information to the family service worker about her abusive husband, she expected that everyone would be apprised of her situation. Yet she found out that the staff had not been informed of this, and because of this oversight, they might have inadvertently allowed her son to leave with his abusive father. He was only allowed to see Jordan under supervised conditions, so this lack of support upset her.

> I wrote it down. The woman who was here as the social worker at the time told me that she was only here temporary. But I thought that the fact that I wrote everything down, that they would review that and the teachers would know. But it doesn't work that way. It's in the file and it's private and personal and that's the end of it. I also wrote down that his father was not to pick him up here, he only sees his father on Saturdays. And I don't think any of them know that! My impression is, well, if the social worker is not there all the time, what happens if that happens? Even though I wrote that stuff down, nobody ever did anything with it. I put it down to say "hey, I got a problem," and I wasn't called. I don't know. It may sound like I'm really negative about the system, but I can't afford not to be when it comes to Jordan. You know? So if I expect more from the school, if I think I deserve more, well, Jordan deserves more. (Heather, parent, Harbor Street Center)

Information and Encouragement

Along with staff support, parents expected that they would be made to feel welcome at their center. Yet, parents' experiences in this regard were highly variable. Depending on the teacher to whom their child had been assigned, and the center they attended, they might be given a warm welcome or a cold shoulder. Heather shared what happened when she brought her son into the center on his first day, and how it set the tone for her and her son's entire experience at Head Start:

> The people didn't really extend themselves, at least to me. Not at all. Nobody asked me who I was the first day. When I walked in, they just spoke amongst themselves, saying, "is this your new one?" No, I think it's Miss Winnie's. "Okay, what's his name?" And I said, "Jordan." And they said, "Jordan, you have to go sit over there." And I'm like, I can't believe this!

> Then I was told to remove myself. . . . I was told, like, shoo, with their hands . . . and I sat in this parking lot and I was mortified. Nobody asked me my name, and they never told me who they were. I had only met Miss Winnie, and I had met the nurse, and that's it. So here I am, his first day, dropping him off with strangers. There was no one else in there, he was the only child, it was his first day, and I was told to get out. He was crying, and it really hurt me. I understood later that they are on guard for the kids, and you can't be sensitive, but I still believe, especially the first time, the first few times, but they don't guide you through it. So, right off the bat, it was a terrible feeling. It really was, especially coming from my situation. So, I'm like, they just don't put that extra whatever out. (Heather, parent, Harbor Street Center)

Heather also had the expectation that the staff would genuinely care about the children. This view was common among all parents. This included the expectation that the staff enjoyed working with children, and that they would strive to make it a place of learning where children would feel good about themselves. Some centers had wonderful reputations for working with the children. Unfortunately, this could not be said for all teachers, nor for all centers. Some teachers were considered less than excellent, even harmful. In fact, the parents at Harbor Street expressed many problems in this area, and several commented that they felt some staff were just plain mean to the children. As one parent discussed:

> There's been a lot of problems this year, with teachers and aides, and things like that. You hear certain things about this teacher being mean, or not speaking to the kids right. You know, all these things kind of scare you, and you don't know what to do. It's just, I heard too many things this year, that made me, you know, like wonder, why are some of these people in these positions? You know, if they don't want to be there, or they don't like kids, they have no business being there. (Christine, parent, Harbor Street Center)

When love and concern wasn't present, parents sensed that "something was lacking." Heather agreed with Christine's perspective, but felt more strongly about it, for she was troubled by the way that her son's teacher, Rhonda, treated the children. Having come from an abusive environment, she did not want her son in another one.

> I understand that they, you know, have to set the mood or atmosphere for the child, and if it's anything less than that, they won't listen. So it

> has to be disciplined, so I understand that. But it just, it's lacking. That's it, there's something lacking. I believe that there should be a lot more love, and a lot more expression. I just love children, and I think that they are very precious. So, when I see them being reprimanded in such a fashion that, well . . . I don't think that kindergarteners should be treated like that. Not even first or second graders.
>
> I saw a couple things happen with Rhonda. She was extremely, I thought, abusive. The way she grabbed clothing off the child, because the child wasn't listening. And I said to myself, she ain't got permission. . . . My personal feeling about Head Start is, this is only coming from a mom now, but I love children. I don't believe that they should be so regimented. (Heather, parent, Harbor Street Center)

Theresa shared Heather's views about the lack of consideration and gentleness provided to the children at Harbor Street.

> [One day] I brought cupcakes for the whole two classes. I said to the teacher's aide, "Nicholas doesn't like chocolate." He was too scared to tell her that. So the aide takes his cupcake off his plate, and she slams it back into my Tupperware plate, and then takes another one and slams it down onto his napkin. Three parents saw that, and they all commented on it. Then, my son pours too much milk in the cup, the cook is calling him by his last name, and yelling, hey, that he better drink all that! What's going on over there, what's going on?
>
> [On the Halloween trip] when we got there, the children just got off the bus. They weren't even allowed to go down to the pumpkin patch to get their own pumpkin. Rhonda handed each kid a pumpkin and she yelled that you can't touch the pumpkins. Now, why did they spend a hundred and some dollars to take the kids on a pumpkin trip, for her to pick up a pumpkin, put it in their hand, and go back to the bus, take it out of their hand, put it in a basket?
>
> Then they boarded the bus and they go home. There were little things for the kids to see there. They had little cut outs [characters] and things. She should be doing that with them, allowing them to go and pick out their pumpkin, to fiddle around with the pumpkins. I mean, it's a pumpkin patch, it's not the mall!
>
> I was also there the day they were taking class pictures. When it came to taking a sweater off a little girl for a class picture, they were so angry. I just felt that, if it were my daughter, I would only hope they would take my kid's sweater off. I mean, you're putting the child in a fancy dress.

> But no, they couldn't take the sweater off, they couldn't be bothered. And the little girl's hair was sticking up. I wanted to fix it. This should just come natural to the teacher. (Theresa, parent Harbor Street Center)

Bobbie saw the staff's lack of affection for the children and their rude demeanor as being related to a lack of training.

> To me, you know, they need to take the time to understand some of these kids' problems. I was in the classroom, I think it was November, and a parent was in the hospital. Now, she did get a little obnoxious 'cause she called every day, but in the beginning she had called to say that if her child was acting up a little bit more than usual, it was due to the fact that she was in the hospital. And one of the aides said to me, "well, if they think that they're gonna use that as an excuse, they've got another thing coming." And I didn't feel that's what the parent had meant.
>
> This child, I watched for awhile, he would run from one side of the room to another, and he would grab things out of peoples' hands, but the situation he was in, the way I saw it, living with his uncle, I looked at it as them teasing him and taking things away from him, and this is how he was reacting in class.
>
> I said somethin' to the aide, and [she said] "oh, I never looked at it that way." This is what I mean about not takin' the time. I'm not saying they have to accept the fact that this child's gonna be like this and that's the way it's gonna be, but at least try and understand the situation. Some of the kids have been through a lot. Separations, you know, whatever the situation.
>
> Well, parents think that some of them shouldn't be teaching children, 'cause they don't think they are qualified. And they feel that they [parents] should be involved and be allowed to be involved. . . . We just don't get treated like we should, and our kids don't either. (Bobbie, parent, Harbor Street Center)

While parents at Harbor Street had frequent complaints about Miss Rhonda and the two teacher's aides, the other teacher there, Miss Winnie, was dearly loved. Indeed, she seemed to be a good teacher, and was caring and gentle with the children. Unfortunately, she was out sick most of the spring. Since they needed help, I volunteered with her class one morning. In doing so, I understood why parents had complaints. I also realized why parents felt they were not welcome: I, too, was made to feel uncomfortable and unwanted.

Silence and Discomfort

That spring morning was chilly as I arrived at the center. I entered the building and found the staff in the cafeteria; the children were eating breakfast, and the staff were standing over them, arguing among themselves about the day's schedule. The children quietly ate their cereal while furtively glancing up at the staff, looking from face to face as they yelled at each other.

I went up to the staff and said hello. Candice had told me that the staff knew I was coming, but upon greeting them, no one said anything; instead they just glanced my way. So then I said, "I am here to help in the class today. Where should I go?" Again, no response. Feeling quite awkward, I then said, "Well, I'm going to run upstairs to the bathroom, and I'll be right down." Again, silence.

As I was leaving the bathroom upstairs, I said hi to a young woman across the hall, and told her my name. I asked if I would be helping her today. She said, "No, Letitia." Then she turned and walked away without telling me her own name, or who Letitia was.

The other classroom was empty, so I went back downstairs to the cafeteria. I found Miss Letitia sitting at a table with the children. She was loudly scolding them, so I waited until she was done before I again introduced myself, telling her that I would be helping her today. Again, I received no response. I then asked her, "What can I do?" She said "Nothing. Just sit." I took a seat.

During breakfast, Letitia spoke to the children only if she did not like something they had done. I watched this silently for a while, and then asked her to tell me the children's names. She swiftly went around the table, saying each name, and then in silence, we all cleaned up the table together.

Throughout the morning, no directions or explanations were given to me regarding what to do with the children. Miss Letitia was continually curt with the children, and seemingly uncaring. She and the other staff were cold to me as well, and talked to me only if I asked a direct question. I felt as if I were intruding on their space, and it was very uncomfortable.

At midmorning the class went down to the basement of the building to watch a video. It was freezing down there, and although I had on warm clothes, I was cold. The staff and I sat in chairs, in the back of the room; the children were seated on floor mats in front of us. Most of the children were dressed in appropriate clothing for the cool morning, but one little African-American girl wore only a sleeveless shirt and shorts. In a short time, she began to shiver. It was obvious that she was freezing, but no one assisted her. Instead, Miss Letitia just yelled at her to "quit squirming!"

After watching her discomfort for about ten minutes, I felt I had to act. I asked the little girl if she would like to sit on my lap to get warm. She nodded yes, and climbed up. Her skin was like ice. As I wrapped my arms around her, she snuggled up against me and gave me a big smile. When Miss Letitia saw the two of us, she left the room and came back with a big sweater. Without a word, she gave it to the girl.

The rest of the morning was uneventful. The staff remained aloof. After lunch, as I waited for a parent to arrive, Bobbie came into the center. I heard her tell the staff that if they needed her, she could help them that afternoon. Although they were short-staffed — indeed, without the additional help the staff/child ratios would be out of compliance of state rules — they told her no, they did not need her help. Bobbie then came over to the table where I was sitting. I told her that the staff had said the same thing to me, they did not need me that afternoon. Bobbie had this to say about the contradictory nature of the program:

> See, they don't want anybody around, even though they are short staffed. They just don't want us around. Joyce asked me why more parents don't help out at the center. Some people work, and you can't hold that against them; others have little ones, or are pregnant.
>
> A lot just don't feel good about the center, and how they get treated when they come in. The staff treat them like dirt, like they aren't wanted. The program says that parents are supposed to be welcome at anytime, but they aren't. It's like, drop your kid off and get the hell out.
>
> And then they act like, you know, one day they say we should be down there twenty-four hours a day, and there's nothing in the contract that says we have to be down there twenty-four hours a day. But then, at other times, they don't want us around at all. When the bigger people from administration are down [here to visit], they complain that people aren't involved, but then when you try to. . . . But they'll tell the head center that we don't want to volunteer. And that's not the case, not the case at all.
>
> They want to pick who they want to pick. Because they like them. They don't like you, they don't want you there. That's the bottom line. (Bobbie, parent, Harbor Street Center)

Expressions of Anger

Theresa had a different negative response as a parent volunteer. In the previous year, Theresa's son had been in Miss Winnie's class, and Theresa had volunteered there a lot. This year, however, her son was in Rhonda's class, and Rhonda wanted nothing to do with her.

> Last year, I was called up, often, to go in and help out. Miss Winnie would call me and Miss Lynnette, her assistant, called me. They welcomed you. Winnie and Lynnette, they were more than happy to have you there.
>
> Rhonda just doesn't want anyone around her. Whether it be on a little trip, or helping out in the classroom, or a holiday. You know, the first time I met you, Rhonda greeted me with open arms [that night], and I knew something was up. And sure enough, [she was nice because] you were there.[3] I thought that you were just a mother, you know, just one of the mothers, with your little baby there. And sure enough, I put two and two together when I met you, and that's awful. . . . (Theresa, parent, Harbor Street Center)

Parents felt that this situation had to do with respect, and they were not getting enough of it.

> I don't know how to put this. I guess, more respect for the parents, more respect for the kids [is needed]. Letting parents know that getting involved is for their children, and then having the staff welcome their involvement, asking for it. . . . Maybe more open arms would be nice, maybe some people need that to get involved. (Christine, parent, Harbor Street Center)

Heather had worked in business for years, and she viewed the lack of respect for the parents as the result of poor management. The way she saw it, since the staff were treated badly, that was how they treated the parents; it all trickled down.

> They just don't put that extra whatever out. Sometimes, you know yourself, in a work environment, it trickles down. How management handles things, you handle things. If people feel shafted, or if they feel misused, then they kind of carry that same personality out. (Heather, parent, Harbor Street Center)

In expressing the need to feel respected and welcomed, parents were also stating that they wanted to feel needed. While the Downtown Center had few complaints regarding harmful or malicious behaviors against children or parents, it was true that some teachers there were clearly better than others. Furthermore, some teachers were welcoming to families, while others tried to put parents off. April was one of those parents who felt that her child's teacher was not welcoming.

> They make it hard to get involved here, it's like they don't want you around. My daughter's teacher doesn't make any effort to talk to me. You know how teachers are supposed to want to get you involved, and tell you how they are doing and everything. She doesn't. I think she's just stupid, and she doesn't know what she's supposed to do. (April, parent, Downtown Center)

As April concluded, since the program had said that volunteers were needed, parents expected to be called to help. But the staff did not always utilize parents; in fact, it seemed that parents had to be specifically invited, and if you were not liked by the staff, you would not be asked to participate.

Many parents told me that they did not get the opportunity to participate in the way they had hoped. Some said that they had specifically told the teacher of their interest, or that they had noted it on the registration form. Yet, they were never called upon to help. Cynthia shared these comments with me regarding this situation:

> I've told the teacher that if she ever needed assistance, to let me know. Because I'm home during the day. Like each day, I don't leave till two o'clock. I gave them my work schedule, and said, "if you need me, let me know prior and before the time, and then I could work something out." I told her that if she needed anything to feel free to call me. And I never received anything. (Cynthia, parent, Downtown Center)

Maura and Natalie did not get invited either, but they sometimes came in anyway. Both women clearly would have liked to have been more welcomed.

> I would of liked to prepare work for the kids to do. I sent a note saying that I would prepare work for them, and I never got a chance to do that,

> to help prepare. Or whatever they needed, I could come in. I used to come in on my own, not that they told me. (Maura, parent, Downtown Center)

> I would have liked to have come in more. I asked if they wanted me as a regular volunteer, you know, and they didn't really say. (Natalie, parent, Downtown Center)

Both staff and parents recognized that some parents were invited and not others. Francine and Fran and I chatted about this dynamic one day as we sat in the family service office.

> Sometimes the staff here is very short-handed. But rather than call on a parent to fill that spot, utilizing the parents who are willing to volunteer, they just walk around here and complain how short-staffed they are, how tired they are, how much they need help. (Francine, parent, Downtown Center)

Fran concurred, saying: "I agree with Francine on that one. I just think that they don't really want them involved." She also made a point to tell me that the staff only "want the parents to do what they say," therefore it is only "the mild ones" who are asked to participate, not those parents who make waves, or have complaints. Therefore, she concluded, few parents do complain if they want to be a participant: "You know, a lot of parents aren't like Francine, 'cause they are afraid. They think if they say the wrong thing, that they'll kick their kids out of the program."

"GETTING OUR RIGHTS": LINKING INFORMATION AND OWNERSHIP

According to Fraser (1989), to be a client in a welfare program is to be a recipient of services, but not a purchaser. While both may be consumers, the purchaser chooses options and has rights related to exercising that choice. The purchaser acts by the choice that is made, and by the laying out of valued resources — money. The client, on the other hand, rather than acting, is acted on, and is dependent upon the largesse of the system. And, while certain rights for recipients might be structured into the bureaucracy, clients are dependent upon the "formal bureaucratic procedural rationality" for their rights to be upheld. Often not knowing or understanding these rights, and with little information or power, recipients' benefits and their very lives are affected by the whim of "administrative caprice" (p. 152).

It was the capriciousness of some of the actions of staff that angered and frustrated the parents the most. As the year progressed, word began to get around that parents were not only supposed to be welcomed as participants, but have a measure of power in the program. Some parents took this expectation a step further, and expressed the view that their lack of a meaningful role was a violation of their rights in the program. Francine had this to say about parental rights and parent input:

> A couple weeks ago I went around to all of the teachers asking them what problems or issues they felt needed to be addressed. I got some things from them, and they seemed to be glad that I asked. But when I brought it up to Policy Council, Valerie jumped all over me and said I had no right to do that. I told her I damn well did have the right to. She said that there were appropriate ways for parents to get involved, and that wasn't one of them, that dealing with issues and staff was her role, not mine.
>
> I told her, right in that meeting, that she had better look up the guidelines, and that as a parent I had the right to deal with personnel and programming. She didn't want to hear that. We never did get to act on it though, but we never do anything important in Policy Council. (Francine, parent, Downtown Center)

According to Francine and others, the rights of parents in the program included having a right to information, a right to contribute ideas and energy, and a right of ownership in the program. As they saw it, having access to information about the program, and about what was occurring with one's child, was the right of every parent in the program. Furthermore, parents were supposed to be told that they had such rights. Parents were seldom told anything regarding rights, however. "You know, this was the first year that they gave them their rights on the Policy Council. Every other year they were left in the dark, but Francine pressed it this year and they let them see it." Fran thought she knew the reason why previous parents had not been told of their rights: " 'Cause they really don't want them to know about the program. There's too many things wrong with it now, and if parents find out, they'll want to change it."

Marilyn talked to me about what can happen when parents do not know that they can take an active role.

> If you don't know what your rights are, then you can't foresee. . . . You can't focus on anything. We need to have guidelines so that parents could actually see what is going on, and what is required of them in

> order to make this parent group a good group and a forceful group. Then you can make requests. Parents can demand and make requests. And let parents know, you can request anything. You have guidelines, but you can request anything for your children. But they don't know that. They don't. (Marilyn, parent, Downtown Center)

While the administration appeared to be at fault in this regard, so were the family service workers. For example, while this type of information was neglected completely in the orientation, there was a lack of information about other critical areas as well. In particular, nothing was given to parents about how the money that they acquired through their fund-raising efforts was managed. While Harriet might announce at a meeting that toys had been purchased, or a field trip arranged, a detailed accounting of how the money was spent, and by whom, was never presented at the meetings. Instead, only the result of each fund-raiser was mentioned. Josephine had something to say about this situation:

> What happens to the money that is made from these fund-raisers? They do not know. These parents don't even know where this money goes to. They're out there selling this stuff, so that their kid can get a bicycle, or a radio, you know, they're selling it so that their kid can be rewarded, and that's where it stops. It's the parents' fault for not asking, for not coming to the meeting and being involved. Alright? They have to have a better way. (Josephine, parent, Downtown Center)

Other parents had concerns about their right to know what went on in the program, and what they could do as a parent in the program. "Knowing I have the right to approach Miss Kathy about my daughter helps my situation, but what about the other parents who aren't informed of their rights? It's a problem." These situations frustrated parents, for they saw their contributions as being important. Furthermore, as a result of their concern, many felt a sense of ownership in the program, and wanted to make sure that it was the best that it could be. So, despite parents' criticisms, at both the Harbor Street and Downtown Head Start centers you could often sense their pride as they talked about the program. Some of the criticisms they expressed were due to their desire to have a top-notch program for their children.

> It might be selfish of me to want that [power], but you work hard and then get told you can't have any input. We're the ones who know our kids, we should be able to decide. (Theresa, parent, Harbor Street Center)

> There are times I feel like a bitchy mother, and I know that they can't stand to hear from me one more time, but things got to be run right, you know. If I don't stand up for our kids, who will? (Bobbie, parent, Harbor Street Center)

> I'm here all the time, so teachers see me around. I think they get threatened, thinking that I'm looking over their shoulder to make sure that they do right by the children. Well, I am watching them, I'm doing this for the kids, you know. (Francine, parent, Downtown Center)

CONCLUDING THOUGHTS

In summary, it appeared that even though the staff blamed the parents for their nonparticipation, staff also weren't giving parents clear invitations to become involved from the outset. And the messages that parents did receive were muddled, unorganized, and ineffectual. Furthermore, the rejecting and unwelcoming actions of the staff often negated what little invitation parents did receive.

Therefore, the perception of individual parents in the program was that the staff typically did not want their participation. Taken separately, each of the instances that parents described here are disturbing for the way in which their needs, desires, and hopes for themselves and their children were ignored, and the way in which their expectations of being assisted by informative, competent, loving, welcoming, and respectful staff members were frequently dashed. Yet, these poignant and tearful episodes cannot be thought of as separate instances. Instead, when taken together these powerful stories add up to a systematic dynamic of deterrence, a reality that emanated from and was grounded in the poor material conditions of a lack of facilities for parents, inadequate numbers of staff who were overworked and underskilled, and too little training and understanding of the importance of involving parents. Such conditions were then manifested as a lack of respect and outright disregard for families.

Furthermore, not only had parents clearly articulated this dynamic of deterrence with depth and passion, but some staff also acknowledged it. I too had felt its debilitating power. Thus, the feelings as articulated by these parents are another reality that cannot be denied. When promises are made and not kept, when assistance, access, encouragement, and advocacy are denied — regardless of whether it is due to the lack of staff, facilities, supplies, or money, or due to human frailties of ineptitude, inefficiencies, or inattention of the staff — then unease, anger, and outright resistance is the result. And, in a program that is supposed to be organized, supportive, informative, and collaborative, division and distrust grow.

As Bolman and Deal (1991) have so aptly pointed out in their work on organizational politics, "the elements of a revolution include . . . a period of rising expectations followed by disappointment of those expectations" (p. 231). Furthermore, they remind us that "the level of trust that the group has in the leader is essential to their authority. . . . When trust is high, they are unlikely to become mobilized . . . when trust is low and the group expects the decisions of the authority to be bad, then they will try to wrest power away if they believe they can do so" (p.195).

Many of the parents at the Downtown and Harbor Street centers recognized the limitations of the information they received about the program. They also saw that through the encouragement or discouragement of parents, participation, input, and involvement, the staff were exerting power and control over them.

The following chapter addresses issues of the nature of the staff's authority and the various forms of domination that were manifested as a result. For in addition to the control of information, the program had a variety of mechanisms that also functioned to "keep parents in their place." In this next discussion we will see that unless parents acted "appropriately," and in ways that the staff approved, their participation was not desired, and attempts were made to constrain their involvement. Furthermore, these efforts, which used information as control, were grounded in structural forces that served to accommodate and reproduce unequal relations of power in the program.

NOTES

[1] The Head Start program year was mid-August to mid-June.

[2] See Chapter 1.

[3] I first met Theresa at a parent meeting where Rhonda was present. I had brought my infant son with me, which is why Theresa thought I might be a Head Start parent. During that meeting I introduced myself as a researcher, which is when, as Theresa notes, she "put two and two together," as she realized that Rhonda may have been acting nice to her in order to look good in front of me.

CHAPTER 6

Defining "Appropriate Behavior"

Power and Control Issues in Parent and Staff Relations

The official message about parental involvement in Head Start was one of encouragement. Parents were supposed to be welcomed into the centers, their input was to be sought, and their contribution to both their children and to the program was to be considered valuable. Yet, as has been illustrated in the preceding chapters, this policy of inclusion was tempered by the way in which staff actively discouraged parents' participation. Because of the reality of mixed messages in the program, it is not surprising that parents were disturbed and upset, for as Blase (1987) has observed, contradictory, nonsupportive, or overly controlling behavior in organizations leads to conflictive relationships marked by distrust and alienation. He also found just the opposite to be true, however. Respectful, trusting, supportive relations lead to collaboration and positive interactions.

Such interactions and their results — both positive and negative — are the result of the micropolitics inherent in social and organizational settings. While definitions of what constitutes micropolitics in a given setting can differ (Hoyle, 1986; Blase, 1991a; Iannaconne, 1975, 1991), Ball's (1987) work on micropolitics in education reveals seven distinct concepts or factors that affect sociopolitical relations in organizations, including power, goal diversity, ideological disputes, conflicts of interest, political activity, and control. While power is but one of those seven components, Blase's (1991b) remark that "Central to all perspectives on micropolitics is the use of power to achieving goals in organizational settings" (p. 185) emphasizes this as a key issue affecting all other components.

In fact, the recognition that social relations in educational settings are framed by issues of power and control has been a source of much educational theorizing in the past thirty years. Analyses of relationships of power between teachers and administrators,[1] among teachers,[2] between teachers and students,[3] and among students and in communities[4] have begun to illuminate the way in which power is constructed and utilized in a range of educational settings.[5] Analyses of this type are also beginning in relation to interactions between teachers and parents,[6] although most literature regarding parent involvement does not explicitly position power and control as being central to these social relations.[7]

Power has been defined in different ways.[8] From a functional, structuralist perspective, power is a noun, defined as "any force that results in behavior that would not have occurred if the force had not been present" (Bacharach & Lawler, 1980, p. 16). In this framework, power is a tangible function or action that is carried out within institutions and society to control or manage individuals (Etzioni, 1975). Giddens (1979) refers to this conception of power, noting that "action only exists when an agent has the capability of intervening" (p. 256); thus power is the capacity to act in a way that influences some action or behavior.

Conceptions of power have typically referred to actions being wielded over others (Pollard, 1982; Marshall & Scribner, 1991). Kreisberg (1992), however, has further expanded the concept of power as not simply power *over* individuals, but power *with* them as well. Having the capacity to access resources (status, connections, materials, information) lies at the heart of the notion of power (Szilagyi & Wallace, 1987). In fact, Ball's (1987) work posits that it is this connection between resources and relationships that creates the foundations of collaboration or conflict; in other words, the patterns of influence and the expressions of power in educational settings. Ginsburg, Kamat, Raghu, and Weaver (1995) concur with this view, and contend that "what educators do occurs in a context of power relations and distributions of symbolic and material resources" (p. 7). Thus, if one is to be an advocate for equitable resources and just mechanisms of access, then, as Giroux and Freire (1987) have argued, educators must explicitly consider issues of power and domination, for only then can education help the powerless overcome the hegemonic structures that keep their voices, their needs, and their very presence marginalized.

This chapter focuses on the way in which the relations of power and control between staff and parents were constructed in this setting, reveals some of the structural foundations of the staff's power and authority and describes five of the strategies or uses of power that the staff utilized to keep parents marginalized. These include manipulation (controlling of information), the establishment of norms for parents in the program ("appropriate involvement"), social domination (distancing), routinization (limiting choice), and regulation of activities (gatekeeping). While examples of each of these mechanisms will be provided, it is important to note that many instances are indicative of a combination of multiple, overlapping strategies. Following this, a discussion of the possible sources of the staff's power will be offered, as a way of explaining the selection and use of these strategies by the staff. In doing so, this discussion attempts to unravel the "hidden curriculum" of power and control at play within the program, and articulate the real objectives of parent programming at the Morrison County Head Start.

POWER PLAYS AT MORRISON COUNTY

Every story has a beginning, a middle, and an end. Chapter 1 of this book began the saga of parents' attempts to organize a graduation for their children at the Morrison County Head Start. The middle of this story is presented here, and is a documentary of manipulation, half truths, and the controlling of information, all under the guise of democratic principles and "maximum feasible participation."

We take up the middle of this story at the meeting that Desmond had promised to parents one month earlier, on the night they had assembled at the Downtown Center to make their initial request to Valerie. On that night, Valerie had been both resistant and absent. Desmond, while present then, had been evasive. Now both were present, but visibly annoyed that this issue had not gone away.

MANIPULATION: "THEY JUST WANT TO CONFUSE PEOPLE"

At the end of March, the meeting that Desmond had promised finally took place. Eight parents who acted as representatives from the seven Head Start centers in the county were present, along with Valerie and Desmond, both of whom made it clear by their comments and body language that they didn't want to be there. The parents also wondered why they were there to discuss this issue, for several Head Start centers had held graduations in the past, and nothing had ever been said about it.

> We don't understand why this is such a big controversy all of a sudden. This was always up to the parents, and it doesn't come out of Head Start's money, it comes out of what we make during the year selling

> things. So what it boils down to is that the teachers don't want to do it. (Bobbie, parent, Harbor Street Center)

As was typical, when I arrived nothing had been set up for the meeting; the room was in disarray, and the meeting started forty-five minutes late. Desmond opened the meeting by saying that the purpose of the meeting was to talk about what end-of-the-year activities were "appropriate" for children. He also stated that he wanted to create a "menu of appropriate activities" from which each parent group could choose. But parents did not want to discuss a "menu"; instead they cut to the heart of the matter, as Marilyn asked point-blank: "Could it be a graduation ceremony with caps and gowns?" At this, Desmond looked at Valerie, saying, "Acceptable things include singing songs, playing games, having a clown, things like that." Valerie also deflected the question by stating: "Anything that excludes a kid, or has toys or games that are violent, is not appropriate."

With that comment, the parents rationalized that "of course" caps and gowns were acceptable, particularly since they had been used in the past. When Desmond tried to dissuade them from this argument, saying, "we are here to address the future, not the past," the parents cut him off. "I want ideas about what worked in the past," said one parent. So he let the group discuss the types of things that had been done in years previous — picnics and games, clown shows, T-shirt painting, and caps and gowns. Some parents thought caps and gowns were a fine idea, others wanted to stress activities that they thought would be more fun. This discussion - largely reminiscing about years past — went on for about a half an hour. Finally, a parent asked, "So, can we assume that caps and gowns will be on the menu?"

Desmond paused, and then said yes. Marilyn and Francine looked delighted. Valerie looked tense. Desmond then said that since the meeting was running late, it would be he and Valerie who would draw up a survey of ideas and distribute it to the parents for a vote. Desmond summed it up this way:

> Part of the process is to get maximum feasible participation. What this means, then, is that you need to politicize your issue and get people to want to do it. . . . The staff will follow *the lead of administration*[9] and will cooperate fully in whatever activity is decided. (Desmond, executive director, Morrison Head Start)

The meeting then concluded with a parent commenting that "it had been a positive meeting." Valerie agreed, saying, "I think so, too. It is nice to see that everyone feels that the closing activity should be a good time for children and families."

The parents at the Downtown and Harbor Street Head Start Centers left the meeting that night feeling energized and successful. By all appearances, parents were being given a chance to have a graduation with caps and gowns, as long as a majority of parents agreed. As Desmond had instructed them, it was time to "politicize their issue and get people to want to do it." The next step was theirs: it was time to get out the vote.

Politicizing Their Issue: Survey Night. As any informed citizen in a democracy knows, the success, vitality, and validity of the democratic process lies in the checks and balances of power, and the legitimacy of the vote. Each of these areas were problematic at the Morrison County Head Start as it related to the "maximum feasible participation" that parents were promised in relation to determining the end-of-the-year activities for their children. Part of the problem lay in the timing — one month later the promised "menu" still had not yet materialized from Valerie and Desmond. Finally, two weeks after that, in mid-May, the survey came out. By this time, however, rather than just being excited and energized, parents at both the Downtown and Harbor Street centers were now angry about having to struggle against an administration that, while promising them full cooperation, appeared to be putting up barriers instead. In response, the parents at the Downtown Center took Desmond at his word, politicized their issue, and organized themselves around the end-of-the-year survey.

"Shush," Marilyn yelled, trying to get the parents under control in the crowded classroom. There were not enough seats and the adults were trying to get settled, while most of the children were playing noisily in the corner of the room. While other parent meetings had not been well attended this year, tonight was different. The survey that Desmond and Valerie had promised about the end-of-the-year activity had been distributed to all parents in the program. It had been sent home on the bus in the usual fashion; yet, when Harriet, Fran, Francine, and Marilyn saw it, they knew they had to act, and act quickly. So, about twenty-five parents and their children had assembled tonight to discuss it, and to make their selections. They were also urged to encourage others to vote for a graduation.

Francine, as chair of the parent committee, had asked Marilyn to lead the meeting. She began with a few comments, and thanked everyone for coming. Then she and Francine distributed copies of the survey forms.

I took a few minutes to look at it. The letter was three pages long, and two of those pages were a lengthy cover letter from Desmond and

Valerie. It rambled on about how parents had met with them to discuss options for the last day of school. It explained that the result of their meeting was the attached survey, which they were then asked to complete. Based on the survey, the letter explained that "the opinion of the majority of parents at each center will then be used by that center's Parent Group and staff in planning its closing activities."

The letter was long-winded and hard to read, since it was not only riddled with typing and grammatical errors, but was also poorly reproduced: the text was dim and fuzzy, as if it had come from a mimeograph machine that needed more ink. The survey itself was awkwardly inserted in the middle, between the two pages of the letter. It was entitled "Head Start End of Year Activities Survey," and it offered no instructions for how to complete the form. Instead, there were simply three sections, "What to Do," "What to Wear," and lastly, "What to Serve." Several choices were offered under each section.

I glanced at the "What to Do" section. While each item sounded fun, I noticed that the graduation was not listed as an option. Instead, the following items were specified:

_____ Family Picnic/Party

_____ Magic Show

_____ Tee Shirt Painting

_____ Clown Show

_____ Circus Fun Day (art activities, clown hats, games, face painting, balloons, spin art)

_____ Children's Sing-a-long/Play

_____ Puppet Show

_____ Folk Singers or Music Group Performance

_____ Exercise Fun Day (have local gym school come to center for parent/child activities or go to local gym school)

The section on "What to Wear" was confusing, since it offered no explanation about what the options meant. Caps and gowns were listed, but it was not clear if the parents would have to purchase them with their own money. This was the extent of the "What to Wear" section:

_____ Our clothes

_____ Head Start/other T-shirts (purchased by parent group)

_____ Caps and gowns

_____ Home-made

_____ Purchased

_____ Other:_______________________________

The last section listed food items: hot dogs, hamburgers, cold cuts, or a potluck lunch supplied by the parents.

After briefly letting the group read the survey, Marilyn explained that the form was unclear, and confusing. She noted that they had called the meeting tonight to remedy this. Both she and Francine discussed each activity, and what they should vote for in order to have a graduation ceremony. They also voiced their opinion that Desmond and Valerie had purposefully made the survey misleading, for the survey implied that the parents would have to pay for caps and gowns themselves, which was not the case, as the parent group had sufficient money from their fund-raisers.

Parents then discussed the graduation, and agreed on red as the color of caps and gowns. Then each one filled out their forms, and turned them into Francine and Marilyn. As the meeting ended, Francine asked me not to talk to Valerie about what had just taken place at the meeting, explaining that:

> We were not supposed to try to organize parents around this, or try to sway their opinion. At a meeting with Valerie this week, she told us that this was not to be a topic for discussion at tonight's parent meeting, but we felt it was important that we talk to them, and get them together on it. So we tried really hard to get people out tonight so that they could understand this thing. (Francine, parent, Downtown Center)

I asked her why she felt this was important.

> Because the survey form is written like they want to make parents not choose the caps and gowns. It's confusing and looks like they are trying to manipulate us into not doing it. That's why we had to cover it tonight. (Francine, parent, Downtown Center)

I reassured her that I would not tell Valerie. Harriet, the family service worker, then came up and asked me the same thing:

> All the staff were told not to bring this up tonight, or discuss it in any way. Valerie called me into her office alone, too, just to tell me that. But you know, that really pissed me off. Francine too. So, we got together

> and drafted a letter, copied it, and sent it off asking the parents to come tonight to talk about it. (Harriet, family service worker, Downtown Center)

She said that she knew that taking this action was a very chancy thing to do; she could get into a lot of trouble for it. Despite this, however, she laughed it off.

> We aren't supposed to send anything out to parents that is not approved of in advance. It sure wasn't authorized, so I could get in big trouble. But with the copy machine in our office now, we have power. (Harriet, family service worker, Downtown Center)

I then asked her if she really thought that administration worded the survey to keep parents from choosing caps and gowns. She said yes, and explained how and why.

> Oh yeah, the way they worded it, it looks like if you want them you have to pay for them. It also looks like the other choices you don't have to. . . . They just want to confuse people so they won't vote. And that's another problem with the survey. There's no instructions on it, how to fill it out, or when or how to send it back. So you know they don't really want them to respond. (Harriet, family service worker, Downtown Center)

By the end of the meeting, Harriet and the parents seemed even more motivated to see their dream of a graduation ceremony with children wearing caps and gowns come to fruition. In fact, the obstacles they were facing just seemed to charge them up. Francine rationalized it this way: they had done just what Desmond had challenged them to do: "to politicize their issue, and to get the vote out." As the parents chatted excitedly among themselves, I could tell they were relishing the fight.

Norms for Parent Participation: "Appropriate Means Not Raising Hell"

Parents readily apprehended the fact that roadblocks were being put in place to thwart their desire for a graduation ceremony. Furthermore, as they organized against the actions of the administration, they expressed their understanding that Desmond's call to action could not be taken at face value, and that their parental input and authentic choice were limited. While this situation was dramatic, this dynamic of being silenced was a subtle, yet stable fixture in the setting, a fact that parents also recognized. Clearly, despite Desmond's comment about "maximum feasible participation" from parents, many felt that the administration did not want their full involvement. Instead, they wanted them to simply be good volunteers who did what the staff said, and when they said it, and nothing else.

The notion of what a good volunteer was could be found in the concept of "appropriate involvement." In the same way that Valerie had stated that there were certain "appropriate" activities for the children, the parents as volunteers also were constrained by certain norms. For instance, activities that were appropriate for parents were those that helped the staff with the children, and those that taught parents about parenting and teaching. Valerie had clear opinions about this issue:

> There are appropriate and legitimate ways of involving parents. Appropriate things for parents to do are things like parenting education classes, or things that enhance mental health. Having positive experiences with their children, and with the school. Like doing a parent activity that's productive, learning how to make toys or creative play. Besides the social service work with parents, the goal here should be to help parents learn how to interact positively with school personnel. . . . It's not [appropriate] if it means fund-raising and graduation ceremonies. (Valerie, Head Start director)

Thus, the construct of "appropriate involvement" — as Valerie articulated it — meant that there were normative expectations about the behaviors and actions that parents should be engaging in, and those that were outside those norms. The institutionally sanctioned actions of parents were child-focused activities that fit in with the labor needs of the Head Start program. This meant assisting staff in the classroom, on field trips, and at home in a variety of ways, or assuming the organizing role of "class mother,"[10] to plan holiday activities. The rationale for this form of parent participation was that it gave parents a chance to see their child interact with others, to understand their activities, and to note their child's progress.

Other meanings regarding "appropriate involvement" were related to this "helping" role, however, for while it meant being an active parent who was interested in her child's education and who participated in traditional classroom activities, this was not the only way to interpret it. As noted by Elizabeth, the special needs coordinator of the program, "Our job is to help parents learn how to appropriately interact with the institutions that serve their children." Therefore, appropriate involvement also referred to the ways that parents interfaced with the staff.

This notion of appropriate involvement had ramifications about issues of power and authority, and clearly it was expected that parents would defer to the staff. For example, while an active parent who helped at the center was "appropriate," one who was there too much or "too involved" was not desired, and therefore was, in fact, bad. Miss Virginia's comment about Marilyn was telling in this regard. Marilyn had been coming in to the Downtown Center almost daily, working in the classroom, and organizing the fund-raisers and graduation. "You'd think she owned the place," Miss Virginia sniffed one day when I was asking her about parent participation at the center. Intrigued, I asked other staff if they thought that parents could get "too involved."

> You have to hold some of them back, 'cause they get very strong about the things they want to do that aren't always in the best interest of the program. (Miss Alva, teacher, Porterstown Center)

> Of course, some parents can get too involved. Some of them begin to think that, since parents have a say, that when they suggest something that it will automatically happen, and if it doesn't or cannot, they get angry. (Consuelo, family service worker, Porterstown Center)

Furthermore, some parents, and some staff, were explicit about the way that they understood the term "appropriate involvement" to be a euphemism for not rocking the boat. The real unstated rule was that parents were not to criticize the program, regardless of the legitimacy of their complaints or concerns.

> To them, appropriate means not raising hell. We [she and Harriet] don't tell parents that though, we tell them if they have an issue that they need to raise, to go for it, to carry out whatever it takes to address it. If they need the resources to deal with it, we'll help them. (Fran, family service worker, Downtown Center)

Parents felt that the program only wanted them to be supportive of staff. Parents were not to criticize, bring up concerns, or try to make changes;

instead they were to be there to assist the staff — passively, silently, and without discord.

> They don't like it when a parent sticks up for their center. You know, they tell us, they tell us it's basically our school. But it seems like everybody down there doesn't want to be bothered with anything. They kind of like throw it all on the parents. And when you complain, you're a picky parent. But, like I said, the bottom line is politics. Financial politics. You know, the tables always get turned. If they don't want to deal with an issue, they'll find a way to get out of it. (Bobbie, parent, Harbor Street Center)

A few took that view even further, noting that the word "appropriate" meant having no power in the program at all:

> Parents can say what they want, but the staff will only use it if they want to. The staff will run things the way they want to, as they see fit. Parents have no power here, they don't run nothing. (Lily, parent, Downtown Center)

> You're okay when they want something, and when you say yes to that. It's the same being on Policy Council. Yes them to death, and agree with everything they say, and you're okay. Give them an argument and you're not. (Bobbie, parent, Harbor Street Center)

> Policy Council is a group of yes people. The administration does the work and they want you to just say yes, and not challenge them. (Marilyn, parent, Downtown Center)

Francine had some particularly angry comments about the lack of parents' input. Her comments focused on Raymond, who she felt did nothing to ensure that parents have a part in running the program.

> They say we can do a lot, okay? That's what the guidelines say, but when it actually comes down to it, they don't want you to really do a lot. They tell you that because they have to.
>
> The problem with the Policy Council chair is that I call him and Desmond to complain about something, and alert them to the fact that we need a meeting, and nothing gets done. Raymond, he just does what they tell him to do. . . . People say he is so good, but he just sits there,

> they do all the talking. That's why they like him, 'cause he doesn't make waves and he lets them do whatever they want. (Francine, parent, Downtown Center)

As discussed in Chapter 2, the Policy Council was supposed to act as an advisory body of parents and community representatives that assisted the administration in making policy, personnel, and service-delivery decisions. Parents were elected from each center; the number of elected representatives from each differed, depending on its size. For example, the large Downtown Center had three parent representatives, while the smaller Harbor Street Center had only one parent representative. At this Head Start program, sixteen people were on the Policy Council; ten were parent representatives.

Yet instead of having the power to make meaningful decisions about the program, and actively provide leadership to the program, parents on this decision-making body were consistently disempowered, thwarted in their efforts, and otherwise ignored. Examples of some of these situations were offered in Chapter 2, but other ways that the staff manipulated this situation were also evident. These types of "obstacles" and "walls" were effective ways of keeping parents compliant, or out of the way. For example, the staff often tried to prevent parent activities from taking place. While this could be seen in the case of the graduation efforts, it was also true in other areas, such as Policy Council.

> Like, for example, they were supposed to have a Policy Council meeting every month, but when they saw that they had an active bunch this year, they only had three meetings. Valerie and Desmond, they run everything, they control it all. (Harriet, family service worker, Downtown Center)

Only three Policy Council meetings were held all year: in December, March, and June. The first one in December was a two-day weekend orientation that almost no parents attended. Because they were given only a few days' notice, most could not get child care for an overnight meeting. And, the rest of the year, it seemed that the parents on Policy Council never knew if, or when, a meeting was going to be held. Therefore, many had a hard time making plans to attend. Francine thought she knew what was happening in this regard.

> They [the meetings] are supposed to be held every month, but they aren't. And as the representative to the board of trustees for the Policy

> Council, I try to get them to have meetings. I'll call up Valerie and ask about a meeting, and she'll tell me that she hasn't heard from Desmond yet. So, I call up Desmond and I tell him, schedule a meeting, schedule a meeting, schedule a meeting. Then, when they do schedule one, they give you three days' notice, or they get canceled, or there's some other weird circumstances. I think they do it that way so parents can't get organized around complaints. (Francine, parent, Downtown Center)

Francine and I also talked about a situation that occurred the night that the Policy Council's personnel committee recommended that Candice be promoted from education specialist to education coordinator. She had been doing both jobs all year long, and the parent personnel committee felt that she was capable and deserving of this promotion. Other parents on Policy Council agreed, but their vote was overruled by Valerie. Clearly, the administrators had already made up their minds about this, and the parents' contrary opinion had little value. Thus, even when parents made attempts at genuine input and involvement, they were put in their place. Francine was livid:

> Like, for example, with this thing with Candice being education coordinator. The personnel committee decided that they wanted to move her into that position, but Valerie said no. So, then Raymond says no, it's not a good idea. We didn't get it, and it made a lot of people mad. They're supposed to do what the personnel committee wanted. If we can't even do that, then we can't do nothing. (Francine, parent, Downtown Center)

REGULATION AND CONTROL: GATEKEEPING OF PARENT ACTIONS

Thus, even when parents acted in ways that were indicative of "appropriate involvement," staff changed what it was they were attempting to do. The staff would tell parents what to do, or bypass them and make decisions without their input. For example, although the parents were supposed to be the ones to plan their own activities (and be an integral part in planning the center's activities too), and were supposed to be able to decide the way that they would spend their parent money, the staff frequently told them what to do, or carried out the exact opposite of a request that parents had made to the staff. Often these situations did not seem to be rooted in outright maliciousness. Instead they appeared to stem from a lack of training and consciousness of the way in which they, as staff members, were acting. Other instances, however, did seem to have clear objectives of keeping them in their place, and with little power. In these instances, the rationale for not allowing them power was, as the staff described it, related to "efficiency" or "good practice."

Joyce and Rhonda, the family service worker and branch manager of the Harbor Street Center, respectively were a case in point. Parents sensed that these two staff looked down on them and gave little credence to their opinions. Theresa's comment expressed a common view:

> She [Joyce] treats us all like children, all of them do. They are just a big clique. They don't think we have any legitimate concerns. It's always, "everything is okay." Well, it's not okay. (Theresa, parent, Harbor Street Center)

Parents also had the view that staff sometimes "overstepped their bounds." For example, Rhonda would often upset the parents by ordering supplies for the children and then telling the parents that they needed to pay for them.

> Rhonda has stepped over her bounds when it comes to telling us how to spend money. That is supposed be totally up to us, yet she is always telling us what to do. It was the same thing with the readers [books]. Parents voted on buying them, but it was after the fact. It made them feel guilty, like they had to vote yes. It took $218 for those readers, which meant that it had to come out of any fund-raiser money that we made. We started out the year in the hole. That's a heck of a way to start the year. Parents get treated like dirt here. They don't want to be here. The bigwigs wonder why and are told by staff that parents aren't interested, but it is due to the staff, not them. (Bobbie, parent, Harbor Street Center)

Joyce would also change the parents' activities without any regard to them, and sometimes in ways that they did not even realize. Her actions regarding the Harbor Street parents' vote about the end-of-the-year activity were telling in this regard.

Like the Downtown parents, the Harbor Street group also had wanted to have graduation for their children. When the survey forms came out, they too had organized themselves around the issue. A group of parents telephoned families to explain the form, and based on their discussions, agreed that they would work on a graduation, and on getting caps and gowns for the children. After the vote, Bobbie, who had cultivated a relationship with a local seamstress, had approached her and got her to agree to make some caps and gowns for the children.

Joyce was very annoyed that Bobbie had done this. In fact, Joyce told me privately that the administration did not want the parents to organize graduations, so she would have to "clear up this problem" by talking with the seamstress to tell her not to make the caps and gowns. She did just that, and never informed the parents — the result of which blew up later in the year, as will be explored in Chapter 7.

Another type of roadblock that parents and staff spoke of consisted of rules and regulations regarding their participation in the program. For example, parents were often told that something they wanted to do "was against the rules," but were never shown the specific policy. Marilyn had this to tell me about her fight over the cap-and-gown issue:

> I have been fighting every step of the way about this thing. I'm sick of it. I can't wait until this thing is over. I think that has been one of the biggest accomplishments, because we were told that we could not do it, and there were so many obstacles in the way, but no proof of these obstacles. We asked, where is this stipulated that we cannot have this? Show us this in black and white, and then we'll leave it alone. Or then we'll take it to the further step.
>
> They had no proof. I was told, verbally only, that it was in some book, guidelines that was made up eighteen or nineteen years ago. When I asked to see this, nobody could show it to me. So, I figured that, since you cannot prove this, who is it to say that we cannot have it? (Marilyn, parent, Downtown Center)

Bobbie summed it up well when she said there were always "reasons as to why something can't get done." For example, at one point in the year the Harbor Street parents decided to invite Matthew, a family therapist on contract with Head Start, to their meeting to have him explain his services to the program. Yet when they requested that Rhonda arrange this, the parents were initially told they could not invite him. They did it anyway, and he agreed to come.

> I tried to get Matthew to come and do a workshop, but was told that he couldn't come to give a workshop, 'cause we would have to pay him, and you can't pay staff. I don't really know what the problem was, but all I know is that I was told we couldn't use him. The staff always seem

> to have reasons as to why something can't get done, but then don't help us to do something else. I've just had it. All we want to do is do good things for the children, and what do they do, but put roadblocks in our way. What's the use, if every idea you come up with is messed up by the staff? (Bobbie, parent, Harbor Street Center)

In another such situation, Harriet noted that she and Francine had been trying to set up child care for parents, so that they could come help at the center. They "hit a brick wall," however, and could not get any straight answers from the administration about how to go about it.

> The HHS guidelines encourage bringing children into the center while a parent is volunteering. Some of the staff let them, and others do not. Some of the staff say that day-care licensing in the state does not allow it. We hit a brick wall trying to get something going. . . . Our job is to get obstacles out of parents' way, so that they can get active, work with their children, change their lives. As I see it, it's our job to help them learn the channels and procedures that it takes to working with the system. If we don't even let parents have their say, then what are we doing? (Harriet, family service worker, Downtown Center)

Other roadblocks were related to the administration's mandate that all notices to parents be approved prior to being sent. The result was that staff had to wait days to get them back. Bobbie complained that sometimes they never got them back. Without these approved notices, they were not supposed to have meetings.

> It just seems like administration hampers our efforts at every turn. Do you know that we don't even get our minutes back from them? The minutes of the parent meeting are supposed to be approved before they are sent out, and they never get approved. They just sit in their office and get buried. So what happens is that minutes don't get sent out. Parents get angry, and don't know what is going on. How are we supposed to get people involved when this place is like this? (Bobbie, parent, Harbor Street Center)

The bureaucratic rules at the program did seem irrational, nonfunctional, and at times, contradictory. They also were applied differently, depending on the center. For instance, as a volunteer in the classroom, I was always encouraged to eat lunch with the children. In fact, it was a policy of Head Start nationally to urge that parents and volunteers do this, and while parents visited the Downtown Center during lunch time quite infrequently, when they did so they were offered a meal. This was not the case at the Harbor Street Center, for the parents there complained that the staff told them this was not allowed.

> I need to eat if I'm at the center all day, but they won't let me eat. I thought they were supposed to, you know. . . . I can see why a lot of parents aren't down there. I mean, how many times do you go back and get treated bad? You don't. . . . (Bobbie, parent, Harbor Street Center)

Rules about the bus also differed, with some parents having the opportunity to ride the bus with their children and others not. At the Downtown Center, parents were rarely encouraged to volunteer for field trips, but when they were included, they were allowed to ride the bus. At Harbor Street, however, the rules were different. Theresa talks here about Rhonda's rigidity in this regard, and her disappointment about what she felt was "just plain mean" behavior aimed, not only at her, but at the children.

> [At Halloween] we went over to that pumpkin patch. I asked "may I go on the trip?" "Sure! But you have to have your own transportation." I said okay. I talked to Wenda, and she said, "you could fit on my bus." Rhonda wouldn't let me board the bus. There were more than enough seats on the bus for me, but Rhonda wouldn't allow me to sit on the bus. I was the only parent to go on that trip. (Theresa, parent, Harbor Street)

ROUTINIZATION: "WE ALWAYS DO IT THE SAME, EVERY YEAR"

Ironically, even Harriet, who was a vocal advocate of parents, would also attempt to put up roadblocks against parents' involvement. In fact, there were many contradictions in the program as it related to the idea of genuine parent involvement and programmatic routines. According to the Head Start policies: "Head Start programs must develop a plan for parent education programs which are responsive to needs expressed by the parents themselves." Indeed, the staff's role was to be a resource of information and assistance to the parents. A key aspect of this role involved ascertaining the kinds of information and education that parents needed and wanted. As illustrated in Chapter 5, however, while the staff polled parents about their needs and interests during the registration process, they did not act on this information. This situation was especially ironic since, as Candice (the education specialist) noted, "the prevailing attitude among family service workers as it relates to parents is this: if the parents didn't pick it, why provide it?" Thus, the staff spoke the party line about active parent involvement, but instead of offering authentic choice to parents, the family service staff steered parents toward activities that were "routine."

Several factors appeared to influence whether and to what extent or level any aspect of choice was an option for parents in the program. These included each staff person's style of leadership, their desire for routine, their abilities in facilitation, and their controlling manner.

Another important factor that affected parents' ability to have choices was related to the size, configuration, and culture of each center. Indeed, the types, and number of activities available to parents differed at each of the centers. The staff felt that each center had a different personality and that its programming emphasis was based not so much on parents, as on the leadership of the staff assigned to it, and its size and facilities.

> Well, every center is different, you do what needs to be done. I like the small centers better, Downtown is too big. You know, some people have told me that I change when I go over to the Penderville Center.[11] I don't know if that's good or bad, I'm not sure what they mean, but I do like it better there. (Fran, family service worker, Downtown Center)

Harriet's former center had been smaller, and she felt it was a better facility. She thought it affected parent involvement. "At my former center, we had sewing classes and cake decorating going on. We had food classes, "ethic [ethnic] dinners where everybody came in and brought a dish and shared their culture." Lillian also thought that the size of the center mattered. Since there were so many students at the Downtown Head Start, she had little time to organize parent workshops. "Other centers are different though; I think that the size has something to do with it, and the staff too, of course. We're just too big. Everything takes longer here."

Staff's perceptions in this regard resonate with the findings of Brush, Gaidurgis, and Best (1993, in Washington & Oyemade, 1995), who found that programs with smaller enrollments reported a greater level of parent participation. An exception to this dynamic in Morrison

County, however, was the Porterstown Center, which was the second-largest center in the county. Approximately half the size of the Downtown Center, it served over one hundred children, most of whom were Hispanic, and was known for its high level of parent involvement. I asked Consuelo about this, and she indicated that she thought participation was high because people considered the center to be such an integral part of their community.[12]

> We have the most participation of any of the centers in the county. The regional people, whenever they come to evaluate the program, they always say that this center is the way a Head Start should be, a friendly, family atmosphere where people feel welcome. (Consuelo, family service worker, Porterstown Center)

The Porterstown Center also offered the most educational programming of any of the other centers. And, unlike the other family service workers, Consuelo was adamant about the fact that she did indeed take into account parents' preferences of educational workshops and learning needs as offered on the registration materials. The fact was, however, that she offered the same programs each year. I spoke to a parent who had been at that center for several years. Nora talked favorably about her experience there. She said she was pleased that staff asked parents what they wanted, yet she also admitted that the workshops were always the same:

> The Center is great for parents. They are flexible and try to find out what the parents want. I go to the meetings, but sometimes the topics are the same from year to year, so I don't go 'cause I know the information. In fact, I could probably present the information myself now, that is how well I know it. (Nora, parent, Porterstown Center)

Programming at each center was also different because of the leadership of each family service staff member. Their interests, skills, concerns, and resource levels influenced the development of programming and activities, and because they had such a small repertoire of knowledge and skills, it was common that family service workers had parents do the same activities, year after year. Marilyn talked about how staff reacted if parents wanted to do something new:

> If you haven't been organized for a while, and you just are used to going through a certain routine, then when somebody tries to come to

> organize something, it's like, [they say] what are you doing, you're confusing us, it's just not working out. (Marilyn, parent, Downtown Center)

The family service workers did not recognize that they did the same things each year. For example, while Harriet explained that "each year is different, with a new set of parents. So what happens one year might not happen another. With a new year, you get a new group, and new ideas." In reality, parents really did what she wanted. For example, one event held "every year" at the Downtown Center was the carnival. Harriet described it as "really good." They would hire a company to arrange carnival rides, ponies, a petting zoo, and games. It cost approximately $2000, and therefore parents had to raise a great deal of money every year to finance it.

> We are going to do the carnival, even though the graduation may take place. The staff get so excited about this, even come to expect it, that I think that is one reason why they were reluctant [to have something else]. Also, they know that something like that will take work on their part, and they don't want to give any extra time. (Harriet, family service worker)

Many staff felt that Harriet put too much emphasis on fund-raising and entertainment. They felt that she should focus more on important educational programming, and activities and projects that benefited more parents.

> Harriet gets excited about certain activities, the carnival, orientation, holidays, but not the other things that can be more meaningful, like things they can learn in the classroom, how to do things with their children. (Marlene, branch manager, Downtown Center)

It was true that the family service workers put very little emphasis on this area. As a result, the other staff felt that something critical was missing in the program. It was a source of tension among the staff in the program.

> We need child care for the parents, and transportation too, to get them in here. We do need more resources to get parents involved. They should have workshops on budgeting, shopping, the importance of

> keeping the child clean, hygiene, that kind of thing. (Miss Billie, teacher aide, Downtown Center)

> I wish that we could find ways to get parents out. Different activities and things, you know? They say that they give them a choice of things to do at the beginning of the year, but they don't really. They talk about fund-raisers. They need different things to attract them. (Miss Anita, teacher, Cedar Heights Center)

This year, it turned out that the "thing" that was attracting parent involvement was the idea of the graduation ceremony. Yet, Harriet too had at first attempted to keep this from happening. It was at one of the first parent meetings in the fall that Marilyn had brought up the idea of caps and gowns, and at that meeting Harriet had attempted to shut this line of discussion down immediately, stating that "this was not the time to talk about it." The idea intrigued the parents, however, and Marilyn's brief question turned into a lengthy, animated discussion among the group. All the while they were chatting, Harriet was shouting that they were to drop the topic. After realizing that she could not make them stop, she gave up.

The day following that meeting, she expressed her anger that Marilyn would "even bring up this issue now! It was only November, and the end of the year was not until June." Clearly, this discussion did not fit into Harriet's plans of how the year should progress, and she did not want Marilyn's idea to mess up how she thought the year should go. After all, as Harriet put it, they "always do it the same every year," and the fact that a new parent would come in and want to do something different annoyed her. She did not want to be bothered with it.

SOCIAL DOMINATION THROUGH DISTANCING

The notion of not wanting to be bothered was not uncommon among the staff. I noted many times where the staff simply did not want to be troubled by parents' questions or concerns. It was as if parents were in the way, and the staff manifested this view by putting on the role of "authority figure" that both figuratively and literally kept parents in their place.

One way of expressing their authority over parents was evident in the pattern of making parents wait. For example, day after day, I noticed that if a parent came to the family service office for help, they were initially ignored. Rather than saying, "Just a minute, I'll be right with you," the staff would simply let them stand in the doorway, shifting in their shoes as they waited for Harriet or Fran to finish something. Other times, family service workers would not even open their door when parents knocked.

I felt their lack of responsiveness to be offensive and disrespectful, as if parents were beneath their "important" time and attention. An illustration of this lack of respect occurred one day while I sat alone in the family service office, filing some papers. A Latina woman came to the door; she had two children in a stroller and another preschooler by the hand. She asked me a question in Spanish. Since my Spanish does not exceed "no hablo espanol," I called upstairs on the telephone to summon Consuelo, the family service worker from Porterstown, who was upstairs going through boxes of old files with Harriet and Fran.

No one answered upstairs, so I indicated to the woman that she should wait. When I found them they were sitting in the office laughing, and they looked annoyed when I asked them to come downstairs to see this woman. They did not want to, and told me to tell her to come up to them. When I explained that she had a stroller (the building had no elevator), they still said no, they would not come downstairs. Their rationale in refusing to do so was that "she's probably on the waiting list, wanting to find out if her child will get in." Yet, none of them could have known what it was she wanted, and whether she currently had a child in the program. Instead, they just dismissed her need to talk.

I stood there a moment, not knowing what to do. Neither Consuelo or the other workers would budge. I was finally told that they would agree to pick up the phone to talk to her, if I went back downstairs and once again called upstairs. I went back downstairs, and did just that. Finally, the woman got the information she needed, and left.

Distancing behavior was seen in several other types of circumstances as well. For example, one day I was sitting on the steps of the Downtown Center, talking with Nina. As we sat there, Matthew, the family therapist for the program, pulled up in his car, got out, and walked toward us to go into the building. He and I exchanged hellos, and he stopped to chat. As we talked, Matthew never looked at Nina, even when she asked him a direct question about what he did at Head Start. Incredibly, instead of attending to her and answering her question, Matthew gave his answer to me.

Distancing was also seen when staff members welcomed some parents in and discouraged others, in the way that the staff talked about parents,[13] when staff refused to come to parent meetings, and when parents such as Theresa and Bobbie were denied the opportunity to ride the bus or eat with the children. Perhaps the most obvious example of physical distancing was the fact that the staff refused to do the required home visits. As they adamantly resisted the act of entering a family's physical space, and as their supervisors supported them in their refusal, the program as a whole, and individual staff in particular, emphasized authority, superiority, difference, and distance, rather than equality, solidarity, and connection.

SOURCES OF POWER

Thus, the strategies and uses of power and control at the Morrison County Head Start were readily apparent and recognizable by the staff and the parents. The program staff manipulated and controlled information, established and enforced behavioral norms of appropriate involvement for parents in the program, dominated parents through distancing behaviors and language, limited their choice of activities through routinization, and applied rules and regulations around activities, which functioned as a gatekeeping mechanism to impede participation and involvement.

While such mechanisms were evident, we are left to ask from what source did the staff acquire their power? From where did they derive their authority? After all, many had, just a few years prior, been parents in the program themselves, but were now playing a part of reproducing it.

Sources of power have been conceptualized in several ways. Early in this century, sociologist Max Weber (in Willower, 1991) theorized power as both stemming from and legitimated by veneration, tradition, expertise, and law. More recently, French and Raven (1959) and Bolman and Deal (1991) describe the roots of power as being located in six specific areas. The first of these resonates with Weber's typology, this being the "legitimated" position of authority that stems from an individual's standing in a hierarchy. Other sources include an individual's expertise or specialized knowledge base; the capacity to formally reward or punish others; and referent power, which is derived from being close to others in power. The access or control of information and agendas, and the control of symbols or meaning in an organization, have also been cited as sources of power for individuals (French & Raven, 1959; Bolman & Deal, 1991). In each of these areas, having the capacity to access resources (status, connections, materials, information) lies at the heart of the ability to wield power over others (Szilagyi & Wallace, 1987). Alternatively, these resources are also essential assets that enhance the capacity of groups and individuals seeking to transform power relationships into a shared dynamic, characterized as having "power with" others (Kreisberg, 1992).

As evident in this setting, four key elements shaped the staff's power over parents. These involved culturally derived ideas about schools and teachers as authorities, the presumed expertise of the staff, their power to reward or punish parents, and their control of information and agendas. The first of these to be addressed here are concepts about the profession of teaching, schools as institutions, and the intersubjective meaning systems that both staff and parents held about them.

SCHOOLS AS LEGITIMATE AUTHORITY

The schools in which educators work and teach derive their authority, in part, from their role as transmitters of knowledge and values, and their capacity to shape the lives and worlds of their students (Stevens & Wood, 1994). Critical theorists in education (Apple, 1982; Giroux, 1983; Feinberg, 1983) refer to schools as being agents of social control because of the power that these institutions have in socializing students to societal needs and expectations.[14]

Thus, the very essence of a school is the transmission of knowledge from those who are "learned" to those who are needing or wanting the information. Relatedly, as purveyors of knowledge, schools not only represent authority as legitimated by knowledge, but gain it through their positional power of leadership in communities (Jarolimek, 1981) and by their status as "institutions" (Boocock, 1985) with their authoritarian, bureaucratic structures. Authority of schools is also granted legislatively through state laws around obligatory public schooling. These assumptions about authoritative "learnedness" are reinforced by the "common language" (Berger & Luckman, 1967, p. 154) that individuals hold about schools in our society. Berger and Luckman (1967) note that the meanings a culture holds about this "authority," particularly as it relates to knowledge, are difficult to diminish, once established.

In a similar way, Head Start functioned as an institution of learning that had the power and authority of government behind it, and a socially accepted reputation for providing a genuine service to the community. In fact, the entire reputation and mystique of Head Start — what Skerry (1983) calls its "charmed life" — is based upon the tenet that the preschool years are a critical time for learning, and that having a preschool learning opportunity for children is extremely important

(Zigler, 1973). The logic followed, then, that Head Start was a vitally important learning opportunity for low-income children — a message that was printed in bold directly on the recruiting materials distributed throughout the community. Embedded within this message of the critical role of Head Start in low-income children's lives was the assumption, therefore, that the teaching staff and support personnel in the program would be especially knowledgeable and helpful, since the children and families the program targeted were recruited with the expressed goal of making these supportive resources available and accessible to them.

The language in use in the setting also legitimated its role as an authority, as a school, and as a program of the federal government. Children and families were being served in "classrooms," by "teachers," "teacher aides," "social workers," and "nurses." There were even "school buses" to transport the children, and, as many parents referred to the parent group, a "PTA." Thus, Head Start was endowed with all the trappings, meanings, and structures of a venerated system rooted in tradition, expertise, and legalistic policies.

Therefore, as parents entered the program, they did so with a set of sociocultural meanings and understanding about the function and authority of schools, and by extension, about Head Start as an authoritative entity. Because of the collective symbolism inherent in this setting and the assumptions they held about it, they considered this program to be a school in its fullest sense. As a result, parents expected that by enrolling their children it would be a valuable experience for them. Furthermore, parents expected that "the school" would be staffed by "teachers" with the appropriate expertise, skills, and knowledge.

Expertise

In the same way that schools are seen as having authority, those designated as educators are commonly considered to be knowledgeable experts in their field. As a person of knowledge, the teacher is looked to as an authority in her or his subject area. In addition to having "book learning" about particular topics, teachers are also seen as individuals who understand the developmental stages and needs of children and/or adult learners, and are also knowledgeable in various teaching or guidance methods that will help provide for those learners' needs. Furthermore, as a helping professional, the teacher is seen as someone who is dedicated to the benefit of the students (Willower, 1991). It is because the role of educator is linked to interests regarding the welfare of the students, to an in-depth, specific body of knowledge, and to notions of autonomy and professional discretion, that teachers derive status and, therefore, their authority (Pollard, 1982; Ginsburg, 1988).

Since parents had been socialized to understand schools as authority, and likewise to defer to authority figures in schools, the result of this meaning system was that parents came into the program predisposed to respect the staff and allow them to have power over them. This respect was manifested in acts of deference or acquiescence to the teachers, the staff, and the administrators. The deference of parents was supported by the staff when they stressed the importance of parents' learning socially accepted patterns of interacting with teachers and schools. They explained that parents needed to learn this behavior, "so that they would fit in with the system." Inherent in this "system" was the authority and control over both students and parents — a basic though unstated part of an educational institution.

In this case, as part of the institution of Head Start, the staff readily took on the role of authority figure that was a critical part of acting as "educator/expert" in a school (Woods & Hammersley, 1977). And yet, as has been pointed out in previous chapters, many did not have the requisite knowledge, background, and experience, nor understanding of the professional norms or codes of behavior that were part of being socialized as an educator (Wells, 1984; Hall, Johnson, & Bowman, 1995). Therefore, despite the fact that the staff were typically not experts with educational credentials, simply by virtue of their title and their prescribed role in the program, they went about the business of issuing authority and control over children, parents, and families. Frequently being cognizant of the fact that they did not have as full a repertoire of skills as they might need or want, they also distanced themselves from parents to avoid being seen as less than skillful. Anita, one of the long-time staff members in the program, summed up the dynamic in this way:

> The staff think that the parents are suspicious of them. They are afraid that parents will be critical of them if they see how they are working with the kids, so staff push them [parents] away before they can see it. I think sometimes it's because they are insecure about their skills to work with the kids. We don't have the training now that they used to. Anyway, some teachers have really hard rules on kids that are really, I think, meant for the parents. Like when a parent comes into the room, a child wants to run to them. A lot of them don't let them. Staff don't like that 'cause then they don't feel in control of the room. (Anita, branch manager, Cedar Heights Center)

Furthermore, the parents themselves accommodated these dynamics by deferring to teachers and staff and by frequently hesitating to bring up problems or concerns. This appeared to be related to the fact that in complaining, parents increased the likelihood that they would be pushed further away from their child's classroom, not closer, since, when parents did challenge the staff, a typical response was to further avoid parents.

Thus, one way that the staff coped with their limited skills, information, and knowledge base was to distance themselves from parents, and to control and delimit their activity. Each of these strategies was an effort to prevent scrutiny by parents. Recognizing this, we can see that resources and power are indeed linked, for when parents tried to become active, to make a difference, or become informed about the program the staff translated their behavior as being pushy, complaining, or selfish. The staff then made attempts to control the type and level of involvement of parents through the imposition of their authority as staff members.

CONTROL OF INFORMATION

Power in this setting was also wielded over parents as staff controlled and withheld information, put up roadblocks, and denied parents' their legitimate role as a partner in decision making in the program. The staff's use of authority limited participation and involvement, and limited of parents' authentic choice in activities and program management. Because parents were supposed to be supportive and never critical, to acquiesce to the staff's authority, and to be silent and unchallenging of their lack of opportunity to participate in making authentic choices about the program, the conduct demanded by these parameters kept parents relatively powerless to successfully assert their needs and interests, and subsequently make changes in the program regarding those desires.

Foucault (1980), who wrote extensively about theorizations of power, explicitly links power and knowledge. He noted that "discourse can be both an instrument and an effect of power, but also a hindrance, a stumbling block, a point of resistance, and a starting point for an opposing strategy" (1980, p. 101). Thus, in the claims of the staff that they adhered to the belief that they provided parents with choices in programming, and in fact carried this out as a matter of practice, we can see their discourse as both instrumental in its claim, and instructive in its contradictions. Kozol (1991), writing in a similarly resource-poor context of schooling, speaks of choice in this way: "people can only choose among the things they've heard of. No less true is that they can only choose the things they think they have a right to, and the things they have some reason to believe they will receive" (pp. 60–62). Hence, if the process of authentic choice consisted of having full knowledge about the options available, the types of resources that are required to pursue this choice, and information about what the potential resulting outcomes would be, then these Head Start parents did not have real choices in the program. However, if they did not recognize these aspects of choice as being fundamental to their actions, then it is not surprising that real choices were not made.

In Morrison County the types of activities that were encouraged were ones that were considered appropriate by the staff — that is, programs and activities in which the staff maintained authority and control. Yet even within these parameters, parents' choice in activities was controlled. Family service staff felt that they were promoting self-determination, and giving parents real choices and options for programming. In reality, they did the same things, year after year, and neglected key components of the recommended programming that were spelled out within the program policies.

REWARD OR PUNISHMENT

In promoting this type of "appropriate involvement," the staff acted as gatekeepers who mediated genuine involvement, prevented parents' development of ownership, and impeded their acquisition of information and skills. Indeed, as many parents tried to get the system to respond to them, they quickly learned that "appropriate involvement" meant the following: "Learn your place; be a helper, not a leader; be silent, and don't raise hell." In some instances, those who stepped out of their place and raised issues or concerns were penalized by not being welcomed into activities with their children. In effect, as they were separated from their children's activities at the Head Start center, they were deprived of their rights to participate.

The message here was that whether or not parents liked it, they were supposed to readily accept, and promote, this culturally derived paternalism and authority of the school and of its staff, regardless of the legitimacy of that authority. They were to learn, without complaint, what their "place" was in the Head Start program, and by extension, in all schools. Other scholars (Stallworth & Williams, 1983; Schurr, 1992; Smrekar, 1992; Fine, 1993; Harchar, 1993) have also noted these types of power relations among schools and parents. Within the field of adult education, Tisdell (1993) found that these power relations were reproduced with teachers and adults within the higher educational setting as well.

In the case of the Head Start program, it was observed that the cultural meaning systems of both staff and parents explicitly promoted the control/deference relationship inherent in the system. These cultural ideas of a powerless parental role were further compounded by the specific organizational culture of this Head Start, which as noted previously, was marked by resource constraints, political tensions, and distrust among its members. Because of this atmosphere of tension and diminished resources, the staff struggled against what they felt were ineffective leadership, secretive fiscal operations, ridiculous workloads, and dictatorial orders. Furthermore, without the necessary interpersonal and organizational resources, communication was limited. As a result, the organizational culture of the program was marked by silence: staff members used what little power each one had by wielding it over each other, and by denying each other's input, relevant experience, and point of view, and "coped with the institution" (Pollard, 1982, p. 26) by replicating it in their interactions with parents.

When the organization was understood from this perspective, in combination with the other mechanisms of authority, it was not surprising that parents' voices were silenced and that their power was limited, for the staff were treated much the same way. Heather hit upon this point as she spoke about the problems between management and staff. She commented that "the way people are treated trickles on down. If you get treated badly, you treat others the same way." This atmosphere then legitimated efforts at infantalizing them and keeping them in their place. This "hidden curriculum" (Giroux, 1983, p. 47) of disempowerment, which was built around the lack of attendance to parents needs, and the resistance to parents' efforts to speak up, formed the foundation of what was the micropolitics of the program.

CONCLUSION

In summary, the staff derived their power and authority from their ascribed roles and titles, and from the symbolic legitimizing elements of the program as a site of schooling, not from their knowledge and experience as experts. This was because the cultural conditions of schooling, which supported the authority of educators, also supported the authority of the Head Start staff. Relatedly then, the staff in Head Start also derived their authority from the deference of parents who yielded to the power inherent in the symbolism of the program. Hence, the parameters over parents in the program were a function of the social and cultural meanings about power and authority between teachers and parents that were inherent in the setting, and were reinforced by both staff and parents. Such parameters or power dynamics were further strengthened by the negative views and expectations that the staff had about the parents.

The staff's expressions of authority over parents were acts that effectively prevented involvement in the program. These acts included putting up roadblocks to participation, and ignoring parents' perspectives, and even their very presence. The staff's attempts to control parent participation and involvement often led to conflicts, and while parents won an occasional battle, the typical result was anger and resentment between the parents and the staff, as well as hostility among the staff themselves. Feelings of animosity against parents were then voiced as the reasons why even firmer parameters regarding parental involvement were needed.

As might be expected, the parents continued to rebel. The next chapter takes up these issues of resistance to these relations of power, as well as the ways in which parents and staff accommodated and reproduced them. As we step into the final days of Head Start in Morrison County, and what took place at "graduation," the results of these dynamics emerge.

NOTES

[1] Examples include: Hargreaves, 1980; Becker, 1980; Blase, 1987, 1991; Marshall, 1991; Marshall & Mitchell, 1991; Noblit, Berry & Dempsey, 1991.

[2] Lortie, 1975; Woods, 1990; and Hargreaves, 1991 have addressed this area.

[3] See Rist, 1970; Giroux, 1981; Pollard, 1982; Lytle, 1991; Kreisberg, 1992; Tisdell,1993; Brookfield, 1995.

[4] Freire, 1970; Gaventa, 1980; Schofield, 1989; Opotow, 1991; and Bingman and White, (in press) have done work in this area.

[5] For in-depth discussions of power and politics in education, see books by Ball (1987, 1990), Blase (1991a), Ginsburg, Kamat, Raghu, & Weaver (1995), and the 1991 issue of *Urban Education and Society*, volume 23 (4).

[6] Examples include Stallworth & Williams, 1983; Schurr, 1992; Smrekar, 1992; Fine, 1993; Harchar, 1993; Nunez, 1993; and Epstein, & Dauber, 1991.

[7] My model explicating the role that relations of power play in participation and the teaching/learning process is detailed in Sissel (1997), "Participation and Learning in Head Start: A Sociopolitical Analysis," *Adult Education Quarterly*, 47:3/4.

[8] Chapter 7 addresses power from an alternative view, namely, the ways in which and reasons why individuals resist or accommodate the relations of power extant in social settings.

[9] Desmond's ironic comment clearly indicates how the power dynamics in the program are configured, and to whose dictates the staff will be answerable: his authority, and not the wishes of the parents.

[10] See Chapter 4 for a discussion on gendered aspects of Head Start.

[11] Fran was assigned to two centers — Downtown and Penderville, which was a small, two-class center about 20 minutes from Downtown.

[12] Chapter 4 raises the issue of the explicit emphasis on ethnic pride and racial uplift as being a possible impetus of strong parental involvement efforts.

[13] See Chapter 4 for distancing language that staff used to refer to parents.

[14] It has been argued, however, that the reproductive process is never complete because of the nature and potential of human agency and the desire for freedom (Giroux, 1983; McCarthy & Apple, 1988; Apple, 1995). See Chapter 7 for a discussion of the influences on this process.

CHAPTER 7

Coming Together and Coming Apart

Accommodation, Resistance, and the Reproduction of Power

The previous chapter addressed the structural foundations of the staff's power and authority in the setting, and discussed the strategies that the staff utilized as a means of attempting to keep parents silent, marginal, and, effectively, in their place. While it is revealed that the social relations among staff and parents in Head Start were constituted around constructs of manipulation, normative expectations, social domination, routinization, and regulation of activities, also essential to our understanding of the micropolitics of staff and parents in this particular Head Start is the fact that individuals within the program altered these power relations in both subtle and profound ways by either accommodating or resisting these relations of power.

Seth Kreisberg (1992), in his work on power in educational settings, observed that "resistance is readily apparent in most situations of domination. While the mechanisms of hegemony are powerful, they are not all-encompassing, and they are always characterized by contradictions and conflict. The dominated rarely consent fully to their own domination. Many reject the dominator's theories of their inferiority, and they resist the notion that their submission is for their own good" (pp. 16–17).

Henry Giroux (1983) has also pointed to both the reality and dailiness of resistance-in-practice in his critique of analyses of the functions of schooling and pedagogical processes within educational institutions.[1] According to Giroux, acts of resistance are forms of refusal against domination and submission. Thus, when explicating the ways in which power and control over others is manifested, the discussion is not complete without an analysis of the ways in which this domination is accepted and accommodated, or rejected and resisted. Furthermore, by focusing on the way in which power is interpreted by and situated in the subject — and how the self and its diverse identities and shifting boundaries are at the center of the discourse of power (Foucault, 1982), then to address power is to describe more than its characteristic sources and outcomes, but to also analyze it from the perspective of how and why it works. In doing so, and by explaining how the individual intersubjectively relates to those "objective" relations of power by accommodating or resisting them, it thereby centers the subject as being part of a broader framework of social realities and identities, and situates the self in race-, class-, and gender-based positions of power and privilege, powerlessness, or oppression.

Resistance has been conceptualized and documented in myriad ways, and includes constructs that speak to both individual and collective action (violent and nonviolent) and inaction. For example, Sharp's (1973) encompassing review of nonviolent forms of political resistance presents a typology detailing 198 separate strategies in six distinct areas.[2] While such a list may be seemingly exhaustive, it is incomplete since the typology focuses only on "collective, public" activities.[3] In Sharp's day, political action or protest had not yet been expanded to include "private, individual acts"; thus, forms of resistance by people considered apolitical and outside of the public sphere (i.e., women, slaves, children) were typically ignored, since they were seen to have had no meaning or value as political actors (West & Blumberg, 1990).[4]

Fraser (1989) and Hart (1995) remind us that socially constructed conceptions of gender influence normative expectations around the roles of worker, guardian, consumer, parent, and citizen. Because the public role of worker/citizen and the private role of child-rearer have been construed as being fundamentally incompatible, societal expectations militate against accepting the notion of women merging these public and private roles.[5] In fact, Ladner (1987) points out that it is expressly because Black women have typically had to function in these dual roles of private/home sphere and public/work sphere, that they have been viewed as nonnormative, unfeminine, and, therefore, suspect.

Katherine Kuntz's recent (1998) historical overview of the way that women were ignored as public, political actors in Head Start adds depth to this analysis. She notes the way in which women's collective political acts in Head Start were consistently discounted by both policy-makers and the press because they were viewed merely as "mothers." Furthermore, she argues that "Head Start mothers' lack of political credibility is significant because it helped to shape Head Start's transition from a community action program to a preschool education program" (p. 22), thus linking the lack of recognition of the value and role of women's activism to the program's shift from a social change effort to one focusing on individual family problems.

Such gendered views of normative expectations of women's roles thus both silenced and marginalized the political acts of resistance located in family and other "private" (and typically female-centered) settings. However, recent analyses of oral histories, diaries, historiographies, and ethnographic studies of women, African-American slaves, students, and others have expanded our understanding of the range of the forms of nonviolent resistance employed by these groups.[6]

Blase's (1991b) work on the range of teachers' individual political responses to school principals has also expanded the concepts of what is considered political resistance. In Blase's study, teachers reported both major and minor strategies of resistance, such as avoidance, use of rational argument, ingratiation, confrontation, coalition building, use of intermediaries, noncompliance, and documentation strategies when faced with policies or programs they rejected. As Blase's work attests, in the same way that domination is never complete, acts of resistance also have varying degrees.

Giroux (1983) points out that oppositional behaviors have differing levels of effectiveness and importance, and differing magnitudes of strength for creating liberatory spaces. In fact, as he and others illustrate, some forms of resistance are actually contradictory and lead to accommodation of oppressive structures and social relations (McRobbie, 1978; Willis, 1981; Giroux, 1983; Apple, 1995), thereby perpetuating conditions of exploitation.

At the Morrison County Head Start, as the staff negotiated the reality of a workplace with inadequate material conditions, such as supplies, space, or staff to do the job, and little other support, strategies of resistance that helped them to work around, challenge, contest, or protest this system emerged. Sometimes small individual gestures of opposition to the status quo were initiated simply as a way of making life a bit easier, such as in the case when the employees purchased the needed cleaning materials themselves, when they brought in extra spoons for the cafeteria,[7] or when they sneaked the children into the forbidden gym to let them get some exercise on a rainy day.

Sometimes this resistance sought to create or broaden emancipatory spaces for individuals. This could be seen in the rumblings of the staff (though short-lived and not fruitful) about the need for the organization of a union after Columbus Day, or when Harriet and Fran worked with parents to print an illicit announcement for parents about the all-important meeting about the graduation survey. Yet in most instances, rather than being collectively organized in their challenge, the resistance of the staff to their conditions typically took individualized and idiosyncratic forms that limited the effectiveness of their strategy. Moreover, the paradox that Apple (1995), Giroux (1983), and others write about, that of oppositional behavior as actually working to support domination and perpetuation of the status quo, could also be found in many instances.

Worn out by the fact that the Head Start organization would not respond to their needs for materials, more staff, or better training, the staff sometimes protested their poor working conditions by resisting the expectations and duties of their jobs. Because their work was directly connected to the provision of services to children, parents, and entire families, such actions or inaction regarding services and assistance not only diminished the level and quality of services, the result was the reproduction of conditions of inequality and disempowerment of parents. Examples of this can be found when, for instance, Harriet became disgruntled because of her reassignment to the Downtown Center and she was, therefore, unwilling to "unpack" and actively do her job of family service worker. Another example can be found in the fact that the family service workers, due to high caseload levels or other reasons, opted to ignore the specific requests for services, education, training, and other forms of assistance that parents had noted on the program's registration forms. Other staff members could also be seen lessening the amount of time and energy that they were willing to devote to an effort, due to the why-bother attitude that they developed when faced with the various types of material resource constraints in the setting. Other examples of resistance-turned-accommodation occurred when the staff locked the door of the center (or the family service office) and refused to answer it when someone knocked, when they refused the participation and assistance of a parent wishing to volunteer, when they limited parental involvement and authentic choice, and when, out of a sense of protest and a skewed sense of the importance of routine, employees exposed families to cold, dark, unwelcoming facilities.

In each of these areas, as the staff resisted the strictures that the organization placed on them and their work, they resisted as a means of asserting some measure of control over their work lives. Yet instead of being liberatory acts, these acts of controlling behavior reproduced the unequal power relations between staff and parents, and the status quo was maintained. Thus it can be seen that as the staff became resigned to the problems, the result was that they sometimes jeopardized the well-being, and emancipatory potential, of the families they were to empower. In these examples it can be seen that the staff not only accommodated oppressive structures through ineffectual acts of resistance, they subsequently reproduced oppressive relations with parents. The contradictory aspects of their resistance and the connection to the notion of the reproduction of dominant relations of control is perhaps most revealing in the fact that the majority of the staff were former Head Start parents themselves. As such, this behavior leads to the question of why, as former parents who had previously struggled with getting their own needs met in the system, they would act in ways that were contradictory to their own stated reasons for being interested in working for the program,[8] and to the interests of those who followed them as clients in the program.

It has been argued that the reproductive process is never complete because of the nature and potential of human agency and the desire for freedom (Giroux, 1983; McCarthy & Apple, 1988; Apple, 1995). In this setting, this desire was expressed in different ways by staff and parents, and was only fulfilled when helpful resources were in place that allowed for the articulation and affirmation of needs and the creation and implementation of procedures that supported collective action for change. Without this, individuals had little power to successfully oppose oppressive conditions, and subsequently were reduced to accepting the programmatic status quo. In this setting there were many reasons why an individual — despite being surrounded by circumstances of inequality — might succumb to the accommodation of unjust social relations.

Sharp's (1973) expansive work on power and struggle in macrosociopolitical settings cited seven reasons people obey or accommodate relations of power in a given social context: habit, fear of sanctions, moral obligation, self-interest, psychological identification with those in power, indifference, and lack of self-confidence. More recently, Garrick and Solomon (in press), using analyses based on the work of Michel Foucault, have identified four forms of discourse within postmodern organizations that function as powerful elements that seduce workers into accommodating to dominant structures. These four forms of discourse are what they call "the language of empowerment, belonging, reward, and difference."

This chapter will address five reasons for accommodation by the staff and parents at the Downtown and Harbor Street Head Start centers. While these reasons support and reinforce the work of Sharp (1973) and

Garrick and Solomon (in press), I discuss them here in a way that resonates with the data in this particular setting. These reasons include identification, acquiescence to authority, cooptation, seduction, and belonging. This chapter also details the modes of resistance that were discerned as parents struggled against the staff and program. Discussion of these forms and strategies of accommodation and resistance will be interspersed with the depiction and analysis of staff members' and parents' efforts in connection with the end-of-the-year graduation, in addition to analyses of other events taking place during the year at Head Start. Feeling strongly that they were in the right and believing that their point of view and their voices were being neglected, parents at both centers struggled against the opposing administration and staff of the program, but with startlingly different results. We begin with the Downtown Center, after they have learned the results of "getting out the vote."

ORGANIZING AND RESISTING TOGETHER: STIRRING UP TROUBLE AT THE DOWNTOWN CENTER

Once the parents' votes had come back in favor of a closing exercise with caps and gowns, the parents at the Downtown Center began feverishly organizing. Marilyn was at the heart of this activity, designing announcements, planning the songs, activities, and timing for the program, handling the acquisition of the caps and gowns, and lining up someone with a Big Bird costume who would present Head Start certificates to the children.

Despite this very organized effort, many staff still felt that the graduation effort was misguided, and they complained about it. Their rationale against it was based on two arguments: they did not want the littlest ones to feel left out on that day, and they did not believe that the children understood the concept of a graduation. They felt that the caps and gowns were merely a symbol that would "make the parents feel good." And, while Valerie and Candice had expressed this point of view all along, the teachers were now the ones complaining. Miss Kathy expressed frustration with both the event and with the rehearsal schedule for the program:

> Don't ask me about parents today! Uh! Marilyn is driving me nuts, this whole thing is stupid. We're supposed to have practice today, and I only have eleven kids. What are we supposed to do with the others that will miss this? I am disgusted by having to do this thing anyway.

Even Charlotte, who was usually a staunch supporter of parent involvement, felt it was not a good idea. "Harriet should have stepped in and guided parents about what's appropriate for children this age. We used to do a fun picnic, and gave the children gifts. This is too much."

In an effort to respond to teachers' complaints, and win their input and approval, Marilyn and Francine, the two parent organizers of the event, along with Harriet and Fran, the family service workers, held a meeting with the teachers and the parents. In early June, fifteen parents and five of the eight teachers at the center assembled in Miss Jinny's classroom to finalize ideas for the big day.

Francine opened the meeting, and then asked Marilyn to lead discussion. Marilyn was well prepared, and carefully explained how the ceremony would progress. She had seating charts that indicated how the children would walk in. She explained the timing, the schedule, and the rehearsals needed to teach the children their songs. Marilyn also stressed that with only forty minutes for the entire ceremony, parents and children had to be on time, and in their seats in advance. Punctuality was important.

The group posed questions about how the day would go. The teachers were concerned with the matter of who would handle which groups of children, and how the three-year-olds might participate. Parents were interested in how many volunteers they would need that day. During this initial part of the meeting, only two of the teachers present participated in this discussion; the other teachers sat silently, arms crossed, with a look of resistance on their faces. Clearly, although they had to be at this meeting, they weren't happy about it. The parents, however, were very enthusiastic. When Marilyn asked for volunteers for the decorations and refreshment committees, parents readily volunteered.

While there was initial tension among staff and parents, some laughter and teasing among the group also began to emerge. And, when Jamal, one of the graduates, walked into the room to model the red cap and gown, the cheers were deafening. With that, the meeting ended, for the group was so excited that no more business could take place. As we were cleaning up Harriet approached me. The pride in her eyes was immense.

> Peg, you should have seen these parents today! We had a meeting about the graduation ceremony with Miss Virginia, Miss Marlene, and Candice. They came with all of their objections and concerns, and I just kept my mouth shut. Marilyn and Francine had answers to everyone's questions. They were so organized. I was so proud of them. And wasn't Marilyn great tonight? She really got it together! (Harriet, family service worker, Downtown Center)

I asked Marilyn to spend a few moments sharing her thoughts with me about the struggle it took to get the graduation off the ground. She talked about her volunteer efforts, and the way that she resisted the roadblocks that had been put up in the attempt to thwart the graduation, and the status-quo mentality of the staff.

> At first I was shot down, and just told by Harriet that it wasn't possible, that we couldn't do caps and gowns no way. And that's all I got at first. I had to fight to even get them to talk about it, and I had all these people mad at me. But I carried it through, and now, we're gonna make it happen. I feel proud of myself and I'm happy that we can do this for the kids.
>
> I know that people talk about me; they thought that I was just stirring up trouble, and wouldn't see it through. The staff think I'm a total pain, and some of the parents didn't think I would do this. But I just kept asking them, is this in writing anywhere? Give me a rule that says we can't do it. And they couldn't. They didn't know what to do with me. Everyone was afraid that I would go right up to meet with regional and stir all this up.
>
> And I was gonna, but I didn't have to. I'm on Policy Council, and I brought it up there. I just kept pushing, and made them see that they had to deal with this at our level, 'cause there was nothing in writing. (Marilyn, parent, Downtown Center)

Francine also had much to say about the effort it took to make this happen.

> I'm too determined on this one. We are going to do it, no matter what. There is no way we are not going to succeed. They can't stop us, no matter what they do. I'll personally make sure that we pull this thing off. It's too important to the kids, and to us. Besides, we got to prove that us parents can do this thing.
>
> If I have to do it all, it's gonna get done. I've always been that way, not only with here, but with everything. I'm just that way. If you tell me that I can't do something, and I know it can be done, then that just makes me even more determined to do what I gotta do. The way I see it, the harder they push, the more I'll push back. When they told us no, we were willing to go to regional offices, we were willing to go over the Head Start director's head, to go to the executive, to go to the board of trustees, we were willing to do all of this. Okay? (Francine, parent, Downtown Center)

So, despite some of the staff's displeasure with the graduation, the day was set to go. While many did not like it, they were cooperating. They were keeping their part of the deal that had been struck by Desmond: "if parents organized themselves and voted for a closing exercise, then the staff would assist them." Keeping staff at their word, however, took competent, determined parental leadership, tenacity, teamwork, a good political strategy, and the dogged support of Harriet.

GIVING IN TO AUTHORITY AT THE HARBOR STREET CENTER: "WE DON'T GET TO DECIDE THAT, EITHER?"

A much different scenario awaited the parents at Harbor Street. Because the parents did not have the solid support of any staff member, they struggled to have their graduation ceremony. After the April meeting with Desmond and Valerie, the Harbor Street parents also began to organize ideas for their own graduation. As they awaited the return of the surveys, they scheduled a planning meeting for early May, anticipating that they would have the survey results by that time. Unfortunately, when the day of that meeting arrived, Joyce, Harbor Street's family service worker, unexpectedly canceled it, without any explanation. Furthermore, when she did so by manner of a message on an answering machine, she also ordered them not to try to meet without her being present. Parents were furious, but felt helpless.

> Now we have no time to plan for the closing exercise. Joyce is just ruining things, and I worked too hard all year to have some staff person who doesn't know shit to come in here and mess things up 'cause it doesn't fit in her schedule. Why can't we have a meeting without her? That's what I want to know. Where does she get the authority to cancel meetings and just change things on us? I told Bobbie [the parent chair at Harbor Street] that if this happens again, we'll all meet at my house, and I don't care what she says. (Gwen, parent, Harbor Street Center)

> Why couldn't we just have a meeting on our own, without Joyce there? I don't know, but to me, it sure shows a lack of trust on her part, like we can't be trusted to do anything, or plan anything, you know? (Christine, parent, Harbor Street Center)

Joyce had thrown up other roadblocks as well, for in the days following she would not let the parents see the results of their survey. Although the parents had repeatedly asked about them, they could not get a straight answer from her. Bobbie did not know if it was an accidental mix-up, or an intentional ploy, but purportedly Joyce had collected the surveys as they came in, and instead of giving them to Bobbie, she turned them in to Valerie. After the canceled meeting in May, parents rescheduled it for the first week of June, but by then the surveys had supposedly been thrown away. So, even if the parents had requested caps and gowns, they would never really know. Now, with only two weeks to go, Harbor Street still did not know what direction they were headed regarding the last day of school.

With little time left to organize, the parents scrambled to plan something special. The early-June meeting was attended by ten parents, Bobbie, the parent chairperson, and Joyce, the family service worker. First, Bobbie told the parents her understanding of what had happened with the surveys. Reactions to this news were quite obvious: it was easy to see that the parents were very angry. Theresa and the other parents present crossed their arms or shifted in their seats, faces glowering, yet no one said a word. Joyce also remained silent. Bobbie's next announcement related more bad news: for some unknown reason, the seamstress who had originally agreed to make caps and gowns was not taking her calls anymore; therefore, they no longer had this resource available. Bobbie, of course, did not realize that Joyce had carried out her plan to call the seamstress and tell her not to make them. Joyce again said nothing.

Trying to make the best of a bad situation, Bobbie recommended that they buy T-shirts and make graduation caps for the children. Parents agreed that this would be a good idea, and they took votes on the colors of the shirts and caps.

During this business, Joyce began to interrupt a lot, and did not let Bobbie run the meeting on her own. Bobbie began to get extremely frustrated with this interference, but she said nothing to challenge Joyce until the group moved on to talk about the food. A parent had recalled that the choice on the survey was hamburgers, hotdogs, cold cuts, or a potluck to be done by the parents. As they began discussing the various options, Joyce broke into their conversation: "Since you were not there, and it had to be in, I made the decision for you and took it over to administration. I hand-delivered it so it would be in on time."

The parents looked shocked. After a moment of silence, Bobbie started to speak. Before she could continue, however, Joyce yelled at the parents, "Listen, you had better get it together. There's been a lot of confusion in the past, but I'm here now, and things will get taken care of!"

Joyce's lecture was quickly drowned out as several parents began shouting. I caught comments such as, "What is the purpose of this meeting if everything is already decided?" and a frustrated and emphatic "We should have started this thing in March!" The group was clearly disgusted, and became even more so when Joyce told them that she had also promised $325 of their parent money to hire a clown. Her excuse was: "the Head Start centers always used him."

The situation became increasingly tense. As the parents realized that there was little left for them to decide, they became combative and rude with each other. In the midst of this, however, they did decide on one thing. Rather than hold two parties — one for the morning classes and one for the afternoon — they would combine them and have one big party for everybody. To make matters worse, Joyce then told the parents that they could not have their party on the last day of school; instead, it had to be on the second-to-last day, because she would be at the Morrow Street Center on the nineteenth, for their party. "Oh, we don't get to decide that, either?" was the question posed by a very upset Theresa.

Between the yelling, Bobbie tried to manage the meeting. She was clearly rattled, however, and began skipping from topic to topic, not coming to closure on anything. Finally, as one of the parents challenged one of Bobbie's suggestions, Bobbie started crying. In a wail of frustration, she said that she had "tried her best, had done all this work, and no one appreciated it." She got up, and ran out of the room.

The parents looked stunned, and sat in silence for a moment. Then the complaints started — but they were all about Bobbie. Esther said, with a tone of disgust in her voice, "Well, this is not even a real meeting, if everything's been decided." Theresa said, "You can't even give an idea, or you're shot down." Then, like a mother hen gathering up her flustered chicks, Joyce smugly took over the meeting. She used this time to criticize Bobbie, and to seek support for her own role as staff.

> She's burned out, and it's been a difficult year, but she's worked hard. . . . I'm just here to guide you through difficult times. Parents can really make a difference, but to do so, next year you have to vote in a competent leader, not someone like Bobbie. . . . Remember, I got it all on me when I got here. We didn't have a social worker for three months, you know, but now that I'm here, we'll take care of all of this. (Joyce, family service worker, Harbor Street Center)

Joyce then adjourned the meeting, and told parents to call her with ideas for the party. The parents gathered up their things, and talked agitatedly among themselves as they left. Christine was silent, however. She had sat there awkwardly, seemingly uncertain of what to do in her role as vice chair. Others, though, were quite vocal about their feelings. Esther summed up the situation like this:

> I'm disgusted. The way these decisions have been made without us, the lack of leadership. Why did I even come tonight? I only got the meeting notice today, and if I hadn't opened it by chance tonight, I wouldn't have even come. Then, I rush here, and look what happens. It's a mess. I am thoroughly disgusted by this whole thing. (Esther, parent, Harbor Street Center)

After the meeting that night, several parents went to Bobbie's house to console her, and to commiserate together about what had happened. They agreed to organize the day as planned; they would have one big party with games, T-shirts, and graduation caps, and they would ask parents to bring in potluck dishes.

Two weeks passed while they worked on their plans, but as the final day approached, Bobbie showed me a flyer that Joyce had sent home about the picnic. It detailed a much different party. Joyce had scheduled two separate parties, instead of one together, as had been voted on at the parent group meeting that night. Bobbie was angry. "Joyce is making the decisions for us; we have no say in what is gonna happen to our kids on that day. It's supposed to be our event, our party. We'll just see about that."

Bobbie tried to get the administration to help them counter Joyce's plans. She first talked to Doris, Joyce's supervisor, who only expressed her outrage at what Joyce had done. Bobbie then complained to Valerie. She was of no help either, for all Valerie told her was "I'm sure it [Joyce's action] wasn't intentional." So, Bobbie and the parents struggled with Joyce alone.

> I told Valerie that she was just lucky that she didn't have a bunch of us marching down there in protest. People are really mad. I said that we had talked about going to Desmond, but we knew he wasn't in town. But I quoted him to her. "The centers belong to the parents, and what you all decide you want for your children is what will be done. The staff are paid to do their jobs on that day, and will implement whatever program you decide. You can be assured of that." Well, that sure as hell isn't the case. (Bobbie, parent, Downtown Center)

The parents also discovered that the other staff at the center were not on their side, either. Bobbie said that as she and several other parents were discussing this situation at the center, they overheard Helen, the cook, say loudly from the next room: "Just who in the hell do the parents think they are? They act like they own the place."

The parents were outraged at her attitude. When they complained again to Valerie, they could not believe her response either. Bobbie shared it with me: "I told Valerie what she said, and she tells me, 'oh, I'm sure she didn't mean it that way.' Yeah, right."

In this scenario it is evident that the parents acquiesced to Joyce because of her role of authority in the program. Joyce, who clearly understood her role as one that was to wield power over parents instead of facilitating their empowerment, did so out of the role expectations and the meanings that she held about her position in the program. Furthermore, the supervisory staff in the program did nothing about her behavior, which legitimized it. This reinforced the present manifestations of unequal power relations, but also sent a message to the staff that indicated that such actions by staff toward parents would be tolerated in the future, as well. Finally, in using her referent or positional power the way she did, she not only usurped the power and dignity of the parents, but she actually created division among them with her "divide and conquer" tactic of blaming Bobbie for all the problems and encouraging the parents to trust her to do the right thing. Thus, her actions with parents reproduced unequal power relations in two areas; they supported patronizing (though problematic and limiting) relations between staff and parents, and promoted distrust and lack of solidarity among parents. These were not the only ways that accommodation to the status quo was, accomplished, however, as the following sections attest.

CO-OPTATION: BEING BOUGHT, OR MAKING SURE THAT PARENTS DON'T "OWN THE PLACE"

Later that month, as Harriet and I stood in the cafeteria at the Downtown Center, watching the children rehearse songs that they would be singing at the closing exercise, she talked about how the staff were reacting to the graduation plans. Many, she felt, had challenged the idea from the very start because they didn't like to be put out, since, as she noted, that is how she had felt at first. "I've been thinking about this whole thing and even though I fought it too at first, I'm glad I took their side and helped them pull it off, since that is what they wanted." She explained that her thoughts on this had to do with her feelings about the need for parents to have a say in the program.

> I guess you could say I take an activist approach with these parents. I tell 'em, if you see a problem, address it. Don't take nothing from administration just 'cause they say so. This year, them parents have done a lot. I'm real proud of them, they learned that lesson well, and ha ha, some of them, they really took it to heart.

She also recalled (as she often did other times that year) how, when she was a parent in the program, she and others had pressed on with their concerns, and challenged the administration.

> At the time, I think that they thought I was pain in the butt. I know that Consuelo (the family service worker assigned to the center where Harriet was a parent) felt that sometimes, especially when the director would call her up and want to know what that Harriet was doing *this* time!
>
> I really got educated when I got involved in Head Start. I was a young mother, only sitting at home and into babies and soap operas. Then I signed up my son and got involved. Head Start got me out and into organizing things and doing activities. I was at Porterstown. We did a lot of things there. We raised a lot of ruckus, getting parents out to protest and everything. I worked with parent committees, the board, the policy council, and even the mayor. We used to hold meetings, and I would organize bus loads of parents to come. I also led protests and marches down to city hall with other parents, so that we could get our point across about the need for services. You know, when I was there, we even got rid of the executive director.
>
> Once when they were trying to get rid of the program, we even called all of the parents and told them that there was an emergency at the center and to get down here right away. When they got there, we all marched down to city hall to complain, and we saved the program.
>
> [So] I went from that [being a mom] to cutting the ribbon with the mayor at the ground-breaking ceremony for the new Head Start facility. It made me feel good. (Harriet, family service worker, Downtown Center)

It also made Harriet feel good when she was asked to become a part of the paid staff at Head Start. In doing so, however, Harriet quickly became cognizant of the fact that she would have to quiet her political activity in order to keep her job. In fact, getting and keeping jobs was a primary way that parents and staff were kept quiet, and encouraged to accommodate the system.

According to Fran and Harriet, the program sometimes made it a point to hire parents who they saw as making waves, seeking changes in the program, or otherwise complaining. Valerie openly admitted that she had hired people for this very reason. While she had first mentioned to me one day in private that she "had hired Harriet to shut her up," she later made the same type of comment in front of the entire Policy Council.

In an effort to do likewise with Francine, upon seeing what an active parent she was, Valerie had urged her to take a job as a substitute teacher's aide — a position that was not full-time, but would still have the desired result — that of limiting Francine's power as a parent. Francine saw through Valerie's offer, however, and told her she was not interested, since it would mean giving up her role as parent chair at the Downtown Center, and her place on Policy Council.

> I've been offered a job here as a substitute teacher. Well, in so many words, it's like, [they think that] I am the big mouth at Head Start. Let's put her to work for us, so that she'll no longer have the [parent leadership] positions that she has, 'cause then I would have to give them up. I just told them no. They tried to shut me up other ways, like they told me that I couldn't bring my child. I couldn't volunteer unless I could bring my child 'cause I didn't have a sitter and they told me I couldn't and I said, yes, I can. I told them if you tell me I can't bring my child, then I suggest you go read your guidelines, and all the other stuff you gave us at Policy Council and told us to read! So, I talked 'em down. I didn't want to give up what I was doing. I didn't want to be shut up. (Francine, parent, Downtown Center)

Head Start policies require that parents, when accepting employment in the program, relinquish their rights to vote regarding parent functions, even though they continue to have children enrolled in the program. And, because in this setting anyway, the staff were not allowed much input or were given little credence when suggesting ideas, they therefore were effectively silenced by the program.

> There are guidelines about that, you know. If you are a staff person, you can't vote or organize as a parent, things like that. As a parent and staff member, you must give up your rights to vote. (Helen, cook and former Parent, Harbor Street Center)

> I started as a custodian in December. I needed the job, and I like it, it's easy. But you know, now my role as a parent has changed. I can still

> come to meetings, but I can't vote. I miss that. I don't think that's fair. (Inez, parent, Cedar Heights Center)

There were other contradictory aspects to this kind of cooptation of parents, however, for as it has been recognized previously, many parents wanted jobs with the program, and didn't care if they had to give up certain rights to get a paying job. Furthermore, for many this aspect did not apply to them because they started jobs after their parent years. Also, many parents had a strong belief in the program; it had provided a needed service to them, and they wanted to be a part of it too. Current staff members whose children had been in the program spoke of how they were excited to have the opportunity to move from parent to staff member. For many, it was their first job outside the home. Miss Anita and Miss Winnie shared their stories.

> Yes, I was a classroom helper, and I used to attend meetings. I began as a volunteer, and then got hired as a teacher's aide. I was an aide for twenty years, and have been a teacher for two. I got my CDA, I got a better job, and I guess you could say it helped me to deal with my own kids better. The trainings helped me know how to prepare my own kids for school, and they all did pretty well. I just wanted to work here. It was a good environment to be in, both as a mother, and as a teacher. It changed my life in many ways, I guess. I learned a lot, and I got a lot of support as a single mother, which was great. (Miss Anita, teacher, Cedar Heights Center)

> Well, I did it, I guess because of being able to work with the young children. I just love that part of it. And the young underprivileged children. I had been a volunteer in the classroom. And one of the staff persons said you really should come on staff, 'cause you do a good job with the children. So, I thought about it, and then I put in an application, and was hired. (Miss Winnie, teacher, Harbor Street Center)

Current parents who had been invited to participate and volunteer also reported wanting to be a part of helping others. Gwen, who had been one of the few volunteers allowed in Rhonda's class, had felt good about being relied upon and a part of the program, so she wanted to become a part of it. While there was no guarantee that she would get the job, she had Rhonda's support and felt pretty good about the possibility.

> I put in an application with Head Start for teacher aide. I'd really like to stay in this part of it. I enjoy the kids. I go to the store now, and I'll see a kid and they'll say, Miss Gwen, Miss Gwen! I enjoy it. (Gwen, parent, Harbor Street Center)

Raymond, as it turned out, also was benefiting economically from his volunteer work with Policy Council. Raymond explained that now that he was nearly recuperated and was ending his Head Start years, he was going to be taking a job with a nonprofit organization. He felt that his experience with Head Start contributed to his marketability in this regard. Clearly, however, his past background and his social strata (and probably his gender) allowed him access to jobs that few other Head Start parents could ever imagine having access to. Still, it was a great feeling of accomplishment for Raymond.

> I've taken these two years of volunteer work that I've got and now I'm getting into management. So, that's a particular jump from one level to another level. So the contribution is still there, you know what I'm saying? And it's still worthwhile. So it's just taking it from one level to another level. I'm proud of that. (Raymond, parent, Morrow Street Center)

In the same way that Raymond recognized that his contribution to the program benefited his next career move, so other parents realized that volunteering (in appropriate ways) was the key to jobs at Head Start. And, while it may appear to be contradictory to say that those who were hired were those who were particularly seen as valuable (i.e., Winnie and Gwen) as well as some troublemakers (i.e., Harriet and Francine), nevertheless, once employed, keeping the job was a strong disincentive to raise problems, even when they did exist. Charlotte, a teacher at the Downtown Center, had related what happened to her when she spoke out regarding problems at the center: "I was told, though, that I had better stop complaining, and that if I didn't, I might be let go, regardless of how good I was with the kids."

Besides the promise of jobs, other economic factors kept parents from rocking the boat. Fran had commented that some parents were too intimidated to complain about problems in the program, believing that they might have their children kicked out, and then they would have no day care at all.[9] For others, the economic assistance that they did receive, although minor, such as food, or toys, and the calls that the family service workers made for them that yielded assistance with furniture, food stamps, and other benefits, also played a role in the suppression of complaints. Parents, even those with complaints, tried to keep good relations so that they would have access to the help when needed. For example, Judy had been a very active parent in previous years, but had lowered her level of participation after several problems with Harriet regarding parent activities. It was easier to do that than to complain and cause problems. Especially because, as she explained, Harriet had helped her, and Judy knew that she would do so if asked in the future.

> Without Harriet and her contacts, I was gonna have my utilities cut off last year. I just could not pay them. I could not pay them. And it was to the point where they wouldn't accept ten dollars, they wanted it paid in full. I called Harriet, and she got in touch with some contact that paid all my utilities in full. And it was such a load off my mind.
>
> I was to the point where I needed food, even just to get me through the week. I was just down and out, so I called Harriet. Every place I called said you had to be referred by somebody, you can't just come in here. Well, it's like, what if your child isn't involved in some sort of organization. What do those people do?
>
> I feel that I could call Harriet even if my children weren't still in Head Start. Yeah, I still feel I could call, and she would say, "Hey Judy!" So, I still feel that she would help out if, you know, anything came up. (Judy, parent, Downtown Center)

Other parents (and former parents) like Judy who had received much help from the family service workers always talked positively about their experience in receiving assistance. In Winnie's case, a former parent and now teacher at the Harbor Street Center, "it gave me an opportunity to get out, and further my education. I would say that maybe I wouldn't have been able, might not have been able to do that, if Head Start hadn't been the force."

THE SEDUCTION OF MONEY: STRUCTURED WANT AND THE LURE OF "A GOOD CHRISTMAS"

The lure of money is a powerful force in promoting accommodation to the status quo. Because money was always lacking at the Morrison County Head Start,[10] it was common, as it is at most schools, for parent participation in the program to center around the raising of funds. At the Downtown Center, the family service staff almost exclusively channeled parents' energies into fund-raising efforts. At the Harbor Street Center, because they were denied their parent programming money, they relied on fund-raising efforts to provide them with a modicum of a budget that they could use for their activities and for their children. Debbie, the family service worker at Harbor Street, had spoken of this need in this way:

> Well, the fund-raiser is something that has always been a part of the whole thing, at least since I can remember. Besides, many of these parents are familiar with different clubs and things, and realize that you have to have money to do activities, and for the children's things.

In addition to meeting a need, the family service workers also saw fund-raisers as valuable activities that promoted leadership development (at least in ways that they prescribed). As Debbie, at Harbor Street, noted: "Some parents gain a lot of skills from those fund-raisers, like leadership, organizing, handling money, being assertive." While this may have been true as an outcome for a few parents, the real structural reason for the need for fund-raisers was related to the lack of money in the first place. Because of the low funding levels of the program, the money for needed enrichment activities such as field trips, or needed materials or equipment, just wasn't there.

As a result, at the Downtown Center, Harriet pursued fund-raising at the cost of excluding almost all other parent activities. While that was the item at the top of her agenda at the parent orientation night at the Downtown Center, it typically was at every other meeting as well. Having been a parent at Consuelo's center, I asked Consuelo about this. She recalled how fund-raising helped Harriet develop leadership experience, but as she spoke, she wrinkled her nose in disapproval.

> Head Start does not want parents to put so much emphasis on this. I don't agree with Harriet's approach, but fund-raising is her thing. Harriet was a parent here years ago, and when she began, she started our first fund-raiser. Then, when she was hired as a family service worker, she put a lot of effort into this, so that the program could get things for the children.
>
> In the old days, when there was more money to get supplies and to take children on field trips, we didn't need to do much fund-raising. Back then, people were more willing to donate things to Head Start as well. Now, it is harder, and Harriet has gotten into this routine of doing this. We only do two small fund-raisers a year, one for Christmas and

> one in the spring, but they do it year round. (Consuelo, family service worker, Porterstown)

To Harriet, and most other family service workers, it was not a matter of choice whether it should be done or not. It was simply a fact of life at the centers — with little money available, funds had to be raised from somewhere if they were to pursue activities and acquire materials supplemental to those budgeted in the program.[11] In fact, in their view, by giving parents a chance to choose the type of fund-raiser, they believed that this fulfilled Head Start's programmatic mandate that parents choose their own activities.

Harriet was very good at getting some of the parents at her center to buy into the idea that fund-raising was a valuable, empowering experience. Some were very emphatic about it, as epitomized in the threatening comment made by one of the former parent representatives on orientation night; she said, "You must sell something, or your children won't get Christmas presents!"

Because of Marilyn's work, the Downtown Center was enormously successful in their efforts at ensuring "a good Christmas" this year. They sold $7,000 worth of cheap trinkets, expensive chocolates, and Christmas cards and wrapping paper for the Christmas fund-raiser, but Harriet still pushed them to do more. The result was that very little else took place. Marilyn alone sold over $1,000 in merchandise, and I asked her why she made such an effort.

> Because this is a government-funded program. And financially, the government won't fund everything, so you have to have fund-raisers or sponsors or something — otherwise where you gonna get these X amount of dollars to come in?

But, just because parents put a lot of work into it didn't mean that it would pay off. In other years, for example, the Downtown Center had not been as successful. Judy had this story to tell:

> Last year, because the year before was so bad as far as the fund-raisers we had, my first two weeks of school, I was calling up every parent in the school to send in fifty cents per child. If they had two kids in the program, they had to send in a dollar. 'Cause we were in the hole $600 dollars from the candy sale. People had taken the candy home and ate it, but didn't send any money back. They just stole it. That's a lot of

> money. So, over the whole year last year, even with all the fund-raisers we had, that money was taken away from what we made. We had to pay it back. That's a lot of money. We had to have fund-raisers just to pay back bills. (Judy, parent, Downtown Center)

Bobbie had similar problems with fund-raisers at Harbor Street. They were a lot of work, and drained energy from other types of possible activities. Many on staff complained about this emphasis on fund-raising. Comments included critiques regarding "too many fund-raisers, and the ones they have are not always appropriate" (Elizabeth, special needs coordinator); "they take up class time to do these things, like collecting money" (Candice, education specialist); and "I wish that we could find ways to get parents out. Different activities and things, you know? They say that they give them a choice of things to do at the beginning of the year, but they don't really. They talk about fund-raisers. They need different things to attract them" (Miss Anita, teacher, Cedar Heights Center). Each of these points was echoed by Valerie, the Head Start director, who nonetheless did little to stop this emphasis on fund-raising.

Instead, the family service workers just kept on, continually pressing the need for fund-raisers. The desire for money was so strong, and family service workers emphasized it so continually, that they and the parents sometimes got into the position of organizing activities that had the potential to be harmful.

An example of this was a trip to a casino. The casinos did promotions in hopes of getting customers, with the idea being that the casino would give every passenger on the bus ten dollars with which to gamble, in the hope that each person would spend that amount, and lose even more. When Francine had brought up this idea, none of the parents questioned whether it was good to encourage low-income people, who have little discretionary money, to gamble. They voted to organize it, without any discussion among them, nor input from Harriet. I asked her about the trip, and her thoughts about it.

> I had a hard time with it at first. But I just didn't want to get in the way of that whole thing, 'cause Francine really wanted it and thought it would be a good idea.[12] Valerie didn't want us to do it, and told me to put a stop to it, but I really fought for them to do it. Sometimes that is just what you gotta do. You gotta let 'em grow. Some of their ideas are kind of kooky, and I may not agree with them, but I think you have to

> be supportive of what they want, and help them see it through. (Harriet, family service worker, Downtown Center)

Harriet's position caused a great deal of anger and disgust from Valerie and others on staff who vehemently opposed it.

> The family service workers here let the parents do whatever they want instead of guiding them. They have no facilitation skills, and no rhyme or reason for their actions. The point is that they let parents make inappropriate decisions for the program, and the public relations result is terrible. Besides the PR [public relations] problem, Harriet should have guided them into doing something different, explaining to them her concerns. Instead, she just sits back and says, "well, that is what they want." (Candice, education specialist)

Despite objections, thirty parents took the trip. They made no money on the fund-raiser, in fact, they barely broke even. Harriet told me what the day had been like; luckily everything turned out okay, and no one had "lost their shirt" gambling.

> I was concerned about who would go, and whether or not people would spend their entire checks on gambling once they got there. I kept a careful lookout on them. It turns out that the people who went were family members, or people who were working. I tried to make sure that nobody went overboard, but they really were a responsible bunch. A lot of people took the opportunity just to get out of town. It rained that day, but a lot of us just walked up and down the area, or went into the mall. I was also afraid that they would run out of money and have to sit there all day, without even something to eat. As far as I could see, that didn't happen. (Harriet, family service worker, Downtown Center)

Parents themselves had complaints to make about the emphasis on fund-raising. Some parents, like Nora, felt that fund-raising was too difficult given the race relations in the neighborhoods in which they lived.[13] Pressured into participating, however, she bought things she could ill afford.

> I hate the fund-raisers. I don't like selling to people, so I just end up buying the stuff myself, like making a donation. The first time I went to sell something, my neighbor told me that once before he had ordered something from a Black person, and they never delivered it. He bugged

> me every day, so I decided I wasn't going to do that again. (Nora, parent, Porterstown Center)

Others simply refused to participate, since they knew that they, or their friends and family, could not afford to buy things they did not need. I had thought about the ethics of this as well. While this dilemma was sharply cast in the gambling case, I wondered about the ramifications of asking low-income folks to spend precious money on expensive candy and cheap trinkets. Parents had opposing views on this. Some, like Bobbie, reported that she sold only to people whom they thought could afford it: "By and large parents sell only to people that they know have the money. My ex-mother-in-law is not poor, by any means. You pick out people like this to sell to." Many, however, pressed their friends and families to participate anyway, and were sometimes disappointed by how the money was spent.

> I am so mad about this whole thing. We've had three fund-raisers this year, and for what? My family bought and bought stuff, when they couldn't afford it, just so my son could have a good trip. . . . And now, no trip. (Theresa, parent, Harbor Street Center)

After being burned several times, however, parents such as Judy, Josephine, and Lynn, limited their activity with the program. They quit participating as a form of protest over the incident noted in Chapter 5, when Harriet had lost the car-wash money.

> But, it's really depressing, and since then I think I'll just say forget it, 'cause it's like, you guys don't give a shit. That money was, I mean, we worked about six hours on a car wash. But nobody holds anybody responsible for anything, and I just, I don't like it. It's not fair. That just tore me apart, and the bite is that nobody is held responsible for this money. And it's not the first time, you know. We have money disappear constantly. And there should be a better system, there's gotta be a better system.
>
> And the other sad part about this thing is that when I gave Harriet the money, not to sound petty, but when I gave it to her, she gave me no recognition for it. This was at the parent group, and she didn't say, "Well, Judy went out and held a car wash to raise money, and this is what she raised, seventy-five dollars." I feel I should have gotten some recognition for it. Okay, so right now, I'm not really involved this year,

> so far. I see other parents getting involved this year, and I think, well, hey, maybe this is my year, you know, I'll just sit back. (Judy, parent, Downtown Center)

Lynn was the parent who had organized the car wash with Judy. After that incident, and the problem with the bus driver that was discussed in Chapter 3, Lynn was no longer willing to be active at all. In support of her, Josephine (her mother, and grandmother to Lynn's children) had also opted to quit. In previous years she had been involved in almost everything, but by the end of the year she had only come in once, to help with Christmas.

> My daughter [Lynn] and Judy spent a whole Saturday on a car wash, making a car wash, just them two. Then the money was stolen. That's another reason why my daughter will not sell anything anymore. Now, okay, things happen. Money does get stolen. But why was that money left in a place that it could be stolen? So, this year we have done nothing in the way with fund-raisers. My daughter just does not have the heart anymore, after what has happened with that, and the bus. She just does not have the heart. She feels she was not helped and she just, well, she feels that she had no one backing her up at all. I have to abide by her feelings. (Josephine, grandparent/guardian, Downtown Center)

In addition to their complaints about the careless tracking of money, I too had noticed during the year that there was no accounting system in place that allowed parents to know exactly how much money was being raised and how much was being spent. Nina had been elected treasurer, yet never fulfilled that duty, and a treasurer's report was never given during any of the parent meetings. So, not only did some parents feel that they were being used, there was never any measure of their success. Edna, now a grandparent with the program who had also had a child enrolled years ago, summed up this situation when she said:

> I know they do their best, but the parent group isn't as informed as they could be, or should be. They don't know that they can benefit the program, or benefit from it for that matter. In the beginning, parents were participants as well, now they're not. They just want to use us to raise funds. (Edna, parent, Downtown Center)

Clearly, inadequate programming budgets for materials and activities lead to the need for money. This lure of money then kept staff and parents from pursuing other activities, and/or possibly getting organized about other problems in the program. Furthermore, if a parent did not want to participate in the primary activity that Head Start centers engaged in — either out of financial constraints, distress over past problems, or other social reasons — then this, in addition to other factors laid out in this research, further limited a parent's potential to belong. This desire for a feeling of belonging was a strong incentive to accommodating the structure of the program. In fact, it was the key reason Consuelo felt Harriet put such an emphasis on fund-raising, so that she could feel like a contributing member of the Head Start family.

> Downtown, perhaps the emphasis is on donations because then Harriet feels that she is doing something. She is good at it, and maybe she feels more comfortable with that. It might also have to do with the fact that Harriet is not from the community. Since she is not from there, she has to compensate for that lack of community by giving people things. (Consuelo, family service worker, Porterstown)

BELONGING: CREATING COMMUNITY OR LESSENING DISSENT?

In the literature and in practice, Project Head Start has been referred to as "a big family,"[14] one that takes care of its own through the provision of needed services to parents and families by former parents. Yet, this idea of family goes beyond that to include the idea of the development of connection, the feeling of belonging, and the knowledge that others will be there for you when you need them. As Judy had noted above, she knew Harriet would be there for her if she needed help in the future. The potential for creating this sense of belonging has been noted as an important feature in the program, for as Parker, Piotrkowski, and Peay (1987) and Leik, Chaukley and Peterson (1991) have found, regular, meaningful involvement in Head Start can, because of this connection, decrease instances of depression among mothers.

This phenomenon appeared to be true in this case as well, for if invited in as part of the team, then parents could derive great benefits. For some parents Head Start was a place where they could feel at home. In fact, many *did* express the concept that being a part of Head Start was like becoming a part of a family. Former staff members and parents who had not been active with the program for several years often came back to visit. They had learned that it was a place to seek help if needed.

It was this sense of family that kept many staff members affiliated with it. And, in reality, many people did have extended families and friends who worked in Head Start. These relationships often played a significant role in helping to get them into the program. One example of this involved a new employee who had been a parent about ten years ago. She said that a friend still in the program had told her about the position, and administration had let her interview before anyone else, since she was an "insider."

Knowing someone also helped to get your child into the program. One night at a meeting, I met two women who did not have children in the program yet, but who were hoping to get them in. One said that a parent had suggested they come and "work on Harriet." This tactic had worked for Kimberly, who told me that Francine had helped influence Harriet for her. Others also indicated that it helped to know someone in order to get your child accepted into the program, particularly since there was such a long waiting list.

> My daughter's got a cousin here, one of the bus drivers, named Tammy. And her cousin told me about Head Start, and that she could start when she is three years old. So I told her "Well, get me an application." So she got me an application and I filled it out and they put me in the program. (Verdine, parent, Downtown Center)

Working together as a team was also vital at Head Start, for many hands were needed to run the fund-raisers, set up meetings, wrap Christmas gifts, or organize the commodity program. If allowed and encouraged, parents rolled up their sleeves and did what was needed. Many, like Kimberly, were thrilled when they got the chance.

> Miss Jinny's been sick, so I been coming in to help out Ms. Billie, 'cause she had a lot of kids, and it just seemed like she needed help. I think it's good when parents and teachers have a good line of communication so they can help one another. 'Cause they help me when they teach my child how to do certain things, or give me suggestions that I might never have thought of, and you might say, "That's a good suggestion." It gives you a chance. Well, everybody's working together to make Head Start more productive. If I help them they help me, and it's like a balance between the two. (Kimberly, parent, Downtown Center)

The reason Kimberly had been so excited to get the chance to volunteer was due to the fact that, as noted in Chapter 4, Miss Billie almost exclusively called on Pamela to help. So, Miss Billie called Kimberly only when she couldn't get Pamela. Kimberly was lucky, for other parents who wanted to have the chance to volunteer also waited to be called, sometimes in vain. In fact, it sometimes took a great deal of interpersonal resources, such as assertiveness, persistence, and thick skin to get past the barrier of not being invited as part of the team, and to try to become someone who belonged.

As Theresa indicated, she didn't have the energy to resist Rhonda's rejection of her that was the result of her complaints about the way her son was being treated. In previous years she had been one of Head Start's most loyal and heavily used volunteers; yet this year, she had continually been deterred from helping in the classroom. By the end of the year, after being beaten down by the teachers and the administration, she was glad to be rid of the program.

> I would have liked to have volunteered more. I wanted to do a lot this year, helping in the classroom. But, I just couldn't, they didn't want you around, you could tell. I wish that we could have ended on better terms. But sometimes, I guess you just have to let things lie. (Theresa, parent, Harbor Street Center)

April, on the other hand, did have success, and shared her story in this regard. April had to struggle with her child's teacher on multiple levels. At the beginning of the year, she had experienced a problem with Miss Sylvia, who had temporarily "lost" the child one day in a mix-up with the bus. The situation placed the child in danger, and created bad feelings between teacher and parent, and April felt that because of it, Miss Sylvia did not want her to become active in her classroom. April was not going to let Miss Sylvia's attitude keep her from participating, however. She shared with me how she eventually made a role for herself in her child's classroom, even though Miss Sylvia did not want her there.

> Yeah, that incident made me very mad at Miss Sylvia, very mad. It made me have sort of a grudge against her for the remainder of the year. But she apologized. I guess 'cause they [administration] called her. For a long time, she wouldn't talk to me. You'd think that as a teacher she would communicate with me. But she wouldn't. Before, she was not open. She was not, like, talking to me as a teacher to a parent, you know?

> But I pushed it a little, till when she saw I was getting sick of it, you know? Even when she didn't ask me, I'd come in. I would just pop in to both observe and help. And I been trying to make every effort to be here for parent conferences for meetings, to be here, you know, for whatever I could be here for.
>
> Now she is talking to me. Just recently, like about a month ago, she's been a little nicer to me. She's more open now. Now, she's asking me to come in, and she's asking me, like, how Jessimine does at home as far as reading, and her different colors? And she's asking me, can I come for trips? You know, little things. She asked me, any time I want to come in, to come in. (April, parent, Downtown Center)

The parents who were welcomed as volunteers in the classroom were subsequently often relied upon heavily. Sometimes when this type of teamwork was established, the staff began to overuse parents, who often then felt that they were being taken advantage of. Harriet said this occurred when she was a parent in the program. Gwen and Francine had experienced this feeling. Bobbie felt this too, although the sense of teamwork that she and Joyce had was not amicable in the least. Bobbie frequently complained about Joyce's reliance on her.

> They have a tendency to forget that I'm not staff. Joyce kept telling me that she needed me, that she didn't know anything about the area, and she needed me to set up her Rolodex. I'm for sure not gonna do her job, they don't pay me. It's like she doesn't know what she is supposed to do. All she keeps saying is "I need you, I need you, I need you." Well, I'm not doing her job and not getting paid for it. One time I was joking with Rhonda and Joyce, and I said that technically, in one way, Joyce is my boss. She said, no, we're one and one. Well, if we're one and one then sweetheart, I get your paycheck. You know what I mean? (Bobbie, parent, Harbor Street Center)

This situation led Bobbie to become selective about which activities she was willing to do at the center. Between her ill health and the demands of being parent chair, she could only juggle so much. But Joyce demanded more and more time from her. One day, when Joyce ordered Bobbie to volunteer in the classroom, she decided that she could take no more.

> I told her no, that I couldn't, 'cause for one thing I wasn't feeling well, and for another, other parents should have the chance to help. She just

> kept saying to me that she wants me there, no one else. I don't know why. Anyway, I want you there, she says. I had to hang up on her. It probably wasn't right, but I didn't have the patience to listen to her anymore. I wasn't feeling well, and she was not listening. She has a real attitude. That morning I walked out and told Rhonda that I would not be in the classroom that afternoon, and to tell everybody. (Bobbie, parent, Harbor Street Center)

Thus, there were contradictions connected with belonging to the Head Start family. While it made people feel good to feel needed, developing this tight-knit team meant excluding many, and those who were included frequently felt used. Other forces oppressed parents as well, for in becoming a part of the team, the penalty for dissenting became more weighty. For to complain meant to risk the possibility of being rejected, which implied the risk of social, emotional, and economic loss.

CONCLUSION: LEARNING WHEN TO QUIT

Thus, it is evident that parents sometimes walked a fine line between accommodating a Head Start system (a system that is part of a broader structure of schooling and parent involvement) that, while unequal, did have its benefits, and resisting it for the sake of themselves and their children. In resisting, some parents actively worked against the issues that they felt were problematic; others chose actions indicative of more passive resistance, such as not participating when the staff sought their help. Giroux refers to this type of behavior as resistance that is "linked to moral and political indignation" and that contains "an expressed hope for transcendence and transformation" (Giroux, 1983, pp. 107–108). Therefore, these parents' acts of resistance were related to an inherently political perspective that involved the desire for both justice and freedom. Thus, regardless of the venue and the scope, to resist domination is to attempt to make a space wherein freedom, however fleeting, is exercised.

Yet it is also apparent how much easier it is to simply give in to a system, to accommodate injustice and inequality, when parents — as individuals, or even as groups — who have little support and real advocacy, are further weighed down by myriad problems such as ill health, lack of transportation, lack of child care, and financial constraints — situations that are all too typical for Head Start parents. Understanding this, the words of Bolman and Deal (1991) are even more salient: "leaders have the capacity to either provide meaning or hope. . . . or convince the powerless to accept and support social structures and decision-making processes that are not in their best interest" (p. 197).

The importance of these messages, and these relationships between staff and parents, are nowhere more apparent than in the battle over the plans for the last day of school. In the final chapter, we will see how staff and parent interactions in the final weeks at Head Start influenced the outcomes for each of the parent groups at the Downtown and Harbor Street centers.

NOTES

[1] Giroux (1983) provides an in-depth critique of Bourdieu's, Bowles & Gintis's, and Bernstein's theories of schools, culture, and schooling, which are depicted as being uncontested, oppressive agents of reproduction of the dominant culture.

[2] These six areas include: nonviolent protest; social noncooperation; economic boycotts; economic strikes; political noncooperation; and nonviolent intervention.

[3] All of Sharp's strategies or actions have as their locus the public/collective group as a frame for activity, including the Lysistratic strategy of a collective of women withholding sexual activity from their men. Thus, in this sense, this private activity is made public through its organized focus.

[4] See West and Blumberg for a fascinating analysis of how scholarship on social protest has changed theoretically over the years. They specifically address the lack of research on women in this area.

[5] The lack of usage of the Family and Medical Leave benefit by men is also an indication that expectations about men's gender roles are also not permeable in relation to this public/private domain of activity.

[6] For example, in the late nineteenth century, the formation of women's social clubs (Hugo, in press) reflected women's resistance of the narrow domestic roles women played, and during the second wave of feminist activity beginning in the 1970s, increasing numbers of women privately resisted household divisions of labor and paternalistic relations by initiating household work stoppages, enrolling in college, divorcing, and not taking their husband's name upon marriage, among other things. Historical analysis has also revealed African-American slaves' strategies of resistance. Acts of resistance ranged from running away, resting surreptitiously in the fields, breaking tools to limit work, stealing food or other items, and use of special sounds or codes to communicate (Escott, 1979; Berlin, 1998) to sophisticated entrepreneurial businesses, plans, and activities that earned dollars that would allow for the buying (and freeing) of friends and

relatives (Smith, in press). Paul Willis's work *Learning to Labor* (1981) details acts of resistance by the "lads," working-class students who work against their own economic and emancipatory interest by rejecting school. Angela McRobbie's research (1978; in Apple, 1995) on working-class girls finds similar contradictions, but through analysis of the intersection of class and gender.

[7] Interestingly, this is an example of the staff's resistance as being manifested in the exploitation of the self and one's own limited resources.

[8] A few of the staff who had formerly been parents in the program indicated that their desire for a job with Head Start had been due to convenience, but the majority reported a deep sense of mission regarding the helping of families.

[9] Despite their fears of children being removed from the program as a result of a parent's advocacy, I saw no evidence of this happening.

[10] See Chapter 1, which details funding and resource problems nationally, resource problems that, in fact, affect not only Head Start but many public schools as well.

[11] In effect, such fund-raising can be viewed as a regressive tax on parents and low-income communities, since they are asked or coerced into footing the bill for a federal programming initiative.

[12] Note that Harriet had initially attempted to thwart parents' efforts regarding the graduation, although they argued that it was a "good idea." Since this situation was a fund-raiser, Harriet readily supported it.

[13] Racial divisions between whites, African Americans, and Latinos in some areas of the county were notably tense. In some areas, gang violence (gangs made up of white supremacists as well as Blacks and others were in evidence) and individual, racially motivated assaults had been occurring.

[14] This term was used in the report of the National Head Start Association's Silver Ribbon Panel, 1989.

CHAPTER 8

Metaphors of Separation and Community

Implications of Micropolitics in Programs

As the year wound to a close, it was apparent that there were vast differences in outcomes between those parents — both groups and individuals — who had the material and symbolic support of the staff in the Head Start program, and those who did not have such resources available to them. Relatedly, the staff themselves had little or no support from the program and each other regarding material, informational, cultural, and collaborative resources for parent programming. In fact, with no clear mission about parent involvement with inadequate staffing levels, equipment, budgets, and facilities; and with the staff's low comfort levels and lack of knowledge regarding working with parents in combination with the various gatekeeping functions in the program that prevented parent participation, the actual numbers of parents and adult family members who volunteered was indeed low. Clearly, staff understanding and support was vital if parent participation and involvement were to be minimally successful, much less liberatory, or transforming experiences for those adults in the program.

These conditions influenced another important reality at the program: divisive relations among parents. When only some parents — and not others — were called upon, invited in, or otherwise accepted as having something to contribute to the program, not only were some parents angered, confused, or saddened that they were not the ones to be sought, but it also fostered the resentment of the active parents toward those who did not participate. And, as was addressed earlier in this text, with such low levels of participation among parents, parents who were openly welcomed as volunteers were often overused, which left them tired, angry, and wondering why more were not involved. Lacking a systematic assessment of the programmatic problems that either promoted or impeded participation, there was little consciousness about the structural factors that prevented their involvement, and the result was a blame-the-victim mentality. For example, many at the Downtown Center felt that low levels of parent participation and involvement simply had to do with other parents' lack of interest and concern for their children.

> Either they ain't too interested in their kid, you know, or they don't care about it. They care about their kids, you know what I mean, but they don't really care about doing things for the kids, like findin' out about them and what they doin'. (Jasmine, parent, Downtown Center)

> Basically I think it's a lack of concern on the parents' part because of the type of people they are, and whatever. But I don't know if that's true. It may not be. You can't plead busy as a factor, because I'm really busy. I belong to two organizations, and I work eight hours a day, and I try to get to the meetings. (Garnet, parent, Downtown Center.)

> Some parents, some are too busy, some of them lazy. Some of them sit at home, lying down on the couch, in front of the television. They could be here. I mean, for some of them, they could be here, and the experience could probably help them get a job, too. I'm mad about that sometimes, because, sometimes, I want to stay home with my child. But instead of sitting in front of the television, it would give them some type of initiative and some kind of experience that they could help the child at home, their children. (Maggie, parent, Downtown Center)

> It always boils down to just a few parents doing everything, and it really is a lot of pressure, and isn't fair. I practically lived there sometimes, because I have done so much in the past five years. Unfortunately, when a parent gets involved, they get really involved. Other parents like to say they're involved, but you don't even know who they are, you never see them. (Judy, parent, Harbor Street Center)

At Harbor Street the low levels of parent activity and complaints against others were much the same. As Pilar stated:

> There are seventeen kids in my daughter's class, and over sixty in the program, and only a handful of parents show up. And that's a shame.

> Because, then they wonder, well, why don't they do this, and why don't they do that. If you don't show up, you can't help, you can't contribute. (Pilar, parent, Harbor Street Center)

Pilar, Gwen, Christine, Bobbie, and a few others were typically the only parents in attendance at the Harbor Street meetings. The feelings of isolation and the huge sense of responsibility of those who were greatly involved resulted in, as Judy had put it, a lot of pressure. Those feelings, combined with all of the painful incidents that occurred over the course of the year with a staff member who was in opposition to her had taken a toll on Bobbie, Harbor Street's parent committee chairperson. Now, as the days passed and the year neared the end, after trying and subsequently failing to organize a graduation for the children, Bobbie was spending a good deal of time reflecting on whether any of it had been worth it. She sensed that her ability to fight was waning, and she also began to question whether or not she would sign her son up for the program next year. If she did, she knew that she would once again want to be an advocate for children in a program that did not always work, and she was not sure if she had the energy to take it on. She mulled this over with me.

> I've got the whole summer to think about it. I don't know if I can do it anymore, that's why I might have to leave. 'Cause I tried my best this year to have them see the light, and they just don't see the light. And of course, a lot of parents don't even want to speak up because they see what has happened to other children or other parents. (Bobbie, parent, Harbor Street Center)

While the wind had been knocked out of the parents' sails at Harbor Street, Downtown was a bluster of activity. Here, too, however, social relations were problematic, for despite the apparent success of a small core of parents in organizing a graduation for their children, the tactical moves that were required in order to get around the administration's efforts at preventing this effort meant that tensions between some of the staff and the parent organizers remained. While the parents had gained personal support from some staff members, most staff were left angry and upset by the entire process. Indeed, outward appearances seemed calm at the two end-of-the-year events scheduled to take place Downtown. Parent-staff relations were strained, however, and tensions among parents were also in evidence during the Downtown Head Start Center's final days.

DOWNTOWN'S CARNIVAL DAY

The Carnival Day was the first end-of-the-year event held at the Downtown Center. Held a couple of days prior to the graduation, it took place on a brilliant summer day, and the parking lot at the center was crowded with parents, children, and all the trappings of a carnival midway. There was a petting zoo, pony rides, a moon walk, and a "tilt-a-whirl" ride. Booths for popcorn, soda, hot dogs, and cotton candy were set up along the perimeter of the lot, and each child got "free" treats.[1] Harriet looked very happy. Francine just looked tired. I caught her in a slow moment as she sold raffle tickets for yet another fund-raiser, and asked her how the day was going. She had been there since dawn.

> Oh, we had to get ice, soda, clear the parking lot. We got the trucks set up to where we wanted them, sold the raffles, set up the zoo, made sure that parents picked up the parking lot; they are the clean-up committee. I don't know, I've done so much today, I can't think. (Francine, parent, Downtown Center)

After lunch, a clown entertained the children and their parents in the center's basement cafeteria. Few could hear or see him, however, for too many people had crowded into the room and the noise level was awful. The magic tricks were bad too, although Kookoo was the clown whom Joyce had described as being the one that "Head Start always uses." The parents began to get angry about the poor quality of the show, and they started yelling at the clown to speak up.

The entire show lasted only fifteen minutes. This was just as well, however, for the word among the staff was that there were too many people in the cafeteria, and they were now in violation of the fire code. Since they had not been allowed to use the "big room" upstairs, this had been their only choice, and no one had considered the problem of cramming this many people into a space this size. Angry, Valerie came looking for Harriet and Francine once she found out about this. I caught sight of her from across the room as she came downstairs, and while I tried to get her attention so I could talk with her, she brushed me away.

In the meantime, the children lined up to get a balloon from the clown and Harriet and Fran began circulating the room encouraging everyone to clear the room and go outside. Seemingly frustrated by the wait and the crowd, one of the moms started to pick a fight with Francine, arguing that she did not want to have to wait in line for the balloon, but wanted it now so she could leave. Francine told her she would have to wait like the rest, and the woman tried to punch her. Then it was Harriet's turn to get mad, and after showing the woman the door, she said to me: "The last thing Francine needs after working so hard on all this is some big mouth complaining. Did you see? She tried to hit her! I told her to take it outside, not in front of the kids!"

"GRADUATION DAY"

Two days later it was graduation day. Finding a parking place was tough on that very last day of school at the Downtown Center. So many people had come to see the children "graduate" from Head Start that the parking lot and the surrounding street spaces were filled. This huge turnout was vastly different from the typically ill-attended activities for parents and families. Furthermore, as I arrived in the building, I noted that instead of the dreary darkness or haphazardly arranged dirty tables, the auditorium was now clean, bright, filled with neat rows of chairs, and bedecked with red and white balloons and streamers. During the planning process, the parents had opted to use part of their fund-raising money to allow them to rent this "big room," and now the lights were on and almost two hundred people were settling into their seats.

It was easy to spot the parent organizers of the event, for Francine, Marilyn, Pamela, Garnet, Carmen, Nina, and Maggie were all wearing red dresses and corsages of red and white carnations. Their outfits perfectly matched the red and white decorations in the auditorium. Interestingly, in a gesture of seeming solidarity, some of the staff had also dressed in red.

These women bustled about, checking the sound system and getting the three-year-olds who would continue on in the program next year seated in their chairs. Finally, they were ready, but just as the "graduates" began to file in with Marilyn in the lead, a crush of people blocked the children's path to take photos. Flashbulbs went off and video cameras whirred as the children streamed into the room wearing their bright red caps and gowns. Marilyn had to stop everything and yell and scream her way through to make a walkway for them.

As a result, the ceremony began about fifteen minutes late. The ceremony ran long, and instead of the maximum of forty minutes that Valerie had ordered, it took about an hour. With the time that it took for the children to walk in and out, the entire program was longer still. Despite these minor glitches, it was very well done. Several community leaders spoke about Head Start, the children sang the songs they had practiced so well, and a costumed "Big Bird" handed each child moving on to kindergarten a certificate as they walked across the stage.

During one point in the ceremony, as Marilyn led the children in their singing, I overheard two women make a comment about how well trained the children were. One of them asked who that "dynamic" woman was who was leading the children. The other woman told her that was Marilyn, and "she is a parent too!"

The ceremony ended with Harriet giving flowers to the outstanding volunteer parents for the year, who not so coincidentally, were the parents dressed in red. Then, after Marilyn managed to get the parents out of the aisles again, the children filed out of the auditorium and went up to their classrooms to share lunch and a celebration cake.

Afterwards the parents were excited and proud as they buzzed about, congratulating themselves. A shadow fell over them, however, when they learned from Harriet how angry Valerie was that the program had gone too long. Yet Francine, who looked wonderfully cheery and optimistic in her new red dress, hoped that this day would start a tradition: "This closing exercise, hopefully it will be for years to come. After this, every parent group will want to do it for their children."

THE HARBOR STREET PARTY

Harbor Street's parties had taken place the day prior to the Downtown Center's graduation ceremony. The parents had not had any success in changing the plans from two separate events into one, so the morning classes had their party first. When I got to the center that morning, Kookoo the clown was just starting his routine. Twenty-five parents watched from the back of the lunch room. The children sat in a semicircle, at the front.

Bobbie waved as I came in, and I took a seat with her. She looked awful. Her hair was a mess and she had big dark circles under her eyes. She had not even bothered to put on clean clothes or a bra; she wore a pair of denim shorts and a dirty yellow halter top that exposed her midriff. She wearily filled me in on what was happening:

> They all went to the park earlier, before I got here. But I had a lot of the games with me, so they must not have done much there. Christine is still out shopping for toys for the kids. We ran out of money, and couldn't get everything we wanted for the kids. Plus, we wanted every-

> body to get the same thing, and we couldn't find enough of some things, like bubbles. (Bobbie, parent, Harbor Street Center)

Between puffs of her cigarette, she told me of her recent decision.

> You know though, I've made a decision that I'm gonna stay on next year and be Valerie's worst nightmare. I'm gonna ride her so hard she won't know, pardon my French, her ass from her elbow. (Bobbie, parent, Harbor Street Center)

After Kookoo concluded, Miss Rhonda led the children in some songs. Then she handed each child a T-shirt and a certificate. With that, the first party was over. As the families filed out, Bobbie gave each child a bag of toys. As she was leaving, Theresa caught my eye and signaled that I should step outside. We hugged each other and said goodbye, and she told me what leaving meant to her.

> I feel bad leaving. I guess I'm too nostalgic, but this was Nicholas's last year of preschool and I wanted it to be real good, for him and for me. It feels like something was taken from me, something I'll always miss.
>
> But now, however, I just thank God that my children are rid of Head Start. I will put something in the paper eventually. I should have done it months ago. An editorial or something, just so everyone can read it and see what it's all about. (Theresa, parent, Harbor Street Center)

As this first group of parents and children left the center, the next group began bringing trays of food and refreshments. Heather was one of the first parents to arrive, for she had volunteered to help set up for the afternoon party.

I had not seen her in about a month. It looked as if things were starting to turn around for her, for she looked great. In fact, she seemed confident, upbeat, and even feisty. She was a very different Heather than the one I had first met. After greeting me, she complained about all of the mix-ups and problems that the parents had been having in the last few weeks. She also told me that, like Bobbie, she too had made a decision to stick it out, and to stay in Head Start next year and fight.

> I'm gonna have Jordan in the program again next year, and I want to see some changes made. Bobbie and I and a bunch of parents are gonna

> get together this summer and get organized. We're gonna make sure that things change around here. One thing's for sure. We're gonna find out what our rights are: what parents can do, and what teachers can do. They tell us that this is our center, our center, but it isn't true. Not if we can't even have a say in what kind of party our kids have. So, we'll see, next year better be different, that's all I have to say. (Heather, parent, Harbor Street Center)

Christine came in next with her husband and two sons. She looked drained from running around all morning. Karen also arrived, and became angry when she saw that Christine and some of the other parents had brought their non-Head Start children. Karen explained that Joyce's flyer about the party had said "no siblings" would be allowed to come. She wished that she had also ignored Joyce's order, and brought her baby with her to the party.

Joyce finally arrived. Instead of interacting with the parents, however, she went into the kitchen, sat down, and watched the group from afar. Elizabeth, the special needs coordinator, also came in. She told me that she was there acting as the representative from the administration, for neither Valerie nor Desmond attended, despite the fact that it was typical for one of them to stop in to each Head Start center during the end-of-the-year activity.

The room eventually filled with about thirty adults and sixty children. Once the buffet table was set up, people started eating. As the group was eating, Helen, the cook, began running around the room shouting, "He's coming, he's coming!" "Who?" we all asked. "The governor," she whooped. She quickly explained that, since she had read in the morning paper that he would be in the area touring a factory, she had called his staff to ask if he could stop by their party. Now he was on his way.

Everyone talked excitedly of this prospect. Within five minutes the governor arrived with his staff. He stayed only about ten minutes, and gave a brief speech about the value of Head Start and the importance of teachers and parents working together. Before he left, he had his picture taken with several of the children and their parents. During this photo opportunity Bobbie turned to me to say: "So, should we tell him what it's really like here?"

SAYING GOOD-BYE: METAPHORS OF SEPARATION AND COMMUNITY

Rene Nunez (1993), writing about parent involvement in bicultural settings, has said: "It's politics to cover up politics so that it seems as if all people get the same opportunity" (p.135). At the Downtown Center the kind of "equal" opportunity for parents that the staff wanted to reinforce was limited, repressive, and proscribed. This was evidenced by the protectionist politics that quickly emerged after the graduation event, politics that separated staff and parents, even more clearly, into camps with different motivations, different interests, and different levels of power.

A few days following the graduation, I returned to the Downtown Center to say my good-byes and to say thank you to those who had been so generous with their time and input. The staff were busy cleaning up their offices and classrooms, readying to take off for the summer break. Several of the usual parent volunteers were also present, helping out as needed. As I made my rounds to various parts of the building, chatting with staff and parents alike, I found that the parents were totally enthusiastic about the graduation, seeing it as a great success. The staff felt just the opposite, however, and in fact, many said that a graduation should never again take place. They considered it a waste of time and money, and a big failure.

As I talked with Candice, the education specialist, and Elizabeth, the special needs coordinator, about this situation, the ironies of the social dynamics inherent in this setting were readily apparent. In their conversation with me several issues stood out, that while not directly addressed, nevertheless were embedded in what they expressed about the graduation. These included the pervasive finger-pointing and blame present in the program, the lack of a common focus, unequal relations of power, underlying conflict, and the fact that authentic discourse among them was missing. Furthermore, implicit within their comments was the belief in the need to maintain power over parents, to rein them in and not allow them to act except in carefully proscribed ways. The dialogue went as follows:

> It was awful, it went too long, they didn't consider the needs of the kids, they spent way too much money for the caps and gowns, it was a terrible idea. We all talked about it today at staff meeting and we don't ever want to see it again. We discussed why, if it was never allowed before, why now? Some centers had done it, that's true, but there hasn't been any consistent policy. (Candice)

> Desmond didn't manage that Policy Council right. They needed to be educated about the issue, and then the center reps should have gone back and educated the parents. (Elizabeth)

> Desmond seems to think that parents can do anything they want. Through this whole thing he has been overriding Valerie, and that's bad. (Candice)

> This cap and gown thing would have been taken care of if the Policy Council had dealt with it correctly and then reported back to the parents. (Elizabeth)

> The key thing here is educating them. They never understood the developmental needs of the children. (Candice)

> Head Start is supposed to be a start, for godsakes, not an ending! (Elizabeth)

As we talked, I told them that I had heard that the parents loved it. I also shared that in response to what had occurred this year, some of them wanted to organize themselves, and find out what their rights were in Head Start. Elizabeth responded by saying, "That's exactly what they need!" Candice followed with, "Just that point was made at staff meeting today. Everyone wants to know, clearly, what their responsibilities are."

Candice then got up to leave, and she and I said our good-byes. Elizabeth and I chatted a bit longer, however. We talked about the year and what had occurred with the staff and the parents, and their many struggles. Elizabeth again wanted to reiterate to me what she believed was the cause of so many of the problems in the program: the quality of the family service workers who were supposed to guide parents. As she saw it, when adequate expertise and guidance were missing, problems resulted. Relatedly, she also dwelled on the unfortunate happenings at Harbor Street, and how the parents had been given no support whatsoever. She recognized that without a family service worker to help them for several months, all of the problems had fallen on Bobbie, whom she both excused for her deficits and inadequacies, but also blamed for her advocacy.

> Bobbie was left in the dark without Debbie [the family service worker who left]. And because she didn't have anybody to help her, Bobbie took on a role that was not appropriate. She took on too much, without

> knowing the proper channels for complaining. (Elizabeth, special needs coordinator)

Elizabeth also realized that Joyce only compounded the tensions. She told me that she was amazed at the distant way in which Joyce had acted toward the parents at Harbor Street's party. "Did you see Joyce at Harbor Street last week? She cruised in and sat on her butt. She didn't lift a finger to help, much less talked to any of the parents who were there, to get to know them."

As Elizabeth shared this with me, I realized that her remark went beyond the specific problems between the parents and Joyce. I found her comment to be a fitting metaphor for the experience of many parents in the program who struggled with staff to be seen, heard, and truly welcomed into Head Start.

From there, I went down the hall to Valerie's office. Although it appeared that she was in no mood to see me, she was expecting me and offered me a seat. I had come with a brief report for her, one that she had asked for midway during the year. Since I had spent a good number of years as a volunteer coordinator, she had asked me to think about how they might better utilize volunteers, not only the parents in the program, but community members as well. I handed her my analysis and suggestions, and she flipped through it, threw it in the corner, and then lit a cigarette. I thought to myself, "Well, that was that."

"So," I asked her, "how do you feel the year went?" At the top of her mind was the graduation, of course, and she echoed the comments of Candice and Elizabeth, vowing that it would never happen again. She commented that she was tired of parents who just wanted to push through their agenda, no matter what. She also wished they would work on "more important matters." Then, with no apparent irony, she then went on. "One thing that I would like to see is political involvement. Community political involvement is definitely within the scope of parent involvement, but they never get involved in the problems of the community."

I then queried, "What would you say if I told you that I saw a lot of political organizing going on this year, not in the community, but here in the program, and that both as individuals and as a group, I've seen a lot of growth because of this cap and gown issue?"

"Hmmmmm . . . you really think so?" she replied. "Political, huh? Well, yes, I guess you could say that they have organized themselves, but it's wrongheaded . . . Hmmm . . . I'd have to think about that."

With that, she took another puff from her cigarette and picked up what looked like a memo from her in-basket. Recognizing that our meeting was over and I had just been dismissed, I thanked her and left the office to go downstairs to see Harriet.

Busy at work with Marlene in the cluttered family service office, Harriet acted gruff and matter-of-fact as she said good-bye. "You know, I've been thinking about this past year, and looking back. At first I thought it was gonna be trouble, having you here. All these questions, questions, questions."

"Why did you think it would be trouble to have me here?" I asked. She answered:

> It was a hassle, watching us, asking all those questions! But then, you got people to thinking. It really made us think about how parents get involved. And it reminded us what it used to be like, and what it should be. And not just us either, I mean the others too — the teachers, and upstairs [administration]. Well, you brought up a lot of stuff and made us think about it. I think you being here and asking questions made the parents think about it too! (Harriet, family service worker)

In this, Harriet confirmed what I, too, had discovered. By the posing of questions, they began to reflect in a way that they had not done before. Furthermore, I realized that the questioning was at times both powerful and connecting, for them as well as for me.

My final stop was to the basement classrooms. Charlotte was in her room alone, packing boxes. We talked about the year, and her hopes for the program. While Charlotte wished me well, she also wished I could stay. She asked me to make sure that the story of my year with Head Start was told.

> This used to be such a good program, Peggy, but you've seen some of the problems. I wish you could stay a little bit longer, another year, with us, so that you could see all the problems. We need an outside voice like you. Maybe what you write will make a difference. (Miss Charlotte, teacher, Downtown Center)

As I was leaving the building, I ran into Pamela. In a hurry to pick up her daughter, she told me to be sure to call her the next day so that we could talk some more. With a quick hug, I assured her that I would do that. Yet, when I telephoned her the following day, I did not get the chance to say my good-byes. Instead of hearing Pamela's cheerful voice, the recorded message told me that the number had been disconnected, a situation that many families in the program experienced when they did not have adequate resources to pay their bills on time. A fitting ending, I thought to myself as I hung up the phone. Disappointed, I worried that she might think that I had let her down.

This too, was a metaphor, I thought. For sadly, and in too many ways this year, parents and families had frequently been disconnected from staff, and from each other. The result was disappointment, alienation, and a lack of communication. Finally, and perhaps most essentially, the frequent outcome was missed learning opportunities and missed potential for making change for themselves, their children, the program, and their community.

IRONIES AND IMPLICATIONS

The parent involvement component of Head Start began from a vision grounded in principles of justice. While, as Chapter 2 points out, this programmatic element has shifted focus over the years from a radical social-change perspective to a humanistic, deficit-based approach, to one that could now be articulated as a human-capital framework, this antipoverty program is still chartered with the role of advocating for the needs of the poor. And, although the seeking of change with them and for them has moved to the realm of individual change and away from collective struggle for social change, within even this narrow interpretation of programming the principles of justice, fairness, and respect must be held true. And yet, as a result of this research, and other emerging, critical scholarship on Head Start (Ames & Ellsworth, 1997; Ellsworth & Ames, 1998; Spatig, Parrott, Dillon, & Conrad, 1998; Mickelson & Klenz, 1998), we must question how a program can work towards justice at any level when the system and those within it engage in and support actions that are oppressive, and that further marginalize those it is supposed to empower. This final section expands on this contradiction, and focuses on the need to develop new paradigms and practices that recapture and build on the dignity, strength, attributes, and promise of Head Start parents.

LISTENING TO WHAT HAS BEEN SILENCED

Twelve years ago Washington and Oyemade (1987) argued that the philosophical frameworks that undergirded the parent involvement emphasis of the program had not been shown to be effective: cultural-deprivation approaches to parent education did not engage parents nor address the strengths they have; social-disenfranchisement theories that advocated for providing parents with decision-making power in the program only affected small numbers of parent leaders; and the economic emphasis that made attempts at increasing parents' buying power though job acquisition typically included only placement in Head Start jobs. Yet they, and others (e.g., Ellsworth & Ames, 1998) would argue that perhaps the most pervasive and debilitating framework guiding practice and programming is the one that has been the ongoing rationale for the entire program: the deficit approach. This perspective negates the strengths, knowledge, and attributes of parents, and instead replaces these parts of themselves with questions about what they don't have or don't know. When parents, already buffeted by the realities of racism, classism, and sexism, are rarely asked what they are good at, or what they could offer, or when they are put in volunteer positions that are regressive or exploitive, they are put into positions that deny their holistic selves. By not maximizing on the experiences that they have had, their often heroic acts of survival are not made legitimate. By mirroring to them a negative, deficient likeness, a contested, "partial image" of themselves is all that is taken stock of, thereby reifying their belief that they are outsiders, that they are the other.

If, on the other hand, the normative assumption in Head Start[2] was that parents in the program had a host of life skills, lived experiences, and perspectives that were important to build on and share, then the structure of the program would ensure that their desires, preferences, skills, and needs would be noted and enhanced or built on. Conversely, in the frame of the present ideology of the program, although parents may be superficially asked about their needs, these needs may be ignored or not authentically addressed. Clearly, they are not thought to be important enough to require the most creative, potent resources possible. Furthermore, their needs and concerns are not placed into a broader context of classist, racist, and sexist constraints within their community, culture, and society — contexts that could promote solidarity and community among parents in a program that now divides and conquers them. Writing of the need for such a space, bell hooks (1990) reminds us that all who are made marginal by race, class, gender, disability, sexual orientation, or otherwise labeled as the other, need a safe space, "a homeplace" wherein they can seek support and solidarity and promote resistance among the poor, people of color, and the otherwise marginalized. Only within such a space can the marginalized "return for renewal and self-recovery, where we can heal our wounds and become whole" (p. 49). For some parents — those who have been welcomed in — the Head Start "family" has met, at least in part, and within unequal conditions, their need and desire for such a homeplace. For other parents, however, having been further marginalized by being left out and left behind, the metaphor of a "head start" is little more than an unkept promise.

The relations of power and control that were discerned between the staff and parents in Morrison County were grounded in this deficit approach, and subsequently reinforced the patronizing and limiting dynamics between them. This is evidenced by the fact that parents who had tried to do good were shot down for both their effort and advocacy, and the choices they had made as parents in the program. These included parents like Nina, who was blamed not only for her lack of literacy but for attempting to do something about it; Theresa and Bobbie, who were literally rejected for their attempts at acting as advocates for children; Marilyn and Francine, who were reviled for promoting the importance of pride in an education; Bess, the good mother who was branded as bad because she chose to stay home with a sick child rather than come to the center; and Raymond, who was ridiculed by both administrators and parents as he bravely carried out the only role available to him in an unequal system: a powerless figurehead on an impotent Policy Council.

In light of this context, the true nature and meaning of parent participation and involvement at the Morrison County Head Start lay not in the successes or failures of individuals or groups of parents, although these personal and collective experiences may encourage certain changes in the program simply because of their powerfully gratifying or tragic lessons. Instead, the real significance can be found in the very acts of parental resistance and in the staff's responses to that opposition. As parents contested the established boundaries of "appropriate involvement," the reactions of the staff — the manipulative behaviors, attitudes, and verbal exchanges — were indicative of the depth of the hegemonic relations of power and oppression in the program. With the staff's anger and turf mentality overriding any broader articulation of goals for families, they not only missed the parents' desire for a graduation as being a celebratory belief in the power, importance, and potential of education,[3] they also did not (or refused to) recognize that one result of the graduation at the Downtown Center was that a small group of supposedly wrongheaded, deficient women had gotten more parents and families into the school at that one event than in all other parent activities combined throughout the year.

In this example and in a variety of other instances that took place in the program that year, it was apparent that the deficit perspective about parents not only functioned to negate the reality of parents' efforts at maintaining a presence, it worked to invalidate their voices as well. Viewing their desires as ill-conceived or illegitimate, the staff could not or would not hear what it was the parents wanted to say and do. Even when seeming to listen, in seeking to maintain power and control the staff did not actually hear. Instead, they continually reinterpreted parents' needs and desires into what it was that they themselves wanted to happen, and what they themselves thought was "best." Fraser (1989), in writing about this reinterpretation as a function of power, has pointed out that "dominant groups articulate need interpretations which are intended to exclude, defuse, and/or co-opt" (p. 166). Furthermore, she notes that such counterinterpretations are political, explaining that "a matter is political if it is contested across a range of different discursive arenas and among a range of different discourse publics" (p. 167). The politics and power embedded in the staff's efforts at reframing parents' needs and desires was evident in the Downtown Center's success and the Harbor Street Center's failure at organizing a graduation, for only a great deal of concerted effort and solidarity among parents could thwart the staff's reinterpretation of what that final day would hold.

ON MANAGEMENT FIXES AND STATUS QUO MENTALITIES

Within this book, I have attempted to articulate the social phenomenon of the unequal relations among staff, between staff and parents, and among parents in this particular Head Start program. I have also sought to depict and deconstruct the material, symbolic, and social conditions that fostered and promoted these inequalities and contradictions in practice. And, while I have pointedly illustrated some of the forms of dysfunction and dis-ease[4] that existed within this Head Start family, as I noted in the introductory sections of the book, I have sought to offer these findings in the spirit of inquiry as well as advocacy. Thus, I wish to point out that this analytical deconstruction of the lived experiences of the staff and parents in the program is not, and should not be used as, an argument for Head Start's destruction or dismantling. As Skerry (1983) and, most recently, Ellsworth (1998) have pointed out, given the reality that Head Start has retained its solid base of support throughout the years despite having been soundly and regularly criticized by a host of scholars and studies, this is not likely to happen in the near future at least.[5] Indeed, the fact that Congress reauthorized Head Start in October 1998 and increased its funding, the majority of which has been stipulated for quality improvement,[6] speaks to its popularity and resiliency.

In years past, however, efforts at responding to critics' call for increased quality have included Band-Aid approaches that, while involving what appears to be significant appropriations of money nationally, actually involved minor amounts when divided up among the hundreds of programs and thousands of centers and employees. And, while no one can dispute the fact that increased skill development (albeit for only some employees), (minor) increases in wages, and the upgrading of (select) facilities are valuable, and in fact should be a given, when core aspects of the system need to be replaced, such efforts may yield little significant improvement.

For example, a policy shift that appears outwardly significant as it relates to parents is the new language in the *Head Start Performance Standards*[7] that emphasizes the auditing of parents' assets, and which encourages them to develop a contract, with the assistance of the Head Start staff, which spells out their responsibilities as a parent and in the program, and their desired outcomes in terms of work, learning, housing, etc. While this appears to be a hopeful policy that could begin reversing the deficit-based approach to parents, given the fact that because of a lack of programmatic resources, parents' stated needs[8] were ignored in this program and their spoken desires were usurped and manipulated through dynamics of power and control, this opportunity could in fact be a danger for parents. Without a radical change in perspective, and without significant levels of resources put in place that would truly support both parents and staff in making this policy shift prove fruitful, not only will it stand as a mere footnote within the broader text — and context — of Head Start and result in little or no change in either parents' lives or present staff practices, it will reinforce the ideology of deficiency, as parents time and again could be thrust into the position of rationalizing why they couldn't fulfill their contract. Thus, instead of offering a real promise of maximizing on strengths instead of focusing on weaknesses, one could surmise that the *de facto* deficit assumption of the program will remain: that regardless of their expressed needs, most parents could not constructively engage in significant change-making processes and activities anyway — so why even try?

Another improvement attempted by Head Start has been new and better management initiatives. Yet, such reformist management approaches have resulted in rigid management styles that emphasize more accountability but little or no real involvement by parents or the Head Start staff on the front lines of service delivery. While an emphasis on accountability may be a seductive fix in a program fraught with management problems, as Neuharth-Pritchett & Mantziocopoulos (1998) and Ames & Ellsworth (1997) point out, these forms of management are in contradiction with Head Start's stated goal of programmatic flexibility[9] and the participation of parents in the management structure. In fact, as this research has shown, and as others have noted (Spatig, Parrott, Dillon, & Conrad, 1998), parents typically act as mere bodies which rubber-stamp the decisions of the administrators, a function that Ames and Ellsworth (1997) define as "ceremonial" participation.

As Cervero and Wilson (1994) have pointed out, "whenever people act in an organizational context, they do so within sets of power relations" (p. 249). Such actions and their social implications are grounded in issues of material concerns and constraints, conflicts and differences in ideology, and are manifested in social dynamics of power and control. The irony and pervasiveness of the social dynamics that can exist when tighter, top-down management structures are placed within Head Start are illustrated by a comment made to me by Raymond, the chair of the Morrison County Head Start Policy Council. When I inquired about what he thought the program could do to get more parents involved, his reply seemed to parrot the management philosophy of negating the importance of parents. He said: "You just can't call each parent individually. *Priorities*, you know."

Thus, to remedy this situation, to make whole a program that is grounded in principles of justice, more than mere administrative or management fixes are required.[10] Rather, if the program is to authentically seek to empower parents and change the conditions of communities it will require nothing less than perspective and programmatic transformation — transformation mediated and supported by critical reflection, mutual dialogue, and collective action that is grounded in democratic principles and practices.

RECONCEIVING THE DIALOGUE

As a host of social philosophers and educators have articulated (e.g., Brookfield, 1995; Freire, 1970; Freire & Horton, 1991; Shor, 1987, 1996), key to the promotion of justice is the fostering of a reflective stance that is committed to the constant questioning of one's own as well as others' practice. Concomitantly, to be *critically* reflective is to open oneself to the possibility of changing one's (or others') practice in ways that promote more equitable relations of power. Harriet, in her own way, pointed to the importance of this reflectivity in her good-bye to me when she noted that my questioning promoted their questioning, saying: "You got people to thinking. It really made us think about how parents get involved." Addressing this phenomenon in a different way, Stanage (1987) has said, "our attempts at articulating the phenomenon and reflecting on it alters it, not only because of the way in which we come to define it, but perhaps how we act on it" (p. 94).

By necessity, in order to engage in critically reflective practice — what Freire (1970) has termed "praxis" and Shor (1987, 1996) and others call "critical pedagogy" — attempts will need to be made to engage all members of the Head Start community — including parents, staff in all areas and at all levels, and policy-makers — into the dialogue. Involving everyone in this dialogue is vital, since, as has been made evident in this research, a diversity of publics, a variety of opinions, and a range of interpretations of practice exist within Head Start centers, administrative components, programs, and the system. As has also been illustrated, when diverse opinions are repressed, when needs and desires are termed illegitimate or reinterpreted, and when strengths, experiences, and viewpoints are negated or ignored, the marginalized become further disempowered. Furthermore, when staff and those parents who become employees accommodate to a closed system that oppresses others, they proscribe and reinforce their own unfreedom by buying into structures that negate the possibility of liberatory reflection and action. As Giroux (1983, p. 165) has pointed out: "Human agency and structures come together most visibly at the point where oppositional practices and meanings contribute to the very nature of the hegemonic process. Such resistance reveals not only the active side of hegemony, it also provides the basis for a radical pedagogy that would make it the object of a critical deciphering and analysis."

Even in its most superficial and individualistic manifestations, Head Start's mission has always been about human agency. Yet, mere action does not equate with agency. As illustrated in the forgoing pages, the casting of blame, the uncritical parroting of platitudes, and the reproduction of the status quo through the copying of dysfunctional corporate cultures are, indeed, examples of action. These forms of action did little, however, for the Head Start family in Morrison County. Instead, they simply wore down the best intentions, the heartfelt motivations, and the dreams and aspirations of the staff and parents who sought refuge in and made commitments to Head Start out of a desire for a better tomorrow and a more just world for themselves and their children.

In the same way that mere action without thoughtful reflection on that behavior does not open one up to the possibility of change, it is equally true that critical reflection without engaging in action is also devoid of the prospect of any real emanicipatory meaning. Furthermore, while reflection can be a solitary experience, action, on the other hand, because of its overt nature, has not only social, but political implications. Therefore, if Head Start is truly committed to meeting the needs of low-income families and making change — in communities and with families — then critical reflection and authentic listening and dialogue will not only necessitate action toward change in the program itself, but will cause change as well.

It may take great courage and hope to start this process. But as programs and communities struggle over establishing a need as being legitimate or illegitimate, over interpreting and defining it, and over determining ways to satisfy it (Fraser, 1989, p.164), they must begin to pose to all who are connected to the program — the powerful and powerless alike — the types of questions that Sheared (1994, 1998), Swadener and Lubeck (1995), and others have framed for us as they focused on developing the promise of those who have been marginalized. Indeed, we must ask ourselves and each other how we can best hear those whom we have always spoken for, and how we can "give voice" (Sheared, 1994) to those who have been silenced.

I began this volume by asserting the need to bring the private, political world of Head Start into the public view for the purpose of developing a dialogue about the relevance of those politics to the lives of low-income families. I end with a call for change that is grounded in the reality of the lived experiences of those parents and staff who struggled to connect to the program's promise of hope. In seeking this change, Fraser (1989) reminds us that "the best needs interpretations are those reached by means of communicative processes that most closely approximate ideals of democracy, equality, and fairness" (p. 182). Only by throwing open the door of opportunity to all who wish to engage in the dialogue will the connections and contradictions that exist between the private politics of programs and broader public policies be fully revealed, and real change be pursued.

In closing, I offer the words of Nina, for in Nina's voice we hear the profound desire of parents who want to count and be counted as individuals with wishes and dreams of hope and challenge. In her voice, however, we also hear their wish to enter into this dialogue.

> There's a lot of things in my mind . . . you know, you act like you happy and everything, but it's like, deep inside, you going through a rough time and you don't wanna tell nobody. You just keep it inside. . . . But like you came up and said I'd like to ask you some questions, stuff like that. Well, they don't do that. I think they should do the same thing like you did. (Nina, parent, Downtown Center)

Nina's comment also provides us with one final metaphor about the realities of separation and community in Head Start. For if we truly listen to Nina's words, we hear not only a description of the present politics of some programs and their problems, but the ultimate source of their solution as well.

NOTES

[1] Treats that the parents had actually paid for through their purchases of fund-raising items.

[2] And by extension, in all areas of education where the involvement of parents and other adults in the family is sought, including preschool, K–12 schooling, and family literacy programs.

[3] A central tenet of Head Start philosophy and programming.

[4] My term here connotes both the unease that was clearly evident between and among the actors in this setting, and also refers to the structurally grounded, systemic pathology of the social relations inherent in the setting as a whole. In fact, using another medical term, one could say that the poor material conditions of the program served as the "vector" by which this dis-ease was communicated.

[5] Other social and policy factors may change it, however, such as welfare reform and the present and pressing need for full-day-care slots for families, in addition to various ideas currently being posed such as block-grant funding being given to states for child care, with Head Start monies being folded into those grants.

[6] In the reauthorization legislation, 60% of all newly authorized Head Start funding — totaling $35 million — is earmarked for quality improvement in programs.

[7] These new Performance Standards went into effect in January 1998.

[8] Recall that in the registration process parents completed surveys of their needs and desires, which were then ignored by the staff since they had little time to attend to them.

[9] For example, the practice of Total Quality Management strategies and conceptions of the "Learning Organization," while presently much in vogue within management theory, do not appear to be in evidence in recent depictions of Head Start settings.

[10] It is true, however, that some significant changes could be put into effect that would promote enhanced quality of services to children, as well as better ways of organizing and directing programs. The wealth of new knowledge about what constitutes good practice in child development programs, as well as in the management of human services programs, schools, and organizations, is growing.

Bibliography

Abt Associates, Inc. (1978). *A national survey of Head Start graduates and their peers.* Washington, DC: U.S. Department of Health and Human Services, Office of Child Development.

Adams, D. (1976). *Parent involvement: Parent development.* Berkeley, CA: Center for the Study of Parent Involvement. (ERIC Document Reproduction Service No. ED186 511.)

American Association of University Women. (1992). *The AAUW report: How schools shortchange girls.* Washington, DC: American Association of University Women.

American Association of University Women. (1998). *Gender gaps: Where schools still fail our children.* Washington, DC: American Association of University Women.

Ames, L., and J. Ellsworth (1997). *Women reformed, women empowered: Poor mothers and the endangered promise of Head Start.* Philadelphia, PA: Temple University Press.

Andersen, M.L., and P. Hill Collins. (1995). *Race, class, and gender: An anthology.* 2nd ed. Belmont, CA: Wadsworth.

Andrews, P. (1981). Parent involvement: A key to success. *Children Today* 10 (1): 21–3.

Apple, M. (1982). *Education and power.* Boston, MA: Routledge and Kegan Paul.

Apple, M. (1995). *Education and power.* 2nd ed. New York: Routledge.

Arnold, M. S. (1995). Exploding the myths: African-American families at promise. In *Children and families at promise: Deconstructing the discourse of risk*, edited by B. Swadener and S. Lubeck. Albany: State University of New York Press.

Aronowitz, S., and H. Giroux. (1993). *Education still under siege.* 2nd ed. *Critical Studies in Education Series.* Westport, CT: Bergin & Garvey.

Auerbach, E.R. (1989). Toward a social-contextual approach to family literacy. *Harvard Educational Review* 59 (2): 165–81.

Auletta, K. (1982). *The underclass.* New York: Random House.

Bacharach, S.B., and E.J. Lawler. (1980). *Power and politics in organizations.* San Francisco: Jossey-Bass.

Bagnall, R.G. (1989). Researching participation in adult education: A case of qualified distortion. *International Journal of Lifelong Education* 8 (3): 251–60.

Ball, S. (1987). *The micropolitics of the school: Towards a theory of school organization.* London: Methuen.

Ball, S. (1990). *Politics and policy making in education: Explorations in policy sociology.* London; New York: Routledge.

Becker, H.S. (1980). *Role and career problems of the Chicago public school teacher.* North Stratford: Ayer Company Publishers, Incorporated.

Berger, P.L., and T. Luckman. (1967). *The social construction of knowledge: A treatise in the sociology of knowledge.* New York: Anchor Books.

Berlin, I. (1998). *Families & freedom: A documentary history of African-American kinship in the Civil War era.* New York: New Press.

Bingman, B., and C. White. (In press). Resistance and schooling: Challenging notions of adult education practice in Appalachia. In *Making space: Reframing practice in adult education,* edited by V. Sheared and P. Sissel. Westport, CT: Bergin & Garvey.

Blase, J. (1987). Political interaction among teachers: Sociocultural contexts in the schools. *Urban Education* 2: 286–09.

Blase, J. (1991a). Everyday political perspectives of teachers toward students: The dynamics of diplomacy. In *The politics of life in schools,* edited by J. Blase. Newbury Park, CA: Sage Publishing.

Blase, J. (1991b). The micropolitical orientation of teachers toward closed school principals. *Education and Urban Society* 23 (4): 356–78.

Bolman, L., and T. Deal, (1991). *Reframing organizations: Artistry, choice, and leadership.* San Francisco: Jossey-Bass.

Boocock, S. (1985). *Sociology of education: An introduction. 2nd ed.* Lanham, MD: University Press of America.

Borden, E., and K.W. O'Beirne. (1989). False start? The fleeting gains at Head Start. *Policy Review* 47 (Winter): 48-51.

Bounous, R. (In press). Teaching as political practice. In *Making space: Reframing practice in adult education,* edited by V. Sheared and P. Sissel. Westport, CT: Bergin & Garvey.

Bourdieu, P., and J. Passeron. (1977). *Reproduction in education, society and culture. SAGE studies in social and educational change. Vol.5.* Beverly Hills, CA: Sage Publications.

Boyd, V. (1992). *School context: Bridge or barrier for change?* Austin, TX: Southwest Educational Development Laboratory.

Bradley, R., and P. Sissel. (1997). *Father involvement in the lives of head start children and participation in Head Start: A three year study of Head Start families.* Unpublished project proposal. Little Rock, AR: University of Arkansas at Little Rock.

Brookfield, S.D. (1995). *Becoming a critically reflective teacher.* San Francisco: Jossey-Bass.

Brush, L., A. Gaidurgis, and C. Best. (1993). *Indices of Head Start program quality.* Washington, DC: Administration on Children, Youth, and Families.

Cahn, E.S., and B.A. Passett, eds. (1971). *Citizen participation: Effecting community change.* New York: Praeger Publishers.

Cervero, R.M., and A.L. Wilson. (1994). The politics of responsibility: A theory of program planning practice for adult education. *Adult Education Quarterly* 45 (1): 249–68.

Cervero, R.M., and A.L. Wilson, eds. (1996). *What really matters in adult education program planning: Lessons in negotiating power and interests.* San Francisco: Jossey-Bass.

Chafel, J.A. (1992). Funding Head Start: What are the issues? *American Journal of Orthopsychiatry* 62: 9–21.

Chall, J.S., and C. Snow. (1982). *Families and literacy: The contributions of out-of-school experiences to children's acquisitions of literacy.* A final report to the National Institutes of Education.

Chodorow, N. (1974). Family structure and feminine personality. In *Woman, culture and society,* edited by M. Zimbalist Rosaldo and L. Lamphere. Stanford, CA: Stanford University Press.

Coleman, U.R. (1978). Parent involvement in preschool education: A reservation Head Start program. *Dissertation Abstracts International* 39 (56): 3861A.

Colin, A.J., III. (1988). *Voices from beyond the veil: Marcus Garvey, the Universal Negro Improvement Association, and the education of African Ameripean adults.* Unpublished doctoral dissertation, Northern Illinois University.

Collins, P.H. (1991). *Black feminist thought: Knowledge, consciousness, and the politics of empowerment.* New York : Routledge.

Collins, R., and D. Deloria. (1983). Head Start research: A new chapter. *Children Today* 12 (4): 15–19.

Collins, R. (1992). *Head Start facilities study.* Alexandria, VA: National Head Start Association. (ERIC Document # ED353 035).

Copeland, M.L. (1987). *What do parents really learn at the National Conference?* Presentation at the Annual Meeting of the National Association for the Education of Young Children, Chicago, IL. (ERIC Document Reproduction Service No. ED 306 019)

Corbett, H.D., J. Dawson, and W. Firestone. (1984). *School context and school change: Implications for effective planning.* Philadelphia, PA: Research for Better Schools.

Cuban, S., and E. Hayes. (1996). Women in family literacy programs: A gendered perspective. In *A community based approach to literacy programs: Listening to learner's lives. New directions for adult and continuing education,* edited by P. Sissel. San Francisco: Jossey-Bass.

Danziger, S.H., R.H. Haveman, and R.D. Plotnik. (1986). Antipovery policy: Effects on the poor and nonpoor. In *Fighting poverty: What works and what doesn't.* Edited by S. Danziger and D. Weinberg. Cambridge, MA: Harvard University Press.

Danziger, S., and D. Weinberg, eds. (1986). *Fighting poverty: What works and what doesn't.* Cambridge, MA: Harvard University Press.

Darder, A., ed. (1995). *Culture and difference: Critical perspectives on the bicultural experience in the United States.* Westport, CT: Bergin and Garvey.

Datta, L. (1970). Head Start's influence on community change. *Children* 17 (5):193-6.

de Lauretis, T. (1990). Eccentric subjects: Feminist theory and historical consciousness. *Feminist Studies* 16 (1): 115–50.

Derman-Sparks, L., and C.B. Phillips. (1997). *Teaching/learning anti-racism: A developmental approach.* New York: Teachers College Press.

Donovan, J.C. (1967). *The politics of poverty.* New York: Pegasus Publishing.

Dovidio, J.F., and S. L. Gaertner, eds. (1986). *Prejudice, discrimination, and racism.* Orlando: Academic Press.

Edin, K., and L. Lein. (1997). *Making ends meet: How single mothers survive welfare and low-wage work.* New York: Russell Sage Foundations.

Edwards, T.M. (1998). Revolt of the gentry. *Time Magazine* 151 (23). Web site: http://cgi.pathfinder.com/time/magazine/1998/dom/980615/nation_revolt_of_the_gen.html

Ellsworth, J. (1997). Inspiring delusions: Reflections on Head Start's enduring popularity. In *Critical perspectives on Project Head Start: Revisioning the hope and challenge,* edited by J. Ellsworth, and L. Ames. Albany, NY: State University of New York Press.

Ellsworth, J., and L. Ames. (1995). Power and ceremony: Low-income mothers as policy makers in Head Start. *Educational Foundations* 9 (4): 5–23.

Ellsworth, J., and L. Ames, eds. (1998). *Critical perspectives on Project Head Start: Revisioning the hope and challenge.* Albany, NY: State University of New York Press.

Epstein, J.L., and S. L. Dauber. (1991). School programs and teacher practices of parent involvement in inner-city elementary and middle schools. *Elementary School Journal* 91 (3): 289–305.

Escott, P.D. (1979). *Slavery remembered: A record of twentieth-century slave narratives.* Chapel Hill: University of North Carolina Press.

Etzioni, A. (1975). *A comparative analysis of complex organizations. Revised.* New York: The Free Press.

Fagan, J. (1996). Principles for developing male involvement programs in early childhood settings: A personal experience. *Young Children* 51 (4): 64–70.

Feinberg, W. (1983). *Understanding education: Toward a reconstruction of educational inquiry.* Cambridge, England: Cambridge University Press.

Fine, M. (1993). Parent involvement. *Equity and Choice* 9 (3): 4–8.

Flannery, D., and E. Hayes. (In press). Toward more inclusive perspectives on adult learning. In *Making space: Reframing practice in adult education,* edited by V. Sheared and P. Sissel. Westport, CT: Bergin & Garvey.

Foucault, M. (1980). *Power and knowledge: Selected interviews and other writings, 1972-1977.* New York: Pantheon Books.

Foucault, M. (1982). The subject and power. *Critical Inquiry* 8: 777–95.

Fraser, N. (1989). *Unruly practices: Power, discourse, and gender in contemporary social theory* Minneapolis: University of Minnesota Press.

Freire, P., and D. Macedo. (1987). *Literacy: Reading the word and the world.* South Hadley, MA: Bergin & Garvey.

Freire, P. (1970). *Pedagogy of the oppressed.* New York: Seabury Press.

Freire, P., and M. Horton. (1991). *We make the road by walking: Conversations on education and social change.* Philadelphia: Temple University Press

French, J.R., and B.H. Raven. (1959). The bases of social power. In *Studies in Social Power,* edited by D. Cartwright. Ann Arbor: University of Michigan Press.

Freud, S. (1943). *A general introduction to psychoanalysis. Authorized English translation of the revised Edition.* Garden City, N.Y: Garden City Publishing.

Galbraith, M.W. (1990). *Education through community organizations.* San Francisco: Jossey-Bass.

Garrick, J., and N. Solomon. (In press). Technologies of compliance in training. In *Making space: Reframing practice in adult education,* edited by V. Sheared and P. Sissel. Westport, CT: Bergin & Garvey.

Gary, L., L. Beatty, and G. Weaver. (1987). *Involvement of Black fathers in Head Start*. Washington, DC: Institute for Urban Affairs and Research.

Gates, H.L. (1990). Critical remarks. In *Anatomy of racism,* edited by D. Goldberg. Minneapolis: University of Minnesota Press

Gaventa, J. (1980). *Power and powerlessness: Quiescence and rebellion in an Appalachian valley*. Urbana, IL: University of Illinois Press.

Geertz, C. (1973). *The interpretation of cultures: Selected essays*. New York: Basic Books.

Giddens, A. (1979). *Central problems in social theory action, structure & contradiction in social analysis.* Berkeley: University of California Press.

Gillette, M.L. (1996). *Launching the War on Poverty: An oral history*. New York: Twayne Publishers.

Gilligan, C. (1982). *In a different voice*. Cambridge, MA: Harvard University Press.

Ginsburg, M.B. (1988). *Contradictions in teacher education and society: A critical analysis*. London: Falmer Press.

Ginsburg, M.B., S. Kamat, R. Raghu, and J. Weaver. (1995). Educators and politics: Interpretations, involvement, and implications. In *The politics of educators' work and lives*, edited by M. B. Ginsburg. New York: Garland Publishing.

Giroux, H. (1981). Teacher education and the ideology of social control. In *Ideology, culture, and the process of schooling*, edited by H. Giroux. Philadelphia: Temple University Press

Giroux, H. (1983). *Theory and resistance in education: A pedagogy for the opposition*. South Hadley, MA: Bergin & Garvey.

Giroux, H. and P. Freire. (1987). Series introduction. In *Critical pedagogy and cultural power*, edited by D. W. Livingstone. New York and Westport, CT: Bergin and Garvey.

Giroux, H. (1988). *Teachers as intellectuals: Toward a critical pedagogy of learning*. South Hadley, MA: Bergin & Garvey.

Goldberg, D. (1990). *Anatomy of racism.* Minneapolis, MN: University of Minnesota Press

Good, T.L., and J.E. Brophy. (1971). Analyzing classroom interaction: A more powerful alternative. *Educational technology* 11: 36–41.

Gramsci, A. (1991). *Prison notebooks.* New York: Columbia University Press.

Greaney, V. (1986). Parental influences on reading. *Reading Teacher* 40 (8): 813–18.

Greenberg, P. (1969). *The devil has slippery shoes: A biased biography of the Child Development Group of Mississippi*. New York: Macmillan.

Greenberg, P. (1998). The origins of Head Start and the two versions of parent involvement: How much parent participation in early childhood programs and services for poor children? In *Critical perspectives on Project Head Start: Revisioning the hope and challenge,* edited by J. Ellsworth and L. Ames. Albany: State University of New York Press.

Hall, J.L., B. Johnson, and A.C. Bowman. (1995). Teacher socialization: A spiral process. *The Teacher Educator* 30 (4): 25-36.

Harchar, R.L. (1993). *Collaborative power: A grounded theory of administrative instructional leadership in the elementary school.* Presentation at Annual Meeting of the American Educational Research Association, Atlanta, GA. (ERIC Document Reproduction Service No. ED 359 624).

Harding, S., ed. (1987). *Feminism and methodology.* Bloomington, IN: Indiana University Press.

Hargreaves, A. (1991). Contrived collegiality: The micropolitics of teacher collaboration. In *The politics of life in schools,* edited by J. Blase. Newbury Park, CA: Sage Publishing.

Hargreaves, D. H. (1980). "The occupational culture of teachers." In P. Woods (Ed.), *Teacher strategies.* London: Croom Helm.

Hart, M. (1992). *Working and educating for life: Feminist and international perspectives on adult education.* London and New York: Routledge.

Hart, M. (1995). Motherwork. In *In defense of the lifeworld: Critical perspectives on adult learning*, edited by M. Welton. Albany: State University of New York Press.

Hayes, E. (1989). Insights from women's experiences for teaching and learning. In *Effective teaching styles: New directions for adult and continuing education*, edited by E. Hayes.

Hayes, E., and S.A.J. Colin, III. (1994). Racism and sexism in the United States: Fundamental issues. In *Confronting racism and sexism: New directions for adult and continuing education,* edited by E. Hayes and S.A.J. Colin, III.

Hayes, E., B. Sparks, C. Hansman, M. Hart, and V. Sheared. (1998). Talking across the table: A dialogue on women, welfare, and adult education. In *Proceedings of the 39th Annual Adult Education Research Conference*, edited by J.C. Kimmel. May 15–16, 1998, San Antonio, TX.

Heclo, H. (1986). The political foundations of antipoverty policy. In *Fighting poverty: What works and what doesn't*, edited by S. Danziger and D. Weinberg. Cambridge, MA: Harvard University Press.

Hodge, J. (1990). Equality: Beyond dualism and oppression. In *Anatomy of racism*, edited by D. Goldberg. Minneapolis, MN: University of Minnesota Press.

hooks, b. (1984). *Feminist theory: From margin to center*. Boston: South End Press.

hooks, b. (1990). *Yearning: Race, gender, and cultural politics*. Boston: South End Press.

Houlares, J., and S. Oden. (1990). *A follow-up study of Head Start's role in the lives of children and families: Interim report.* Ypsilanti, MI: High/Scope Educational Research Foundation.

Hoyle, E. (1986). *The politics of school management*. London: Hodder and Stoughton.

Hruska, S.W. (1993). Factors related to high and low parent involvement in a Head Start program. *Dissertation Abstracts International* 54 (06-A): 2337.

Hugo, J. (In press). Creating an intellectual basis for friendship: Practice and politics in a white, women's study group. In *Making space: Reframing practice in adult education,* edited by V. Sheared and P. Sissel. Westport, CT: Bergin & Garvey.

Iannaconne, L. (1975). *Educational policy systems*. Fort Lauderdale, FL: Nova University Press.

Iannaconne, L. (1991). Micropolitics of education. *Education and Urban Society* 23 (4): 465–471.

Jarolimek, J. (1981). *The schools in contemporary society: An analysis of social currents, issues, and forces*. New York : Macmillan.

Jongsma, K.S. Intergenerational literacy (questions and answers). *Reading Teacher* 43 (6): 426–27.

Jorde-Bloom, P. (1988). *A great place to work: Improving conditions for staff in young children's programs.* Washington, DC: National Association for the Education of Young Children.

Jorde-Bloom, P., and M. Sheerer. (1992). Changing organizations by changing individuals: A model of leadership training. *The Urban Review* 24 (4): 263–286.

Jurmo, P. (1989). The case for participatory literacy education. In *Participatory Literacy Education*, edited by A. Fingeret and P. Jurmo. San Francisco: Jossey-Bass.

Kagan, S., D. Powell, B. Weissbourd, and E. Zigler, eds. (1987). *America's family support programs*. New Haven: Yale University Press.

Kassebaum, N.L. (1994). Head Start: Only the best for America's children. *American Psychologist* 49 (2): 123–6.

Kennedy, E.M. (1993). The Head Start Transition Project: Head Start goes to elementary school. In *Head Start and beyond: A national plan for extended childhood intervention,* edited by E. Zigler and S. Styfco. New Haven: Yale University Press.

Kennedy, L.W. (1991). *Quality management in the nonprofit world.* Jossey-Bass, San Francisco.

Kinard, J. (1975). The effect of parental involvement on achievement of first and second siblings who have attended Head Start and Follow Through programs. *Dissertation Abstracts International* 35 (9): 5914A.

Kleberg, J.R. (1993). *Quality learning environments. Columbus, OH: Ohio State University.* (ERIC Document Reproduction Service No. ED 354 613).

Knapp, M.L., and J.A. Hall. (1997). *Nonverbal communication in human interaction,* 4th ed. Fort Worth: Harcourt Brace.

Knauft, E.B., R.A. Berger, and S.T. Gray. (1991). *Profiles of excellence: Acheiving success in the nonprofit sector*. San Francisco: Jossey-Bass.

Knowles, M. (1970). *The modern practice of adult education: Andragogy versus pedagogy*. New York: Association Press.

Kohlberg, L. (1984). *The psychology of moral development: The nature and validity of moral stages,* 1st ed. San Francisco: Harper and Row.

Kotelchuck, M., and J.B. Richmond. (1987). Head Start: Evolution of a successful comprehensive child development program. *Pediatrics* 79: 441–45.

Kozol, J. (1972). *Free schools*. New York: Bantam Press.

Kozol, J. (1991). *Savage inequalities: Children in America's schools*. New York: Crown.

Kramer, M. (March 8, 1993). Getting smart about Head Start. *Time Magazine* p. 43.

Kreisberg, S. (1992). *Transforming power: Domination, empowerment, and education*. Albany: State University of New York Press.

Kuipers, J.L. (1969). The differential effects of three parent education programs on the achievement of their children enrolled in an experimental Head Start program. *Dissertation Abstracts International*, 30 (12):5321A.

Kuntz, K. (1998). A lost legacy: Head Start's origins in community action. In *Critical perspectives on Project Head Start: Revisioning the hope and challenge,* edited by J. Ellsworth and L. Ames. Albany: State University of New York Press.

Ladner, J. (1987). Introduction to tomorrow's tomorrow: The black woman. In *Feminism and methodology*, edited by S. Harding. Bloomington, In: Indiana University Press.

Larrivee, R.C. (1982). A comparison of the effects of three parent education programs: STEP, PAT and EP, on the perceptions and interactions of low-income Head Start mothers and their preschool children. *Dissertation Abstracts International* 42 (12): 5068A.

Lawler, E.E., III. (1981). *Pay and organizational development*. Reading, MA: Addison-Wesley.

Leik, R., M. Chaukley, and N. Peterson. (1991). Policy implications of involving parents in Head Start. In *The reconstruction of family policy*, edited by E.A. Anderson and R. Hula. Westport, CT: Glenwood.

Levine, J. (1993). Involving families in Head Start: A framework for public policy and program development. *Families in Society* 74: 4–21.

Levine, J.A., D.T. Murphy, and S. Wilson. (1993). *Getting men involved: Strategies for early childhood programs*. New York: Scholastic, Inc.

Lewis, O. (1968). *A study of slum culture: Backgrounds for LaVida*. New York: Basic Books.

Lieblein, M.A. (1988). Parent involvement in Head Start. *Dissertation Abstracts International* 50 (4): 871A.

Lortie, D.C. (1975). *Schoolteacher: A sociological study.* Chicago: University of Chicago Press.

Lubeck, S. (1988). Nested contexts. In *Race, class, and gender in American education*, edited by L. Weis. Albany: State University of New York Press.

MacKinnon, C. (1981). Feminism, Marxism, method and the state: An agenda for theory. In *Feminist theory: A critique of ideology*, edited by N. Keohane, M. Rosaldo, and B.Gelpi. Chicago: University of Chicago Press.

Marcon, R. (1993). *Predictors of parent involvement and its influence on school success*. Conference Presentation at the 2nd National Head Start Research Conference, Washington, DC. November, 4–7, 1993.

Marshall, C. (1991). The chasm between administrator and teacher cultures: A micropolitical puzzle. In *The politics of life in schools,* edited by J. Blase. Newbury Park, CA: Sage Publishing.

Marshall C., and B. Mitchell (1991). The assumptive worlds of fledgling adminstrators. *Education and Urban Society* 23 (4): 396–415.

Marshall, C., and J. D. Scribner. (1991). It's all political: Inquiry into the micropolitics of education. *Education and Urban Society,* 23 (4): 347–55.

Maslow, A.H. (1970). *Toward a psychology of being*. New York: Van Nostrand Reinhold.

McCarthy, C., and M. Apple. (1988). Race, class and gender in American educational research: Toward a nonsynchronous parallelist position. In *Race, class, and gender in American education*, edited by L. Weis. Albany: State University of New York Press.

McIntosh, P. (1988). *White privilege and male privilege: A personal account of coming to see correspondences through work in women's studies*. Wellsley, MA: Center for Research on Women, Wellsley College.

McKey, R.H. (1983). *A review of Head Start research since 1970 and annotated bibliography of the Head Start research since 1965.* (ERIC Document Reproduction Service No. ED 248 995).

McKey, R.H., I. Condelli, H. Ganson, B. Barrett, C. McConkey, and M. Plantz. (1985). *The impact of Head Start on children, families and communities: Final report of the Head Start Evaluation, Synthesis and Utilization Project.* (DHHS Pub. No. OHDS 85-31193). Washington, DC: U.S. Government Printing Office.

McRobbie, A. (1978). Working class girls and the culture of femininity. In *Women take issue*, edited by the Centre for Contemporary Cultural Studies. Boston and London: Routledge and Kegan Paul.

Mezirow, J. (1991). *Transformative dimensions of adult learning.* San Francisco: Jossey-Bass.

Mickelson, R.A., and M.T. Klenz. (1998). Parent involvement in a rural Head Start and the reproduction of class. In *Critical perspectives on Project Head Start: Revisioning the hope and challenge,* edited by J. Ellsworth and L. Ames. Albany: State University of New York Press.

Midco Educational Associates, Inc. (1972). *Perspectives on parent participation in Head Start: An analysis and critique.* Denver: Midco Educational Associates, Inc.

Miller, D.C. (1990). *Women and social welfare: A feminist analysis.* Westport, CN: Praeger.

Miller, W.B. (1965). Focal concerns of lower class culture. In *Poverty in America,* edited by L. A. Ferman, J. L. Kornbluh, and A. Haber. Ann Arbor, MI: University of Michigan Press.

Monk, R. (1994). *The employment of corporate non-verbal status communicators in western organizations.* Doctoral dissertation. Santa Barbara, CA: The Fielding Institute.

Morris, V.D. (1974). Factors related to parental participation in Project Head Start. *Dissertation Abstracts International* 34 (8): 4576A.

Moynihan, D.P. (1969). *Maximum feasible misunderstanding: Community action in the War on Poverty.* New York: The Free Press.

National Head Start Association. (1989). *Twenty-five voices celebrating twenty-five years: Testimony to the Silver Ribbon Panel.* Phoenix, AZ: National Head Start Parent Association Meeting. (ERIC Document Reproduction Service No. ED 319 501).

Neuharth-Pritchett, S., and P.Y. Mantziocopoulos. (1998). A bumpy transition from Head Start to public school: Issues of philosophical and managerial continuity within the administrative structure of one school system. In *Critical perspectives on Project Head Start: Revisioning the hope and challenge,* edited by J. Ellsworth and L. Ames. Albany: State University of New York Press.

Nickse, R.S. (1990). Family literacy programs: Ideas for action. *Adult Learning* 1 (5): 9–13, 28.

Niemi, J.A. (1985). Fostering participation in learning. In *Involving adults in the educational process*, edited by S. H. Rosenblum. San Francisco: Jossey-Bass.

Nieto, S. (1992). *Affirming diversity: The sociopolitical context of multicultural education*. New York: Longman Publishing.

Noblit, G., B. Berry, and V. Dempsey. (1991). Political responses to reform: A comparative case study. *Education and Urban Society* 23 (4): 379–95.

Nunez, R. (1993). A study of parent involvement and perceptions concerning occupations requirements of their children. In *Bicultural studies in education: The struggle for educational justice*, edited by A. Darder. Claremont, CA: Institute for Education in Transformation, The Claremont Graduate School.

Office of Child Development. (1973). *Head Start policy manual: Head Start program performance standards*. Washington, DC: U.S. Government Printing Office.

Omewake, E.B. (1979). Assessment of the Head Start preschool education effort. In *Project Head Start: A legacy of the war on poverty,* edited by E. Zigler and J. Valentine. New York: The Free Press.

Opotow, S. (1991). Adolescent peer conflicts: Implications for students and schools. *Education and Urban Society* 23 (4): 416–41.

Parker, F., C. Piotrkowski, and L. Peay. (1987). Head Start as a social support for mothers: The psychological benefits of involvement. *American Journal of Orthopsychiatry* 57 (2): 220–33.

Parker, F., C. Piotrkowski, S. Kessler-Sklar, A. J. L. Baker, L. Peay, and B. Clark. (1997). *Executive summary. Final report: Parent involvement in Head Start*. New York: National Council of Jewish Women Center for the Child.

Parker, F., B. Clark, L. Peay, S. Young, A. Fernandez, R. Robinson, and A. Baker. (1997). *Parent involvement: A training manual for Head Start staff.* New York: National Head Start Association.

Payne, J.S. (1971). An investigation of a training program designed to teach parents how to teach their own Head Start children. *Dissertation Abstracts International* 31 (11): 5890A.

Payne, J.S., R.A. Payne, C.D. Mercer, and R.G. Davison. (1973). *Head Start: A tragicomedy with epilogue*. New York: Behavioral Publications.

Pearce, D. (1990). Welfare is not for women: Why the War on Poverty cannot conquer the feminization of poverty. In *Women, the state, and welfare*, edited by L. Gordon. Madison: The University of Wisconsin Press.

Pelligrini, A.D., J.C. Perlmutter, L. Galda, and G. H. Brody. (1990). Joint reading between black Head Start children and their mothers. *Child Development* 61: 441–53.

Persell, C.H. (1976). *Testing, tracking, and teachers' expectations: Their implications for education and inequality. A literature review and synthesis.* (ERIC Document Reproduction Service No ED 126 150).

Phillips, D.A., and N.J. Cabrera, eds. (1996). *Beyond the blueprint: Directions for research on Head Start's families.* Washington, DC: National Academy Press.

Polakow, V. (1993). *Lives on the edge: Single mothers and their children in the other America.* Chicago: University of Chicago Press.

Pollard, A. (1982). A model of classroom coping strategies. *British Journal of Sociology of Education* 3 (1): 19–37.

Powell, G. (1996). Revisiting our investment in quality. *National Head Start Association Journal.* Summer 1996: 34–35.

Pyle, N.S. (1989). *The relationship of parent involvement in Head Start to family characteristics, parent behaviors and attitudes.* Doctoral dissertation, University of North Texas.

Reiter, R., ed. (1975). *Toward an anthropology of women.* New York: Monthly Review Press.

Reynolds, A.J. (1989). *A structural model of first-grade outcomes for an urban, low socioeconomic black population.* Paper presented at the Annual Meeting of the American Educational Research Association, San Francisco, CA. (April 1989).

Reynolds, A.J. (1991). Early schooling of children at risk. *American Educational Research Journal* 28 (2): 392–422.

Reynolds, A.J., M. Hagemann, N. Bezruczko, and N. Mavrogenes. (1991). *Multiple influences on early school adjustment: Results from the Longitudinal Study of Children at Risk.* Paper presented at the Annual Meeting of the American Educational Research Association. Chicago, IL. (April 1991).

Richmond, V.P., and J.C. McCroskey. (1995). *Nonverbal behavior in interpersonal relations,* 3rd edition. Boston: Allyn and Bacon.

Rist, R. (1970). Student social class and teacher expectations: The self-fulfilling prophecy in ghetto education. *Harvard Educational Review* 40: 411–451.

Rist, R. (1972). Social distance and social inequality in a ghetto kindergarten classroom. *Urban Education* 7:241–260.

Rosaldo, M.Z., and L. Lamphere, eds. (1974.) *Woman, culture, and society.* Stanford, CA: Stanford University Press.

Rosenblum, S.H. (1985).The adult's role in educational planning. In *Involving adults in the educational process*, edited by S.H. Rosenblum. San Francisco: Jossey-Bass.

Rosenblum, S.H., and G.G. Darkenwald. (1983). Effects of adult learner participation in course planning on achievement and satisfaction. *Adult Education Quarterly* 33 (3): 147–153.

Rubovits, P.C., and M. Maehr. (1973). Pygmalion black and white. *Journal of Personality and Social Psychology* 25 (2): 210–218.

Sadker, M., and D. Sadker. (1994). *Failing at fairness: How America's schools cheat girls*. New York: Macmillan Publishing Co.

Saranson, S.B. (1982). *Culture of the school and the problem of change,* 2nd edition. Boston, MA: Allyn and Bacon.

Schiller, B.R. (1980). *The economics of poverty and discrimination, 2nd ed.* Englewood Cliffs, NJ: Prentice Hall.

Schofield, J.W. (1986). Causes and consequences of the colorblind perspective. In *Prejudice, discrimination, and racism*, edited by J. F. Dovidio and S. L. Gaertner. Orlando: Academic Press

Schofield, J.W. (1989). *Black and white in school: Trust, tension, or tolerance?* New York: Teachers College Press.

Schurr, S.L. (1992). Fine-tuning your parent power. *Schools in the Middle* 2 (2): 3–9.

Scott, D.M. (1997). *Contempt and pity: Social policy and the image of the damaged black psyche.* Chapel Hill: University of North Carolina.

Shapiro, J., and R. Doiron. (1987). Literacy environments: Bridging the gap between home and school. *Childhood Education* 63 (4): 262–69.

Shapiro, S. (1977). Parent involvement in day care: Its impact on staff and classroom environment. *Child Welfare 56* (1): 749–760.

Sharp, G. (1973). *The politics of nonviolence. Part two: The methods of nonviolent action*. Boston: P. Sargent.

Sheared, V. (1993). From workfare to edfare: An Africentric feminist epistimology of welfare, education, and work. In *Proceedings of the 34th Annual Adult Education Research Conference*, edited by D. Flannery. University Park, PA, Pennsylvania State University.

Sheared, V. (1994). Giving voice: An inclusive model of instruction — a womanist perspective. In *Confronting racism and sexism: New directions for adult and continuing education,* edited by E. Hayes and S.A.J. Colin, III.

Sheared, V. (1998). *Race, gender, and welfare reform: The elusive quest for self-determination.* New York and London: Garland Publishing.

Shor, I. (1987). *Freire for the classroom: A sourcebook for liberatory teaching*. Portsmouth, NH: Boynton/Cook.

Shor, I. (1996). *When students have power: Negotiating authority in a critical pedagogy*. Chicago: University of Chicago Press.

Sissel, P.A. (1993). *Going through changes: Parents, learning, and Project Head Start*. Paper presented at the American Association for Adult and Continuing Education Annual Meeting, Dallas, TX.

Sissel, P.A. (1994). Parents, learning, and Project Head Start: A socio-political analysis. In *Proceedings of the 35th Annual Adult Education Research Conference*, edited by M. Hyams, J. Armstrong, and E. Anderson. Knoxville, TN.

Sissel, P.A. (1995). *Capacity, power, and connection: An ethnographic study of parents, learning, and Project Head Start*. Doctoral dissertation. Rutgers, The State University of New Jersey.

Sissel, P.A. (1997). Participation and learning in Project Head Start: A socio-political analysis. *Adult Education Quarterly* 47 (3–4): 123–139.

Skerry, P. (1983). The charmed life of Head Start. *The Public Interest* 73: 18–39, Fall.

Slaughter, D.T., and V.S. Kuehne. (1988). Improving black education: Perspectives on parent involvement. *Urban League Review* 11 (1–2): 59–75.

Slaughter, D.T., R.W. Lindsey, K. Nakagawa, and V.S. Kuehne. (1989). Who gets involved? Head Start mothers as persons. *Journal of Negro Education* 58 (1): 16–29.

Slavin, R.E. (1989). *Effective programs for students at risk.* Boston: Allyn and Bacon.

Slavin, R.E. (1990). *Cooperative learning: Theory, research, and practice.* Needham Heights, MA: Allyn and Bacon.

Smith, C. (In press). Market women: Successful African American women entrepreneurs of the antebellum era in the United States — Implications for inclusivity in twenty-first century entrepreneurship education programs. In *Making space: Reframing practice in adult education,* edited by V. Sheared and P. Sissel. Westport, CT: Bergin & Garvey.

Smrekar, C. (1992). *Building community: The influence of school organization on patterns of parent participation.* Paper presented at Annual Meeting of the Educational Research Association, San Francisco, CA. (ERIC Document Reproduction Service No. ED 347 674).

Snyder, K.J., and R.H. Anderson. (1986). *Managing productive schools: Toward an ecology.* Chicago, IL: Harcourt Brace Jovanovich.

Spatig, L., L. Parrot, A. Dillon, and K. Conrad. (1998). Beyond busywork: Crafting a powerful role for low-income mothers or sustaining inequalities. In *Critical perspectives on Project Head Start: Revisioning the hope and challenge,* edited by J. Ellsworth and L. Ames. Albany: State University of New York Press.

Stack, C. (1974). *All our kin: Strategies for survival in a black community*. New York: Harper and Row.

Stallworth, J.T., and D.L. Williams, Jr. (1983). *A survey of school administrators and policy makers: Executive summary of the final report.* Austin, TX:

Southwest Educational Development Laboratory. (ERIC Document Reproduction Service No. ED 245 369).

Stanage, S. (1987). *Adult education and phenomenological research: New direction for theory, practice, and research.* Malabar, FL: Kreiger Publishing Co.

Stanlaw, J., and A. Peshkin. (1988). Black visibility in a multi-ethnic high school. In *Race, class, and gender in American education,* edited by L. Weis. Albany: State University of New York Press.

Steiner, G.Y. (1976). *The children's cause.* Washington, DC: The Brookings Institute.

Stevens, E., Jr., and G. Wood. (1994). *Justice, ideology, and education: An introduction to the social foundations of education,* 3rd ed. New York: McGraw-Hill Companies.

Stockard, J., and M. Mayberry. (1992). *Effective educational environments.* Newbury Park, CA: Corwin Press, Inc.

Strickland, D.S., and L.M. Morrow. (1989). Family literacy and young readers. *The Reading Teacher* 42 (7): 530–31.

Strickland, D.S., and L.M. Morrow. (1990). Family literacy: Sharing good books. *The Reading Teacher* 43 (7): 518–19.

Swadener B., and S. Lubeck, eds. (1995). *Children and families at promise: Deconstructing the discourse of risk.* Albany: State University of New York Press.

Szilagyi, A., and M. Wallace. (1987). *Organizational behavior and performance,* 4th ed. Glenview, IL: Scott, Foresman and Co.

Taylor, D. (1981). The family and the development of literacy skills and values. *Journal of Research in Reading* 4 (2): 92–103.

Tetreault, M.K. (1985). Feminist phase theory: An experience-derived evaluation model. *Journal of Higher Education* 56 (4): 363–84.

Thompson, M. (1980). Head Start teaches lessons board members should learn. *American School Board Journal* 167 (6): 31–33.

Tisdell, E.J. (1993). Interlocking systems of power, privilege, and oppression in adult higher education classes. *Adult Education Quarterly* 43 (4): 203–226.

Tisdell, E.J. (1995). *Creating inclusive adult learning environments: Insights from multicultural education and feminist pedagogy. Information series no. 361.* (ERIC Document Reproduction Service No ED 384 827).

Tisdell, E.J. (1998). Poststructural feminist pedagogies: The possibilities and limitations of feminist emancipatory adult learning theory and practice. *Adult Education Quarterly* 48 (3):139–56.

U.S. Commission on Civil Rights. (1973). *Teachers and students: Differences in teacher interaction with Mexican American and Anglo students. Report V: Mexican American study.* Washington, DC: U.S. Government Printing Office.

U.S. Department of Health and Human Services. (1987). *Commissioner's task force on parent involvement in Head Start. Final report.* Washington, DC: Administration for Children, Youth, and Families (DHHS). Head Start Bureau.

U.S. Department of Health and Human Services. (1994). *Creating a 21st century Head Start: Final report of the advisory committee on Head Start quality and expansion.* Washington, DC: U.S. Department of Health and Human Services.

U.S. Department of Health and Human Services. (1997). *Head Start statistical fact sheet.* Administration for Children and Families, U.S. Department of Health and Human Services Web Site. http://www2.acf.dhhs.gov/programs/hsb/html/1997_fs.html

U.S. Department of Health and Human Services. (1998). *Head Start statistical fact sheet.* Administration for Children and Families, U.S. Department of Health and Human Services Web Site. http://www.acf.dhhs.gov/programs/hsb/facts98.htm

U.S. General Accounting Office. (1994). *Early childhood programs: Local perspectives on barriers to providing Head Start services. Report Number HEHS-95-8.* Washington, DC: General Accounting Office.

U.S. General Accounting Office. (1997). *Head Start: Research provides little information on impact of current program. Report Number HEHS-97-59.* Washington, DC: General Accounting Office.

Valentine, J., and E. Stark. (1979). The social context of parent involvement in Head Start. In *Project Head Start: A legacy of the War on Poverty*, edited by E. Zigler and J. Valentine. New York: The Free Press.

Washington, V. (1985). Head Start: How appropriate for minority families in the 1980's? *American Journal of Orthopsychiatry* 55 (4): 577–590.

Washington, V., and U. J. Oyemade. (1987). *Project Head Start: Past, present, and future trends in the context of family needs.* New York: Garland Publishing.

Washington, V., U.J. Oyemade, and D. Gullo. (1989). The relationship between Head Start parental involvement and the economic and social self-sufficiency of Head Start families. *Journal of Negro Education* 58 (1): 5–15.

Washington, V., and U. J. Oyemade Bailey (1995). *Project Head Start: Models and strategies for the twenty-first century.* New York: Garland Publishing.

Watkins, K.E., and V.J. Marsick. (1993). *Sculpting the learning organization: Lessons in the art and science of systemic change.* San Francisco: Jossey-Bass.

Weber, L.C. (1990). Fostering positive race, class and gender dynamics in the classroom. *Women Studies Quarterly* 18 (1 and 2): 126–34.

Weld, L.A. (1973). Family characteristics and profit from Head Start. *Dissertation Abstracts International* 34 (3): 1172B.

Wells, K. (1984). *Teacher socialization in the educational organization: A review of the literature*. Paper presented at a Convention of the Western Speech Communication Association. Seattle, WA, February 18–21, 1984. (ERIC Document Reproduction Service No ED 242 668).

West, C. (1993). *Race matters.* Boston: Beacon Press.

West, G., and R.L. Blumberg. (1990). Reconstructing social protest from a feminist perspective. In *Women and social protest,* edited by G. West and R.L. Blumberg. New York: Oxford University Press.

Westinghouse Learning Corporation. (1969). *The impact of Head Start: An evaluation of the effects of Head Start on children's cognitive and affective development*. Washington, DC: U.S. Department of Commerce.

Whitebrook, M., C. Howes, and D. Phillips. (1989). *Who cares? Child care teachers and the quality of care in America (Final report of the National Child Care Staffing Study).* Oakland, CA: Child Care Employee Project.

Wilgoren, D. (1997). Irate judge closes two DC Schools: Twelve others cleared to open at hearing. *Washington Post,* September 16, 1997, B1:1.

Williams, L.R. (1975). Mending the hoop: A study of roles, desired responsibilities and goals for parents of Head Start children in tribally sponsored Head Start programs. *Dissertation Abstracts International* 36 (3): 1361A.

Williams, W., and J.W. Evans. (1969). The politics of evaluation: The case of Head Start. *Annals of the American Academy of Political and Social Science* 385: 118–132.

Willis, P. (1981). *Learning to labor: How working-class kids get working class jobs*. New York: Columbia University Press.

Willmon, B. (1969). Parent participation as a factor in the effectiveness of Head Start programs. *Journal of Educational Research* 62 (9): 406–10.

Willower, D. (1991). Micropolitics and the sociology of school organizations. *Education and Urban Society* 23 (4): 442–455.

Wilson, L.C. (1977). Basic education through Head Start programs. *Adult Literacy and Basic Education* 1 (1): 6–12.

Wilson, W.J. (1987). *The truly disadvantaged: The inner city, the underclass, and public policy*. Chicago: University of Chicago Press.

Wolcott, H.F. (1990). Ethnographic research in education. In *Complementary methods for research in education*, edited by R.M. Jaeger. Washington, DC: American Educational Research Association.

Woods, G.H. (1994). *Justice, ideology and education: An introduction to the social foundations of education,* 3rd ed. New York: McGraw-Hill.

Woods, P., and M. Hammersley, eds. (1977). *School experience*. London: Croom Helm.

Woods, P. (1990). *Teacher skills and strategies*. New York: Falmer.

Zarefsky, D. (1986). *President Johnson's War on Poverty: Rhetoric and history*. AL: University of Alabama Press.

Zigler, E. (1973). Project Head Start: Success or failure? *Children Today* 3 (1): 2–7, 36.

Zigler, E. (1994). Reshaping early childhood intervention to be a more effective weapon against poverty. *American Journal of Community Psychology* 22 (1): 37–47.

Zigler, E. (1995). Meeting the needs of children in poverty. *American Journal of Orthopsychiatry* 65 (1): 6–9.

Zigler, E., and S. Muenchow. *(1992). Head Start: The inside story of America's most successful educational experiment*. New York: Basic Books.

Zigler E., and S. J. Styfco. (1993). *Head Start and beyond: A national plan for extended childhood intervention.* New Haven, CT: Yale University Press.

Zigler, E., and S.J. Styfco. (1994). Head Start: Criticisms in a constructive context. *American Psychologist* 49 (2):127–32.

Zigler, E., S.J. Styfco, and E. Gilman. (1993). The national Head Start Program for disadvantaged preschoolers. In *Head Start and beyond: A national plan for extended childhood intervention*, edited by E. Zigler, and S.J. Styfco. New Haven: Yale University Press.

Zigler, E., and J. Valentine, eds. (1979). *Project Head Start: A legacy of the war on poverty.* New York: The Free Press.

Author Index

Subject Index

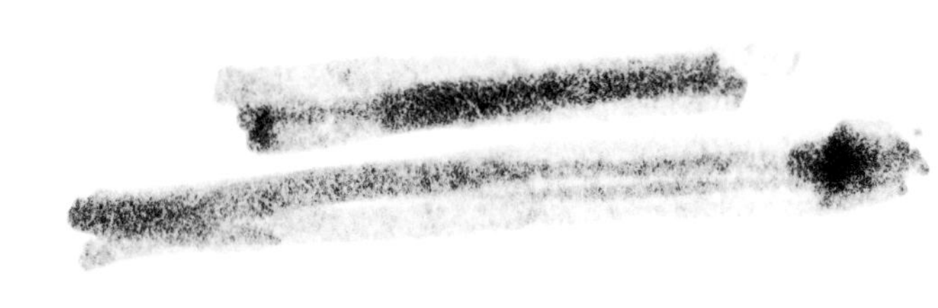